Media Literacy

This volume explores how educators can leverage student proficiency with new literacies for learning in formal and informal educational environments. It also investigates critical literacy practices that can best respond to the proliferation of new media in society. What sorts of media education are needed to deal with the rapid influx of intellectual and communication resources and how are media professionals, educational theorists, and literacy scholars helping youth understand the possibilities inherent in such an era?

Offering contributions from scholars on the forefront of media literacy scholarship, this volume provides valuable insights into the issues of literacy and the new forms of digital communication now being utilized in schools. It is required reading for media literacy scholars and students in communication, education, and media.

Kathleen Tyner is an assistant professor in the Department of Radio, Television and Film at The University of Texas at Austin. She is author, editor, producer, and co-editor of numerous books, articles, documentaries, and curricular materials related to literacy and new media, including *Literacy in a Digital World: Teaching and Learning in the Age of Information*, *A Closer Look: Youth Media*, and the award-winning *Scanning Television II*. Professor Tyner conducts research and evaluation projects internationally about the uses of digital media for analysis and production in formal and informal learning environments.

New Agendas in Communication

A Series from Routledge and the College of
Communication at the University of Texas at Austin

Roderick Hart and Stephen Reese, Series Editors

This series brings together groups of emerging scholars to tackle important interdisciplinary themes that demand new scholarly attention and reach broadly across the communication field's existing courses. Each volume stakes out a key area, presents original findings, and considers the long-range implications of its "new agenda."

Interplay of Truth and Deception
edited by Matt McGlone and Mark Knapp

Journalism and Citizenship
edited by Zizi Papacharissi

Understanding Science
edited by LeeAnn Kahlor and Patricia Stout

Political Emotions
edited by Janet Staiger

Media Literacy
edited by Kathleen Tyner

Media Literacy

New Agendas in Communication

Edited by Kathleen Tyner

 Routledge
Taylor & Francis Group

NEW YORK AND LONDON

First published 2010
by Routledge
270 Madison Ave, New York, NY 10016

Simultaneously published in the UK
by Routledge
2 Park Square, Milton Park, Abingdon, Oxon OX14 4RN

Routledge is an imprint of the Taylor & Francis Group, an informa business

© 2010 Taylor & Francis

Typeset in Sabon by
HWA Text and Data Management, London
Printed and bound in the United States of America on acid-free paper
by Edwards Brothers, Inc.

Library of Congress Cataloging-in-Publication Data
Media literacy : new agendas in communication / edited by Kathleen
Tyner.
      p. cm. – (New agendas in communication series)
   Includes bibliographical references and index.
   1. Media literacy. 2. Mass media – Technological innovations.
   3. Mass media – Study and teaching. I. Tyner, Kathleen R.
   P96.M4M46 2009
   302.23–dc22   2009019073

ISBN10: 0-415-87220-0 (hbk)
ISBN10: 0-415-87221-9 (pbk)
ISBN10: 0-203-86727-0 (ebk)

ISBN13: 978-0-415-87220-1 (hbk)
ISBN13: 978-0-415-87221-8 (pbk)
ISBN13: 978-0-203-86727-3 (ebk)

Contents

Figures

Tables

Contributors

Sanjay Asthana is an associate professor in the School of Journalism at Middle Tennessee State University. His research interests are heterodox and span neo-Marxism, postcolonial theory, media studies, and visual culture. Dr. Asthana received his Ph.D. from the School of Journalism and Mass Communication, University of Minnesota. His book, *Innovative Practices of Youth Participation in Media*, published for UNESCO in 2006, is a seminal text in the emerging field of youth media.

Elizabeth A. Bandy is a research associate at Rockman *et al*, a research, evaluation, and consulting company with offices in San Francisco, CA, and Bloomington, IN. Elizabeth's interests revolve around the role of media and technology in young people's development and learning, both formal and informal. At Rockman, Elizabeth is currently working on evaluations of the Science and Technology Program at Youth Radio, the Advanced Digital Pathways program at the Bay Area Video Coalition, and the QUEST media education project for PBS station KQED in San Francisco. Elizabeth has a B.S. in communication from Miami University, an M.A. in communication technology and policy from the University of Texas at Austin, and a Ph.D. in children, adolescents, and media from Stanford University.

Kristin M. Bass is a research associate at Rockman *et al*, a research, evaluation, and consulting company with offices in San Francisco, CA, and Bloomington, IN. Kristin is primarily interested in the development, evaluation, and implementation of alternative assessments of student learning. Kristin manages evaluation projects primarily related to STEM education at Rockman and consults on the selection and design of project instruments. Current evaluations include the Science and Technology Program at Youth Radio and the Advanced Digital Pathways program at the Bay Area Video Coalition. Prior to joining Rockman, Kristin was a postdoctoral fellow at the Learning Research and Development Center at the University of Pittsburgh and the Berkeley Evaluation and

Assessment Research Center at the University of California, Berkeley. Kristin has a B.A. in psychology from Yale University and a Ph.D. in education and psychology from the University of Michigan.

David L. Bruce is associate professor of English education in the graduate school of Education, Department of Learning and Instruction, University of Buffalo, the State University of New York. Prior to earning his Ph.D., he taught high-school English and media studies for 11 years, during which his students' media compositions won numerous local, regional, and national awards. His primary interest in research and teaching deals with reading and composing with video, particularly the way in which students and teachers can use print and video to complement each other. He has served as director for the Commission on Media for the National Council of Teachers of English and as president of the Ohio Council of Teacher of English Language Arts.

Allison Butler is assistant professor in the Department of Communication at Western Connecticut State University. Her work is focused primarily on integrating media education into secondary schools and the intersection of young people, media studies, and identity development. She holds a PhD from NYU's Media, Culture, and Communication Department.

Aaron Delwiche is an associate professor in the Department of Communication at Trinity University. His current research interests encompass ways in which the Internet can be used to foster education and global dialogue since the early 1990s. His experiments with virtual worlds in the classroom have been covered by publications ranging from *Wired* to *The Guardian* (UK). He co-founded one of the first full-service virtual world consultancies and recently served as co-chair of an international conference (*State of Play V: Building the Global Metaverse*) that explored the implications of transnational virtual worlds

Jennifer Fleming is an assistant professor in the Department of Journalism at California State University, Long Beach. Her current research interests include media literacy, journalism, and mass communication education. Before joining academe, Jennifer worked in the broadcast news industry in Canada.

James M. Mathews is a doctoral student in the Department of Curriculum and Instruction at the University of Wisconsin-Madison. As a member of the Games, Learning, and Society research group at UW-Madison and as a game designer at the Local Games Lab, Jim conducts research around augmented reality gaming and location-based digital story telling. Jim also teaches part-time at a small alternative high school in Middleton, Wisconsin. His communication arts-based curriculum connects students with their local communities through documentary film making, photography, writing, and service learning projects.

J. Lynn McBrien is an assistant professor in the College of Education at the University of South Florida. She teaches courses that fall within social foundations of education, including a graduate course in media literacy. She is the former Senior Education Editor of CNN's education Web site, and she was the project manager and senior editor of a high-school curriculum entitled *Media Matters: Critical Thinking in the Information Age*. Her particular interest in media education focuses on ways in which media can enhance or deter social justice. Additionally, Dr. McBrien evaluates ways in which her own students respond to the use of new media as teaching tools. Dr. McBrien received her Ph.D. from Emory University in 2005.

Alice Robison is an assistant professor of English in the College of Liberal Arts and Sciences at Arizona State University. As a member of the rhetoric and composition studies area of the department, Alice specializes in writing and designing processes; digital literacies and social media; and learning sciences. Alice has also worked on a variety of digital learning grants sponsored by the MacArthur Foundation. At Arizona State University, she is a faculty researcher on the Situated Multimedia Arts Learning Laboratory (SMALLab) Project in the Arts, Media and Engineering program. Her work on SMALLab is combined with a role in the development of the Quest to Learn school, a project run by the Institute of Play in New York City. Previously, she was an academic advisor to the New Media Literacies Project at MIT and a founding member of the Games+Learning+Society research initiative at the University of Wisconsin-Madison. She received her Ph.D. from the University of Wisconsin-Madison in 2006.

Jeff Share is faculty advisor in the teacher education program at the University of California at Los Angeles (UCLA). Previously, Dr. Share worked for 10 years as a freelance photojournalist documenting situations of poverty and social activism on three continents. He spent six years teaching bilingual primary school in the Los Angeles Unified School District and two years teaching in southern Mexico. He worked for several years as the regional coordinator for training at the Center for Media Literacy. His current research and practice focuses on the teaching of critical media literacy in K–12 education. Dr. Share earned his Ph.D. in the Graduate School of Education and Information Studies at UCLA researching critical media literacy.

Kurt D. Squire is an associate professor of Educational Communications and Technology, and director of the Games, Learning, and Society Initiative at the University of Wisconsin-Madison. His research focuses on new media and learning. He is a former Montessori and primary school teacher and, before coming to Wisconsin, was research manager of the Games-to-Teach Project at Massachusetts Institute of Technology and co-director of the Education Arcade. Squire earned his doctorate in instructional systems technology from Indiana University; his dissertation research examined students' learning through a game-based learning program he designed around *Civilization III*. Squire cofounded Joystick101.org with Jon Goodwin and currently writes a monthly column with Henry Jenkins for *Computer Games* magazine. In addition to writing more than 30 scholarly articles and book chapters, he has given dozens of talks and invited addresses in North America, Europe, and Asia. Squire's current research interests center on the impact of contemporary gaming practices on learning, schooling, and society. Along with several other University of Wisconsin-Madison faculty, he runs the Games and Professional Practice Simulations initiative at the Academic Advanced Distributed Learning Co-Lab

Kathleen Tyner is an assistant professor in the Department of Radio, Television, and Film at the University of Texas at Austin. She is author, editor, producer, and co-editor of numerous books, articles, documentaries, and curricular materials related to literacy and new media, including *Literacy in a Digital World: Teaching and Learning in the Age of Information; A Closer Look: Youth Media;* and the award-winning *Scanning Television II*. Professor Tyner conducts research and evaluation projects internationally about the uses of digital media for analysis and production in formal and informal learning environments.

Introduction

New Agendas for Media Literacy

Kathleen Tyner

In June 2008, scholars from across the United States came together with experts in gaming, simulations, virtual worlds, journalism, media production, and education to explore the potential of new media for learning at the *New Agendas for Media Literacy* conference on the University of Texas-Austin campus. Hosted by the College of Communication, the two-day conference was designed to advance the emerging field of media education by fostering intensive dialogue, discovery, and connections between traditional concepts of media literacy and the innovative outlooks from next-generation thinkers. Through presentations of new work from media literacy scholars, academics, educators, community-media practitioners, and media industry professionals, *New Agendas* participants explored topics related to the definitions, purposes, impact, and iterations of media literacy theory and practice found in formal and informal educational settings.

In his keynote address, Digital Media and the Future of Learning (If There is a Future), noted literacy scholar James Paul Gee kicked off the discussion with a provocative view of the disconnect between the burgeoning media literacy skills in contemporary society and their diminished and restricted role in formal learning environments (Gee, 2008). Throughout the conference, discussions addressed this educational gap and its impact on the way that critical media analysis, play, production, and participatory networks accrue social benefits for individuals and societies.

Rodney Gibbs, executive studio director of Amaze Entertainment and chairman of the Digital Media Council of Austin, addressed this gap from an industry perspective in *The Intersection of Digital Media and Learning*, a cogent analysis of the way that games, simulations, and virtual worlds can be used to bridge formal and informal learning. (Gibbs, 2008). This volume in the *New Agendas* series is intended to reflect the conference dialogue and to showcase emerging scholarly work from the diverse field of media literacy.

Literacy theorist Harvey Graff likens literacy to a series of labyrinths, and the metaphor resonates throughout the history of media literacy

(Graff, 1987). In the last century, the concept evolved in fits and starts in tandem with various political, cultural, and educational agendas. Even the most entrenched bibliophile recognizes that new communication devices represent an extension of paper and pen, with all the social capital, liabilities, competing values, and access issues that have been long associated with traditional literacy skills. Typically, the definitions, practices, and theories about the social uses of new technologies have been stuck in debates about the qualities inherent in contemporary literacy. Although the parameters, aims, and purposes of media literacy are still in question, this volume attempts to move beyond partisan debates to explore the wider possibilities for literacy in a digital era.

In addition to the use of qualifiers added to *literacy*, such as *media literacy*, *multimodal literacy*, and *visual literacy*, other terms and concepts used to describe contemporary literacy include theories related to *multiliteracies* (Cope & Kalanzis, 2000; Kress, 2000; New London Group, 1999); *pluriliteracies* (Garcia, Bartlett, & Kleifgen, 2006), which extends the practices of multilingual, global communities to include media and computerized languages and *transliteracy*, which delve further into the role of computer platforms and codes as linguistic structures (Thomas et al., 2007).

In attempting to understand the frameworks for studying new media literacy practices, U.K. scholar Simon Biggs argues that the computing process is essentially linguistic and, like language, evolves and changes over time. As such, Biggs envisions contemporary literacy, including computing, as a dynamic concept that can still be contextualized within traditional, historical frameworks for orality and alphabetic literacy, linguistics, and poetics. In his view, the idea that technologies change cultures is an overstated concept. Instead, computing is an extension of intellectual processing. Biggs sees cultural and linguistic factors as essential to the design and uses of technologies.

> It could be argued that there is nothing new about so called "new media" and that the idea of computation is not novel ... Perhaps culture, like language, can be considered as a network of constantly regenerating relations? If so then the implication is that technology is not the cause of change but rather the material manifestation of the social, technology's most pervasive materialisation being in the form of language.
>
> (Biggs, 2008)

This volume does not attempt to reconcile or resolve debates about the nature of literacy. Instead, it provides iterations of its application across theoretical perspectives, disciplines, and discourses. In fact, when coupled with discussions about the role of literacy in the learning environment, the debates serve only to reinforce Gee's notion that literacy is a "socially contested term" (Gee, 1996). In 1990, Australian scholars Luke and Freebody (1990) developed a groundbreaking model for the uses of multiple, multimodel literacies in educational settings in Australia. In defending their multiliteracies model, they noted:

> To say that literacy is a social practice is to say that it is subject to the play and power relations of local face-to-face contexts—of classrooms, communities, workplaces, places of worship, homes, and so forth ... However, to say that literacy is a social practice is also to say that it is constrained, mediated, and shaped by relations of power—relations that may be asymmetrical, unequal, and ideological ... It was our position that determining how to teach literacy could not be simply "scientific," but rather had to involve a moral, political, and cultural decision about the kind of literate practices needed to enhance both peoples' agency over their life trajectories and communities' intellectual, cultural, and semiotic resources in multimediated economies. Literacy education, then, is ultimately about the kind of literate society and literate citizens or subjects that could and should be constructed.
>
> (Freebody & Luke, 1999)

Media literacy is the term most commonly used in North America, especially in relationship to media education for youth. Its practice draws heavily on the key concepts, academic traditions, and field-tested practices of media educators in Europe, Australia and New Zealand. Even so, the concept is not new in North American educational circles. As early as 1933, Ohio State University education professor Edgar Dale recommended the integration of non-print media, audio-visual resources in the public school curriculum (Nichols, 2006). Ironically, his visual *Cone of Experience* has been plagarized and revised beyond all recognition and is now used as a seminal media literacy exercise for establishing the authenticity and authorship of media texts (Thalheimer, 2006). By the 1960s, the integration of media literacy in the curriculum was recommended by a broad range of scholars and policy makers, including Marshal McLuhan, who promoted the first formal North American efforts in Canada (Duncan, Pungente, & Andersen, 2002). Since that time, its applications cut across artistic, scientific, mathematic, and humanities disciplines in formal and informal education.

Advocates of media literacy also profess a broad range of priorities and competing aims and purposes for learning, from general youth development, workforce development, artistic self-expression, anti-consumerism, civics education, values inculcation, and health education. It could also be argued that in the last century, media literacy efforts at the political and policy level were identified as a response to the perceived need to protect children from harmful media effects. Protectionist approaches of this type, especially in regard to television critical viewing, argue that media education could blunt the effects of media and popular culture through structured critical thinking exercises with children about the constructed nature of media. These views are at loggerheads with traditional literacy theories that envision literacy as a pathway to social capital, independent thinking, and pleasure.

At least, the uses of literacy are various, and media literacy has the potential to engage with its consequences on many levels. For example, media literacy also presents ripe opportunities to study the ethical boundaries for freedom of expression, intellectual property, and the uses of literacy as a pathway to political power and economic gain. More recently, a cadre of scholars make the case that both ends of the technophobia and technophilia continuum are flawed and distracting foundations for media literacy theory and practice. Instead, they envision innovative strategies that leverage students "everyday" literacy skills for learning in an attempt to eschew both moral panics and simplistic notions of technological determinism (Buckingham, 2000; Livingstone, 2003).

As the next generation of scholars engages with media literacy studies, new questions about the aims and purposes for media education provide grounds for investigation of contemporary literacy practices. Many scholars make the case that contemporary students' informal literacy practices are not sufficiently integrated into formal elementary and secondary classrooms (Levin & Arafeh, 2007). This is often attributed to a "hole" in pre-service teacher preparation, especially in media production, which relegates the media skills and knowledge to a basic audio-visual or educational technology, devoid of critical analysis and production. Canadian media educator Barry Duncan critiques these approaches as teaching *through* vs. teaching *about* media (Duncan, 2001).

Even when teachers have ample professional development opportunities, the widespread integration of media literacy across the K–12 curriculum remains a daunting challenge in public schools. Jeff Share provides research from his in-service work with a group of teachers in an urban elementary school art program in Los Angeles. Across the country, Allison Butler uses an ethnographic approach to study the results for a media education focus in a theme-based public secondary school in New York City. Their experiences confirm the inherent challenges as new forms of digital communication are introduced into schools that are still designed for an industrial age.

Authors who explore media literacy practices at the university level in this volume demonstrate that critical thinking about media analysis, reception, and production has moved beyond communication studies programs at the university level. J. Lynn McBrien provides some historical context for the analysis of common online resources that cut across discipline boundaries in higher education courses. Drawing on her own experiences with new tools for learning, her chapter reinforces the need for educators to continually question their own practice and to ask, "Digital access for what purpose?"

Author David L. Bruce presents a case study of video production in his graduate education program to demonstrate the way in which the humanities area can benefit from hands-on creation of multiliteracy texts in university education programs. In a chapter about the uses of media literacy in journalism education, Jennifer Fleming relates her efforts to integrate media literacy tasks to help her journalism students understand the shifting challenges for news media in a digital age.

It can be argued that community-based media programs have the longest track record for field-based work in media literacy across the globe. The first section of this volume showcases two studies about media literacy in community-based settings. Sanjay Asthana investigates international media literacy practices through his study of youth participation with information and communication technology in the Cybermohalla (Cyber-Neighborhood) project in India. In North America, Kristin M. Bass and Elizabeth A. Bandy present their findings from an evaluation of YouthLink, a media production program for youth at the non-profit Bay Area Video Coalition in San Francisco. Each of these chapters presents structured strategies and evidence of impact for community-based media. Their work contributes to conversations about "best practices" in critical media production, the links between analysis and production, and promising strategies to connect formal and informal literacy skills.

Finally, some scholars, notably scholars at Project New Media Literacies (NML), a research initiative based within Massachusetts Institute of Technology's comparative media studies program, have begun to explore the way that Web 2.0 and participatory pedagogies can extend the theoretical base for media literacy (Jenkins, Purushotma, Clinton, Weigel, & Robinson, 2006). In particular, the common uses of social networks, video games, and virtual worlds by youth is fertile ground for investigation. In his chapter on gaming and media literacy, Aaron Delwiche details the impact of gaming in the private sector and recommends important principles for teaching students to become critical consumers and producers of video games and virtual worlds. Alice Robison discusses the role of "gaming literacies" as a fundamental curriculum design strategy for the Game School, set to open in New York City in the near future. Finally, James M. Mathews and Kurt D. Squire round off the volume with their case study of Dow Day, a place-based augmented reality game that uses GPS-enabled handheld devices to transport students back to the 1960s-era Dow Day riot, a controversial day in American history. Their work shows the importance of simulated contexts for learning and provides a proof of concept for the design literacies envisioned by the New London Group (1999).

The scholars in this volume present compelling evidence and innovative approaches that tie into the rapid influx and uses of new intellectual and communication resources. In the process, *Media Literacy: New Agendas in Communication* provides one portal for those who want to investigate new possibilities at the intersection of literacy and learning. It is hoped that this volume will contribute to stimulating conversations about contemporary literacy in all of its contexts.

References

Biggs, S. (2008). Transculturation, transliteracy and generative poetics. Paper presented at the European Electronic Literature Conference, University of Bergen, Norway (September 12). Retrieved January 7, 2009, from http://hosted.simonbiggs.easynet.co.uk/texts/trans.htm

Buckingham, D. (2000). *After the death of childhood: Growing up in the age of electronic media.* San Francisco, CA: John Wiley & Sons.

Cope, B., & Kalantzis, M. (2000). *Multiliteracies: Literacy learning and the design of social futures.* New York: Routledge.

Duncan, B., Pungente S. J., & Andersen, N. (2002). Media education in Canada. (September). Ontario, Canada: The Association for Media Literacy. Accessed January 9, 2009, from http://www.aml.ca/articles/articles.php?articleID=272

Duncan, B. (2001). A media literacy menu: Ingredients for successful media studies. In Sigrid Jones (ed.), *MedienABC: Introduction into Media Education.* IoE: London. Retrieved January 10, 2009, from http://www.medienabc.org/page1/page46/page46.html

Freebody, P., & Luke, A. (1990). Literacies programs: Debates and demands in cultural context. *Prospect: Australian Journal of TESOL, 5*(7), 7–16.

Freebody, P., & Luke, A. (1999). Further notes on the Four Resources Model: Transcript of online conversation with the authors. International Reading Association Online Discussion Forum (October 26). Retrieved January 7, 2009, from http://www.readingonline.org/research/lukefreebody.html#freebodyluke

Garcia, O, Bartlett, L., & Kleifgen, J. (2006) From biliteracy to pluriliteracies. In *Handbook of applied linguistics on multilingual communication* (Fall). Mouton.

Gee, J. P. (2008). Digital media and the future of learning (If there is a future). Keynote address for the New Media Literacy Conference (June 6). Retrieved January 15, 2009, from http://rtf.utexas.edu/medialiteracy/presentations.html

Gee, J. P. (1996). *Social linguistics and literacies: Ideology in discourses.* London: Taylor & Francis.

Gibbs, R. (2008). *The intersection of digital media and learning.* Keynote address for the New Media Literacy Conference (June 6). Retrieved January 9, 2009, from http://rtf.utexas.edu/medialiteracy/presentations.html

Graff, H. J. (1987). *The labyrinths of literacy: Reflections on literacy past and present.* New York: Routledge.

Jenkins, H., Purushotma, R., Clinton, K., Weigel, M., & Robison, A. (2006). *Confronting the challenges of participatory culture: Media education for the 21st century.* Chicago, IL: The John D. and Catherine T. MacArthur Foundation, Digital Media and Learning Initiative. Retrieved January 9, 2009, from http:// www.digitallearning.macfound.org

Kress, G. (2000) *Multimodality in multiliteracies: Literacy learning and the design of social futures.* London & New York: Routledge.

Levin, D., & Arafeh, S. (2007). *The digital disconnect: The widening gap between internet savvy students and their schools.* American Institutes for Research for the Pew Internet & American Life Project. Washington, DC: Pew Charitable Trust. Retrieved January 9, 2009, from http://www.pewinternet.org/PPF/r/67/report_display.asp

Livingstone, S. (2003). *The changing nature and uses of media literacy. Media@ LSE: Electronic Working Papers,* 4. Retrieved January 9, 2008, from http:// www.lse.ac.uk/collections/media@lse/mediaWorkingPapers/Default.htm

Nichols, J. (2006). Countering censorship: Edgar Dale and the film appreciation movement. *Cinema Journal* , 46, 1(Fall), 3–22.

Thalheimer, W. (2006). People remember 10%, 20% ... Oh really? (May). Retrieved January 15, 2009, from http://www.willatworklearning.com/2006/05/people_remember.html

Thomas, S., Joseph, C., Laccetti, J., Mason, B., Mills, S., Perril, S. *et al.* (2007) Transliteracy: Crossing divides. *First Monday,* December 3, 12:12. Retrieved January 7, 2009, from http://www.uic.edu/htbin/cgiwrap/bin/ojs/index.php/fm/article/view/2060/1908

Part I

Literacy in Action
Media Literacy in Community-Based Settings

Chapter 1

Young People, New Media, and Participatory Design

A Study of Cybermohalla from India[1]

Sanjay Asthana

Although scholarship in cultural studies, critical media pedagogy, and youth studies developed a set of theoretical ideas in examining how globalization is reshaping youth participation in media, particularly in the context of the postcolonial world, a certain theoretical disquiet prevails in exploring young people's media engagement through the inter-linked concepts of citizenship, civil society, and public sphere. To overcome the theoretical conundrums, some scholars pointed out that concepts such as citizenship, civil society, and public sphere do not explain the *actually existing* social realities in the postcolonial world (Chatterjee, 2004; Diouf, 2003; Obadare, 2004). The questions raised regarding the non-applicability of concepts, though important, do not explain how certain developments in globalization and media convergence enable young people to create "new politico-cultural spaces" and to refashion notions of participation, citizenship, and civil society in particularly important ways.

A primary purpose of this chapter is to demonstrate how young people from the Cybermohalla (Cyber-Neighborhood)—an alternative education project designed to enable democratic access to information and communication technologies among poor young people in India—not only appropriate and reconfigure old and new media in the process of creating personal and social narratives but understand the refashioning of participation and citizenship and the possibilities for the emergence of youth public spheres. Drawing upon and combining a range of cultural materials—metaphors, symbols, local histories, global ideas—young people produce a range of narratives that are not only bracing critiques of adult-centered conceptions of citizenship, civil society, and public sphere but serve as pragmatic elaborations of the various notions. To these young people, citizenship is not so much a matter of contractual and legal obligations, marked by performative practices, and participation not as consensus but instead as "conflictual" engagement (Miessen, 2007; Mouffe, 2007). Pramod Nayar (2008, p. 2) situates the Cybermohalla Project as "a move towards a postcolonial appropriation of cyberspace, a move facilitated by and through the digitextual nature of the new media of information and communication technology (ICT)." Drawing upon Anna Everett's (2003) formulation of "digitextuality," which refers to "the collage of forms, registers and signifying systems visible in the new media," Nayar examines how Cybermohalla enables the making of "a cyber-public sphere via an audio-visual economy." Nancy Adajania (2006, p. 369) has suggested that Cybermohalla's "young practitioners belonging to different social and educational backgrounds have been exploring the phenomenology of the technological act, as performed in the interstices between pedagogy and creativity." I generally agree with Nayar's overall arguments and find his characterization of Cybermohalla as a "postcolonializing" project quite useful. I propose, following Adajania, that a hermeneutic approach[2] to young people's engagements at the Cybermohalla Project, and the digitextual collage of forms they create, may indeed point to particular elaborations of citizenship, participation, and public sphere and merit closer examination.

To this end, this chapter sketches a praxis-oriented[3] analytic framework by bringing together the idea of a "hermeneutic self" from Paul Ricoeur's (1996) work, the notion of "social imaginaries" developed by postcolonial theory (Gaonkar, 2002; Chakrabarty, 2000; Chatterjee, 2004), and new media studies concepts like participation, remediation, and bricolage (Lievrouw, 2006; Deuze, 2006; Bolter and Grusin, 1999). Within humanities and social sciences, and more particularly in the field of critical media pedagogy, Ricoeur's hermeneutic philosophy had generally played a marginal role (Andrew, 2000; Leonardo, 2003; Nijman, 2007). The proposed chapter argues that Ricoeur's hermeneutic philosophy offers a way forward in understanding the multiple modalities through which young people engage the media as they develop their imaginations and narratives. More important, it presents an understanding of the human subject in terms of an embodied subjectivity that takes us beyond singular conceptions of identity, whether in terms of the abstract Cartesian subject or various other discourse-centered theorizations of subject (Nijman, 2007). Ricoeur has argued that a person's narrative identity can be approached via two interconnected and overlapping notions of identity: *idem* (sameness) and *ipse* (selfhood). Whereas *idem*-identity refers to "sameness of body and character, our stability illustrated by genetic code," *ipse*-identity pertains to our "selfhood, the adjustable part of our identity," and furthermore the two kinds of identities—of sameness and difference—offer coherence to the self and the possibility for change and reflexivity. Indeed, the notion of *ipse*-identity emerges in narrative. According to Ricoeur (1996), hermeneutic philosophy has attempted to demonstrate the existence of an opaque subjectivity which expresses itself through the detour of countless mediations—signs, symbols, texts and human *praxis* itself. The hermeneutic idea of subjectivity as a dialectic between the self and mediated social meanings has deep moral and political implications.

(p. 140, emphasis in original)

The notion of embodied subjectivity developed by Ricoeur offers analytic insights in the study of youth media pedagogies and experimentation, particularly as young people are involved in constructing personal and social narratives through creative and critical imaginaries.

The chapter also considers the contributions of John Dewey and Paulo Freire—two original thinkers of education, democracy, and human development—to sketch relevant models of learning and pedagogy for community-based, youth media efforts. Dewey's (1966) theory of education, with its emphasis on interaction, reflection, and experience, and Freire's (1972) insights on dialogical education (and developing consciousness) have shaped contemporary discussions of media education, learning, and literacy. Consequently, it becomes important to pursue the field of media education and pedagogy as a broad rubric where principles and practices are interlinked in terms of a "constellation" that is dynamic and open-ended. Obviously, new information and communication technologies (ICTs) play a significant role in enhancing youth participation and involvement in media and drive discussions about the potential directions for the field.[4]

Although young people of the Cybermohalla Project share common legacies, of socioeconomic inequity, such as poverty, lack of education and health, and political disenfranchisement, their imagination is shaped not by despair but, to borrow Raymond Williams's (1989) felicitous phrase, by "resources of hope." As Mamadou Diouf (2003, p. 6) points out, youth in African societies—and much of the postcolonial world—are uniquely positioned to mediate across the local and global contexts, particularly in light of the failures of national political enterprises. Diouf remarks that "looking beyond national borders, young people appropriate new technologies (digital and audiovisual)," to produce new narratives of democratic engagement. Appadurai (2002, p. 24) specifically articulates the idea of "deep democracy" in his explanation of the way that poor people in the city of Mumbai, India, mobilize and rework citizenship and "seek new ways to claim space and voice." In a similar fashion, this chapter argues that youth from the Cybermohalla Project not only raise crucial questions about power modalities around gender, poverty, and other generational and socioeconomic inequities but sketch out creative and critical ideas about democracy, citizenship, and participation.

Cybermohalla Project as Participatory Design

Cybermohalla is an experimental project designed to enable democratic access to information and communication technologies among poor young women and men in Delhi, India. The initiative began in 2001 through an experimental collaborative project between Sarai project of the Centre for the Study of Developing Societies and Ankur, a nongovernmental organization involving young people living is slums settlements and working class neighborhoods in Delhi. The main aim is to give a forum where young people not only explore their creativity but comment on the social and moral topics that impact their lives. The media labs of Cybermohalla are located in different parts of Delhi—four informal working-class settlements: LNJP, Dakshinpuri, Nangla Maanchi, and Ghevra—and provide opportunities to young people to work individually and collectively. The four settlements of Delhi, with around 60,000 to 400,000 inhabitants, have had a troubled existence and frequently faced governmental threats of demolitions and evictions. A significant number of inhabitants of the settlements are immigrants from other parts of India in search of work and a better life. In 2006, India's court ordered the demolition of the Nangla Maanchi settlement to pave the way for the construction of several shopping arcades and apartment complexes. The lab and the young practitioners from here have since relocated to the Ghevra settlement. When the Nangla Maanchi settlement was being demolished, several Cybermohalla practitioners wrote and recorded their poignant expressions in the form of booklets and blogs (Nangla, 2008). These printed and online narratives caught the attention of national media and have been quoted as instances of a specific genre of journalistic reporting combined with nuanced political critiques. Since its inception in 2001, around 450 young women and men from the settlements have been involved with the Cybermohalla Project. Their participation spanned a few weeks to a year or two. Some of these young participants continued their involvement serving as peers and mentors to the new practitioners.

The idea of a "mohalla," as a locality and neighborhood, exceeds the semantic connotations implied by the English term. As a social space, *mohalla*, with "its sense of alleys and corners," can be conceived as "dense nodes" where young people from economically deprived and marginalized communities carry out their everyday activities. Formal schooling is out of reach or unaffordable for the youth. They visit the lab out of curiosity but soon get absorbed in the creative possibilities offered by computers and other media. These young participants, mostly school dropouts ages 15 to 20, visit the Compughar (in Hindi, *an abode of computers*), a media lab with several low-cost desktop computers and free software, dictaphones (portable audio recorders), and digital and bromide print cameras to freely express their ideas and imaginations from the mundane to the serious. Working at the media lab, these participants write, draw, and sketch a range of interesting verbal and visual narratives and texts published as books, diaries, magazines, and wallpaper that become available in print and digitized formats.

Cybermohalla can be considered a participatory design project if we understand the concept of participatory design as adaptation and reconfiguration of distinct communication modalities to support the resistance of centralized power and capitalization. Participatory design also implies a "remediation" of existing media content, whether we take this to mean refashioning of collages of found objects or digitextual materials (Lievrouw, 2006). The following account (Cybermohalla) describes the philosophy of the project:

> One can approach the Cybermohalla project from many directions. One can begin with a critique of the technological imagination and the excessive universe of the dominant mediascape, and then go on to map a counter strategy which grounds itself on access, sharing and democratic extensibility. One can see it as an experiment to engage with media technologies and software 'tactically', and create multiple local media contexts emerging within the larger media network that the Internet seems to engender. Still one can see it as an engagement with local history, experiences, modes of expressions and creativity.

From this description, it is clear that Cybermohalla is about adopting alternative strategies to explore and engage the ICTs so as to provide young people opportunities for learning and education. The Hindi-Urdu words that are combined with English to produce terms such as "Cybermohalla" and "Compughar" capture the evocative and open-ended features of new media technologies. These technologies are not rooted in a singular space and place but as de-territorialized forms that offer unique possibilities for informal learning and can be actualized in non-linear ways. For instance, reflections of young participants on the everyday life in the city are sprinkled with personal experiences, creative self-expressions, and commentaries that offer some concrete suggestions on social and political issues. The ICTs also open up "spaces of dialogue" for the young participants: conversations and discussions lead to collective participation in a variety of multimedia experimental works. One of the coordinators and educators of Cybermohalla points out that "what binds them [the Cybermohalla practitioners] together is their experimentation and play with diverse media forms (photography, animation, sound recording, text, etc.) to improvise and create cross-media works—texts, collages, posters, print publications, videos, installations" (Figure 1.1).

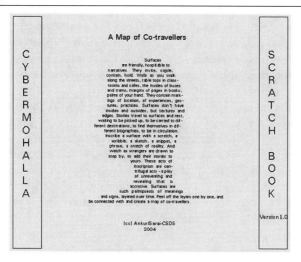

Figure 1.1 Scratch book as collage of forms (copyright Ankur, SARAI-CSDS)

The Cybermohalla Project is constituted in terms of four distinct yet interlinked networks of creative and communicative modalities: *generative contexts*, *minor practices*, *commoning*, and *public domain*. It is interesting to note that the particular words and phrases used to describe these areas have phenomenological and hermeneutic inflections. For instance, generative contexts (Sarai/Cybermohalla) refer to "gathering multiple narratives [that] produce the possibility of a dense and unstable archive of biographies, events and ordinary life," and minor practices "require an engagement with the self ... done in solitude, or with small groups." In commoning, young practitioners bring various forms of resources to the labs and, as part of their activities for the public domain, the Cybermohalla practitioners produce and take back a diverse range of materials—broadsheets, posters, booklets, radio programs, and wall writing, to their respective localities to initiate dialogue and conversations. On the one hand, the Cybermohalla Project places an emphasis on the virtual and the "cyber" (while the name itself suggests Cyber-Neighborhood or locality) aspects of community; on the other, it is about engagement with the poor urban communities and settlements of Delhi through the creative and critical appropriation of cyberspace and other media forms by young people. The Cybermohalla Project has also been characterized as an alternate educational initiative. Instead, it represents a radical pedagogic experiment in terms of how young people refashion diverse media forms to create multiple narratives about personal and social identities. Writing (mainly in Hindi-Urdu and English) is a critical component of the narrative process, although the audio-visual communicative modalities are equally important. On the one hand, the young people seem to appropriate ICTs as "*détournement*": that is, mixing and using dominant media forms toward revolutionary ends, and on the other, as producers and story tellers (*à la* Walter Benjamin) of a diverse range of narratives from the banal to the serious. In many respects, these narratives represent what Markus Meissen (2007) has characterized as "conflictual" participation, a form of critical engagement not soaked in deliberative discourse that seeks to produce consensus.

Anna Everett (2003, p. 7) points out that new media technologies have substantially refashioned our ideas of text. Thus, through the concept of digitextuality, she proposes that "new media technologies make meaning not only by building new text through absorption and transformation of other texts but by embedding the entirety of texts (analog and digital) seamlessly within the new." Furthermore, according to Everett, the various representational strategies of bricolage, collage, and other hybridized forms become more complex in the digital age. Similarly, Jay Bolter (2002) noted that the concept of remediation has analytic purchase in explaining the formal and cultural elements of media theory and, consequently, proposes remediation as a "bridge theory" that straddles the formal and cultural modalities. Indeed, the Cybermohalla practitioners combine the formal aspects of their work—in terms of "designers as producers"—with social and political critiques.[5] Though Bolter and Everett provide useful analytic strategies in examining a range of digitextual materials, I propose that Cybermohalla practitioners produce meanings through *hermeneutic appropriation* of the digitextual materials: that is, the young Cybermohalla practitioners create and develop narratives and stories as collaborators. For instance, the narratives are infused with newer meanings and interpretations acquiring symbolic and phenomenological density marked by colloquial and vernacular idioms of culture and language. These narratives become material artifacts whereby language and writing are woven with the auditory, sensory, and visual imaginaries of young Cybermohalla practitioners. Rather than treating these as semiotic constellations of meanings, it would be useful to consider the wide repertoire of communicative and narrative modalities as embodied practices.

Narrative Identity and Pedagogies of Engagement

Ricoeur's hermeneutic approach opens up a range of analytic possibilities that can be used to examine the multi-layered narratives and texts of Cybermohalla practitioners. According to Sandy Farquhar (2008, p. 8), in Ricoeur's hermeneutic philosophy, an essential feature of dialogue (and necessary precondition of interpretation) is its ability to distance the subject from the production of the text so that it can be viewed anew from different perspectives. It is the moment the text becomes distant, that its dialectical counterpart of appropriation comes into play. It is in the act of appropriation (keeping the text close) that we respond.

(Ricoeur, 1996) argued that the narrative modality of dialogue requires neither a consensus nor an impasse; rather, the hermeneutic of distancing and appropriation are essential features of dialogue. The digitextual narratives of Cybermohalla practitioners, much like what Ricoeur pointed out, do not seek "an easy dialectical synthesis or reduction of meaning" but instead invite creative and innovative interpretations. The narrative forms created by Cybermohalla practitioners as dense, multi-layered texts not only make visible their communicative praxis and their embodied subjectivities but reveal a strong desire to narrate both the banal and the serious in rather uncanny ways.

Talking about their initial experience at the locality labs, two young Cybermohalla practitioners, Neelofer and Babli Rai, point out how their writing has evolved through a deepening of conversations and relationships with fellow practitioners and peers at the labs but also reflect on how the process of writing has led them to a greater sense of participation and involvement with their community and neighborhoods. The reflections of Neelofer (2008) reveal how her embodied subjectivity, particularly the *ipse* part of her identity, had developed through her conversations and relationships:

> The Compughar (Locality Lab) is our own space. We write and share our texts with one another. Conversations, through which we share our ways of thinking and experiences, help expand and deepen our thoughts. Apart from writing, we also do sound recording, digital and analogue photography, and make animations as well on free software image manipulation tool, GIMP. We've also learnt a lot about how computers work. We've been working on creating forms that will help deepen the relationship of the lab with the locality, e.g. wall magazines, and now the locality public events. Our locality, i.e. the neighbourhood, is the link between the deepening and strengthening of the lab, and its extension and spread.

Babli Rai (2008) explains how creative uses of media forms have enabled a deepening of relationship with her own self, with fellow practitioners, and others in the community:

We have many relationships outside our family—relationship with our selves, with our environment, objects around us. Through writing, we allowed for these relationships to emerge, and to relate with them. Earlier, I used to see the walls of my house, the clock, the fan, the iron, the road. But when I started thinking about them, and writing, only then did I realize the intensity of my relationship with them. When we translate our texts into images, making palimpsests through animations, we feel our texts have also been given a new life. Through combinations of sound and text, text and image, image and sound, we give seriousness to our skills in each—just like an artisan gives form to his skills, an identity to the form, and a name to the identity.

The writings, a mixture of reportage, personal reflections, and fragmentary prose, borrow a repertoire of idioms, metaphors, and symbols from the colloquial and vernacular contexts. In describing and interpreting their life-worlds and the neighborhoods, the young people frequently raise questions of social justice, the failure of the state and local institutions in providing adequate shelter, health facilities, and educational opportunities. A closer look at the narratives indicates that their creative and critical expressions are neither contrived nor forced. Several young practitioners, mostly women, begin to express themselves via the computer screens. A bimonthly magazine, *Ibarat* (*Inscription*), explored various meanings of work in women's lives. The magazine in Hindi and English is made available in digital and printed forms. A series of creative writings in the form of diaries have been published into a book called *Galiyon Se* (*By Lanes*). These are a bunch of reflections and thoughts on the everyday life in the city. Here is one such reflection on streets and by-lanes:

> For the last one year now, I have been in regular conversation with the group of young people in Compughar. Amongst other things streets and lanes were discussed many times. Streets make for great conversations. Streets would lead us to think about the harsh and aggressive behaviour of men towards each other and towards women in particular, the total lack of pedestrian pathways or respect towards them, the absence of street lighting, noisy traffic and its uncaring behaviour, or the near-total inaccessibility for disabled people or elder people. Also being amidst strangers, in crowds and moving with crowds.

This young women's narrative account of the streets of Delhi offers some unique insights into what has become of the public places and spaces. Although this reads as a political critique, there are many more writings that offer some interesting solutions to civic life and public infrastructure in the city of Delhi. Some participants write about daily life around streets, some draw and sketch using graphics software presenting multiple perspectives on the topic. The digitextual materials produced become available to all participants and are distributed in the neighborhoods for further commentary and reflections. What emerges here goes beyond content creation to more complex and relevant forms of creative engagement with particular issues and topics that touch the lives of young people. As such, they can be considered important interventions that seek to broaden the terms of political and cultural discourses in some surprisingly innovative ways. For example, the questions of gender insensitivity and discrimination are taken up by various youth members of Cybermohalla in a variety of media forms—texts, collages, graphics, sound recordings, photographs, and video. A conversation between two young women practitioners, Azra Tabassum and Mehrunissa, recorded in the form of a Socratic dialogue called "The Zoo," is a searing critique on teasing in Delhi's public places. Shveta Sarda (2006), coordinator at the Cybermohalla, suggests that linking the broader environments of our digital worlds with the conversational worlds of our communities is central in understanding "publicness":

> The world of the digital surrounds us. In our lanes and by-lanes we live through a dense palimpsest of images, texts and sounds, increasingly accessed and accelerated through the digital—VCDs, CDs, Cable, PCOs, DTP operations (pamphlets, stickers, sign boards), etc. Through our own practice, we are trying to work out an interface between this density and our concerns. We use the digital to create for us a networked platform in our own explorations with texts, images and sounds.

Sixty young participants from three different labs—20 from each—have been involved in sketching ideas around this idea of "publicness." Working with a range of multimedia forms such as animations, booklets, broadsheets, HTML, typed and formatted texts, sound-scape, photo stories, written word, audio and visual juxtapositions or narratives, storyboards, and the like, members develop innovative perspectives on alleys, corners, mohallas, and locality—important metaphors for "publicness." Visiting the city alleys and corners, meeting disadvantaged children and other dwellers in the poor and working-class neighborhoods, young participants begin conversations with a young girl working in a factory, an old woman sweeping the streets of Delhi, to a middle-aged man who runs a photo studio, a shopkeeper, a tea stall owner, and so on.

Several young members have produced a collage called "Hamari Dilli" (Our Delhi) texts.

Young practitioners of Cybermohalla have been engaged in collecting artifacts, documents, and objects and then explore and map through these inanimate materials the life trajectories of poor individuals and families who have settled in the various localities over the years. The narratives rendered *vis-à-vis* through such diverse documents as a ration card, land survey notice, and identity papers are poignant accounts and stories of how the power of state and local institutions disrupts the lives of poor migrants. The fragmentary reflections of Cybermohalla practitioners, describing their personal family narratives caught up in the phantasmic world of documents, interspersed with several longer discussions, are reminiscent of Walter Benjamin's philosophical writings. The image and text reflection entitled "Paper Waits/Weights" was presented by the Cybermohalla Project at an International Colloquium on Information Society in Amsterdam in 2007. The reflection (Documents, 2008) states that "documents determine access to formal networks. Documents tell stories. Stories of broken lives, fragile access, combative claims, capacities of negotiation, dreams of mobility and more are part of the hidden transcripts of documents."

The "Walls" project draws upon ideas of publicness and locality to talk about how walls interact with and shape human experience. The experimental multimedia work being carried out by young participants connects ideas of dwelling and experience.

> Dwellings are made of walls. Our lived experience shows these walls are testimonies of fractured, fragile, contested stories of the everyday struggle to make life in the city. Walls are demolished. Walls get hardened. Fragile lives build themselves and reside along walls. Women gather around walls to share experience, youngsters lean against them to recount the day's stories from other parts of the city, infants rest in their shade.

The Cybermohalla project provides opportunities of self-expression and exploration for the young underprivileged people from Delhi. The new and old ICTs not only enable an enhanced participation in media but allow young participants a creative range of possibilities for commentary, critique, and dialogue. The approach to cyberspace and the new media as open-ended and globalized forms of communication with the ability to connect with localized forms of communication as embodied in the "mohalla" is an innovative feature. This overlapping of the local and global contexts offers media educator's theoretical and practical resources in creating flexible models of media pedagogy. What the young people seem to accomplish here is an important aspect of media engagement that pushes the boundaries of media pedagogy toward eclectic theory-praxis dialectic. Perhaps, an apt term would be to call these instances "pedagogies of engagement." Several years ago, Paul Willis (1996, p. 136, emphasis added) suggested that a great deal of symbolic work by young people needs to be considered educational, particularly when it involves

> making (not receiving) messages and meanings in your context and from materials that you have appropriated is, in essence, *a form of education in the broadest sense*. It is specifically *developmental part of symbolic work, an education about "the self" and its relation to the world* and others in it.

Toward Agonistic Public Spaces?

The narratives produced by the Cybermohalla practitioners, their creative and critical reflections, are marked by particular ideas about the "political" that seem to question the dominant understanding of terms such as participation and citizenship and civic engagement. As a form of radical pedagogy, these go beyond dominant notions of education. As a form of "direct education," they emulate what Paulo Freire had outlined through his philosophy of education: dialogical education through interaction with a focus on practice (or praxis). Indeed, this idea of "direct education" does not imply either romanticizing or privileging young people's experience; rather, experience, following McLaren (1993, p. 7), "is a way in which individuals confront the contingency of the present, the inevitable alternation of oppression, and the politics of daily living." The ICTs that the practitioners appropriate also open up "spaces of dialogue" for the young participants: conversations and discussions lead to collective participation in a variety of multimedia experimental work. It is the idea of the political in the Cybermohalla narratives that maps a more nuanced elaboration of participation and collaboration. This is particularly visible in the numerous writings organized under "Public Domain." Three bilingual books—*Galiyon Se* (*By Lanes*) in 2002; *Book Box* in 2003 and, more recently, *Bahurupiya Shehr* (*Polymorphous City*) in 2007—provide specific inflections to political questions about their neighborhoods, their localities, and the city. Yet, in all these and other collages of forms created, there is a strong *will to narrate* and mediate their subjectivities from the personal to the social in spatial and temporal contexts. For instance, the idea of "space"—whether as a conceptual abstraction, particularly in the reflections entitled, "The Edges of Questions" by Shamsher and a response from Suraj, or as concrete reality of their neighborhoods—becomes a central motif of their narratives (Figure 1.2).

Figure 1.2 A wallpaper by Cybermohalla practitioners

In the hermeneutics of Ricoeur, a narrative modality of dialogue does not seek consensus or impasse, but the act of distancing and appropriation of texts brings diverse perspectives in a state of tension—or as Ricoeur would indicate, a "corcordant discordance." The Cybermohalla practitioners complicate Ricoeur's notion of narrative modality by combining various digitextual media forms to produce multi-layered texts that are reconfigured in the process of distancing and appropriation. More specifically, the narratives of Cybermohalla practitioners point to a form of "critical" participation that cannot be interpreted through either a neo-liberal framework or Habermasian communication ethics. Through the twin processes of distancing and appropriation of the narratives, the Cybermohalla practitioners infuse newer meanings into the notions of participation and collaboration. An important characteristic feature of this is that these meanings are produced in praxis, not theoretical abstraction. Participation here can be construed as what Markus Meissen has termed as "conflictual" as it reaches a political dimension. Rather than seek a consensus through diffusing the tension, what is needed is to provide grounding and recognition of the legitimacy for different perspectives.

How do we make sense of pedagogic practices of the Cybermohalla practitioners, particularly their notion of participation? The work of Chantal Mouffe (2007, p. 5) may offer some provisional ideas in understanding the Cybermohalla Project in terms of an "agonistic pluralism." While distinguishing her approach from other perspectives, Mouffe outlines her concept of agonistic pluralism in relation to public spaces:

> Public spaces are always plural and the agonistic confrontation takes places in a multiplicity of discursive surfaces. While there is not predetermined centre to this diversity of spaces, there always exist diverse forms of articulation among them and we are not faced with any kind of dispersion envisaged by some postmodernist thinkers. Public spaces are always striated and hegemonically structured. A given hegemony results from specific articulation of diversity of spaces and this means that the hegemonic struggles consist in attempt to create a different form of articulation among public spaces.

This chapter argues that the Cybermohalla Project is engaged in sketching out a form of "agonistic" public space where participation and collaboration, following Florian Schneider (2006, p. 572), imply a form of "conflictual" engagement, and where, "collaboration is driven by complex and often diverse realities rather than romantic notions of common ground and commonality of interests."

Concluding Remarks

Although the conclusions offered here are provisional, I noticed the transformative possibilities of media in the hands of young people. Through the study of the Cybermohalla Project, this chapter looked at how the innovative uses and role of technology, particularly the old and new ICTs, provided a baseline for an examination of the way that young people engage the new media forms. Developing media materials in the form of graphics, text, page design and layout, design aesthetics, and digital constructions offered interesting opportunities to the young participants to become media makers. The idea of learning through content creation also includes designing the messages in creative and expressive ways. The combinations of media forms enabled the young people to creatively build media materials on a range of personal and social topics. The conversations between young participants revealed that they are not only capable of understanding complex issues but can act on these as well. The dialogues between the young people, their peers, media educators within the initiative, and the larger community pointed to aspects of participation and involvement that otherwise would not have been possible in other media and educational settings. An important aspect of the Cybermohalla initiative is the critique of the notion of "participation" that can be discerned in the creative and critical work of the youngsters. Through a series of personal and social narratives, young people pointed both to the problems and prospects in theorizing participation.

Through an explorative study of the Cybermohalla Project from India, this chapter points out that media educators continue to play an important role in inculcating and facilitating learning and education among young people through the process of collaboration. However, with the emergence of new media, the roles become increasingly complex and multi-faceted. This chapter argues that the new media forms at the hands of the young people complicate how ideas of education and pedagogy can respond to both local and broader concerns. This offers both a challenge and an opportunity for media educators and pedagogues to draw insights from global approaches while remaining attentive to local and national contexts.

Notes

1 Some of the ideas discussed are outlined in my UNESCO book, *Innovative Practices of Youth Participation in Media* (Asthana, 2006). An earlier version of this essay was accepted to the "Media in Transition 5: creativity, ownership and collaboration in the digital age" conference at the Massachusetts Institute of Technology in April 2007. This essay is based on research funded by the FRCAC Grant from the Middle Tennessee State University.

2 The hermeneutic approach refers to interpretation and meaning making involved in reading and appropriation of texts. More important, it sketches the notion of self and subject in terms of embodied subjectivities. The subsequent sections of the chapter discuss the hermeneutic approach drawing from the work of Paul Ricoeur in specific detail.

3 Praxis is understood "as a social or pedagogical process which enlists human efforts to understand the world more accurately in conjunction with a political will to transform social practices and relations" (Sholle and Denski, 1993).

4 Despite the celebratory tone and positive appraisals of scholars and experts on the role of ICTs in media pedagogy, one needs to be attentive to the fact that ICTs are indeed hegemonic and linked to flows of capital and global finance. In the context of Cybermohalla project, however, ICTs and new media are appropriated in terms of "dêtournement."

5 Ellen Lupton (1998), following Walter Benjamin's formulation of "author as producer" suggests that designers as producers mediate social and material reality wherein language becomes a raw material, theory is seen as practice, and writing a tool for social change.

References

Adajania, N. (2006). The sand of the coliseum, the glare of television, and the hope of emancipation. *Sarai Reader*, No. 6, 364–375.

Andrew, D. (2000). Tracing Ricoeur. *Diacritics*, 30(2), 43–69.

Appadurai, A. (2002). Deep democracy: Urban governmentality and the horizon of politics. *Public Culture*, 14(1), 21–47.

Asthana, Sanjay (2006). *Innovative practices of youth participation in media*. UNESCO, Paris.

Bolter, J. D. & Grusin, R. (1999). *Remediation: Understanding new media*, Cambridge, MA: MIT Press.

Bolter, J.D. (2002). Formal analysis and cultural critique in digital media theory. *Convergence*, 8(4), 77–88.

Chakrabarty, D. (2000). *Provincializing Europe: Postcolonial thought and historical difference*. Princeton and Oxford: Princeton University Press.

Chatterjee, P. (2004). *The politics of the governed: Reflections on popular politics in most of the World*. New York: Columbia University Press.

Cybermohalla (2008). *Cybermohalla* . Retrieved October 10, 2008 from Cybermohalla, http://www.sarai.net/community/saraicomm.htm.

Deuze, M. (2006). Participation, remediation, bricolage: Considering principle components of a digital culture. *The Information Society*. 22, 63–75.

Dewey, J. (1966). *Democracy and education: An introduction to the philosophy of education*. New York: Free Press.

Diouf, M. (2003). Engaging postcolonial cultures: African youth and public Sphere. *African Studies Review*, 46(2), 1–12.

Documents (2008). Retrieved October 10, 2008 from http://www.sarai.net/practices/cybermohalla/minor-practices/collecting-documents.

Everett, A. (2003). Digitextuality and click theory: Theses on convergence media in the digital age. In Anna Everett & John T. Caldwell (Eds.). *New Media: Theories and practices of digitextuality*, 3–28. New York and London: Routledge.

Farquhar, S. (2008). Narrative identity: Ricoeur and early childhood education. (Unpublished doctoral Dissertation, University of Auckland, 2008). Retrieved July 15, 2008 from http://hd1.handle.net/2292/2625.

Freire, P. (1972). *Pedagogy of the oppressed*, London: Penguin.

Gaonkar, D. P. (2002). Toward new imaginaries: An introduction. *Public Culture* 14(1), 1–19.

Lievrouw, L. A. (2006). Oppositional and activist new media: Remediation, reconfiguration, participation. *Proceedings of the ninth conference on participatory design: Expanding boundaries in design*, 1, 115–124. New York: ACM.

Leonardo, Z. (2003). Interpretation and the problem of domination: Paul Ricoeur's hermeneutics. *Studies in Philosophy and Education*, 22, 329–350.

Lupton, E. (1998). Designer as producer. In Steven Heller (Ed.). *The Education of a Graphic Designer* (pp. 159–162). New York: Allworth Press.

McLaren, P. (1993). Critical literacy and postcolonial praxis. *College Literature*, 19–20(3/1), 7–21.

Miessen, M. (2007). The violence of participation. *Eurozine*, 1–5.

Mouffe, C. (2007). Artistic activism and agonistic spaces. *Art & Research*, 1(2), 1–5. Retrieved October 1, 2008, from http://www.artandresearch.org.uk/v1n2/mouffe.html.

Nangla Labs (2008). *Evictions.* Retrieved July 10, 2008, from http://nangla.freeflux. net/.

Nayar, P. (2008). New Media, Digitextuality and public space: Reading "Cybermohalla." *Postcolonial Text*, 4(1), 1–12.

Neelofer (2008). *Our own space.* Retrieved October 15, 2008, from http://www.sarai. net/practices/cybermohalla/public-dialogue/books/book-box/text-imagesound.

Nijman, J. E. (2007). Paul Ricoeur and international law: Beyond 'the end of subject'. Towards a reconceptualization of international legal personality. *Leiden Journal of International Law*, 20, 25–64.

Obadare, E. (2004). The alternative genealogy of civil society and its implications for Africa: Notes for further research. *Africa Development*, XXIX (4), 1–18.

Rai, B. (2008). *Text-image-sound.* Retrieved October 15, 2008, from http://www.sarai. net/practices/cybermohalla/generative-contexts/locality-labs/our-own- space.

Ricoeur, P. (1996). *Oneself as another.* (K. Blamey, Trans.). Chicago/London: The University of Chicago Press.

Sarai/Cybermohalla (2008). *Practices.* Retrieved October 10, 2008 from http://www. sarai.net/practices.

Sarda, S. (2006). *Reflections.* Retrieved October 15, 2008, from Cybermohalla, http:// www.sarai.net/community/saraicomm.htm.

Schneider, F. (2006). Collaboration: The dark side of the multitude. *Sarai Reader*, 6, 370–382.

Sholle, D. & Denski, S. (1993). Reading and writing the media: Critical media literacy and postmodernism. In Colin Lankshear & Peter McLaren (Eds.). *Critical literacy: politics, praxis, and the postmodern.* Teacher Empowerment and School Reform Series. Albany, NY: State University of New York Press.

Williams, R. (1989). *Resources of hope: Culture, democracy, socialism.* New York: Verso.

Willis, P. (1996). *Common culture: Symbolic work at play in the everyday cultures of the young.* London: The Open University Press.

Chapter 2

Digital Pathways to Learning Through Collaborative Media Production

Kristin M. Bass and Elizabeth A. Bandy

Introduction

The emerging new media environment offers a wealth of possibilities for self-expression and communication, participation in social and civic life, and new job opportunities for young people. To take advantage of these opportunities, however, they need access to those technologies and mastery of the twenty-first-century skills required to use them. Through its Digital Pathways program, the Bay Area Video Coalition (BAVC), the nation's largest non-commercial media education and production facility, seeks to provide youths from low-income and minority backgrounds with the skills to contribute to and succeed in this new media environment. The program employs young people to use digital media arts to realize their creative voices, explore career options, and contribute to their communities.

This chapter describes the results of a two-year evaluation of Digital Pathways that assessed the development of twenty-first-century skills in two cohorts of Digital Pathways students and the sustained presence of those skills in program graduates. Analyses of student work demonstrate how youth not only learned how to produce media but also gained information gathering, critical thinking and collaboration skills. Interviews highlight the lasting impact of Digital Pathways on participants' perceptions of media and technology and their personal identities as media makers. The findings highlight the potential for a practical, skills-oriented media education program to enhance youths' critical understanding of media and of themselves as creators.

Media Education for the Twenty-First Century

Among media literacy scholars and practitioners, production- or skills-oriented programs such as this frequently raise concerns. National media literacy organizations such as the Center for Media Literacy (CML, 2009) and the National Association of Media Literacy Educators point out that the ability to produce messages via media, in and of itself, does not render one media literate. For example, the CML Web site (2008) states clearly that "it's not enough to know how to press buttons on technological equipment: thinking is even more important." This idea is especially salient given the rapidly evolving nature of new media technologies. It is increasingly clear that the "buttons" will change, and the skills needed to master and use twenty-first-century media extend beyond following step-by-step directions.

New media technologies are changing the ways people work, get information, and spend their leisure time. They are also changing the nature of media creators and consumers. Nearly two-thirds of online teens (ages 12–17) engage in some form of content creation. Moreover, most of those teens participate in conversations about the content they create and share (Lenhart, Madden, Macgill, & Smith, 2007). To engage with new media in this way, young people need to learn a host of skills that extend beyond the technical to include the abilities to learn from and collaborate with others, to create, share and reflect on content, and to navigate information in multiple forms (Jenkins, 2006).

Though overall access to online media is high among all teens, of those youths who are creating content online only 23 percent live in urban areas and only 13 percent live in households with incomes of less than $30,000 a year (Lenhart *et al.*, 2007). Young people who do not master the technical, cognitive, and social skills required for success in this new media environment will not be able to fully participate in twenty-first-century society on either a social or a professional level.

The Digital Pathways Program

Digital Pathway's model is designed to engage underserved young people in media and technology through media projects that are relevant to the students' lives and their communities. In doing so, Digital Pathways seeks to prepare young people for careers in digital media technology. Digital Pathways also supports young people in their transition from school to career through a media technology internship program in which students help to produce digital media projects at nonprofit organizations and businesses.

All students who participated in the Digital Pathways program were selected through an application and interview process. Between 2006 and 2007, a total of 116 youths in grades nine through college freshman participated in the Digital Pathways program evaluation across three cohorts. The program evaluation included 81 students in the second and third cohorts of digital arts and video tracks. One goal of Digital Pathways was to involve traditionally underserved youths in media and technology production. Of the 81 students evaluated, 44 percent were female, 91 percent were low income (64 percent extremely low), and less than 10 percent identified themselves as Caucasian. The video classes discussed in this chapter included 45 students.

Students who participated in the program during the evaluation period chose between two tracks, video or digital arts. In each track, students took a beginning and an advanced course, followed by an internship. Classes of approximately 15 students met two times a week for approximately two hours throughout the spring (Advanced, Cohort 2), summer (Beginning, Cohort 3), and autumn (Advanced, Cohort 3) of 2006. In the video track, students learned video production and post-production on Final Cut Pro. In the digital arts track, students learned HTML, Dreamweaver, Photoshop, Illustrator, and Flash. This chapter focuses on outcomes of the evaluation of the video track.

In the beginning video class, students created individual pieces designed to help them develop story-telling skills and individual style using technology. In the advanced video class, students worked collaboratively to create a video piece on a community issue. The Digital Pathways program incorporated a sequence of design-feedback-revision as students prepared their final projects. Students pitched story ideas and then worked to refine them using a story, conflict, message, audience, aesthetic (SCMAA) mnemonic. Once they had developed an initial version of their video pieces, students screened their work for teachers, peers, and invited media professionals at a Rough Cut Review, sessions designed for critical feedback and reflection. They had the opportunity to incorporate feedback and revise their work before making final presentations to their classmates and then to invited guests at public presentations.

BAVC's Digital Pathways program infuses its technical production courses with opportunities for students to develop essential twenty-first-century skills. All production activities, from initial planning to final presentations, were designed to help students learn and practice the media literacy skills of analyzing and evaluating their work and others. Each of these steps offered students the opportunity to reflect on the media creation process, culminating in a reflective task known as the *Director's Statement* in which students discussed the goals and outcomes of their final pieces.

Program Evaluation

Rockman *et al*, a research and evaluation firm in San Francisco, CA, worked with BAVC as the external evaluator for Digital Pathways under a grant from the National Science Foundation's Innovative Technology

Experiences for Students and Teachers (NSF ITEST) program. The evaluation activities were designed to investigate the impact of the program on twenty-first-century skills such as communication, media analysis, and community engagement.

Evaluation Framework

BAVC designed the Digital Pathways program to extend beyond teaching production skills to encompass the skills necessary for life and work in the twenty-first century. In designing the evaluation, we turned to The Partnership for Twenty-First-Century Skills (2003). The Partnership has identified the skills necessary for success in education and employment in the twenty-first century, as follows:

1   Information and communication skills

   a   *Information and media literacy skills*: Analyzing, accessing, managing, integrating, evaluating, and creating information in a variety of forms and media; understanding the role of media in society
   b   *Communication skills*: Understanding, managing, and creating effective oral, written, and multimedia communication in a variety of forms and contexts

2   Thinking and problem-solving skills

   a   *Critical thinking and systems thinking*: Exercising sound reasoning in understanding and making complex choices, understanding the interconnections among systems
   b   *Problem identification, formulation, and solution*: Ability to frame, analyze, and solve problems
   c   *Creativity and intellectual curiosity*: Developing, implementing, and communicating new ideas to others, staying open and responsive to new and diverse perspectives

3   Interpersonal and self-directional skills

   a   *Interpersonal and collaborative skills*: Demonstrating teamwork and leadership; adapting to varied roles and responsibilities; working productively with others; exercising empathy; respecting diverse perspectives
   b   *Self-direction*: Monitoring one's own understanding and learning needs, locating appropriate resources, transferring learning from one domain to another

    c   *Accountability and adaptability*: Exercising personal responsibility and flexibility in personal, workplace, and community contexts; setting and meeting high standards and goals for one's self and others; tolerating ambiguity

    d   *Social responsibility*: Acting responsibly with the interests of the larger community in mind; demonstrating ethical behavior in personal, workplace, and community contexts

In the overall evaluation, and in this chapter, this framework guides our data analysis and discussion of outcomes.

The initial evaluation included a series of research questions and encompassed the digital arts and video tracks and the internships. Because BAVC maintains an active database of graduated students, we were also to gather follow-up data from students after they left the Digital Pathways program. This chapter includes data from two areas of the evaluation:

- *Analysis of student work, video track.* What is the nature and quality of student work in the Digital Pathways digital arts and video classes? What kinds of decisions do students make in their work? What is the evidence of twenty-first-century skills seen in (1) students' products and (2) their articulation of the process behind their pieces?
- *Graduates.* What is the impact of Digital Pathways on graduates' (1) college and career choices, (2) understandings of and attitudes toward media and technology, and (3) application of twenty-first-century skills?

Evaluation Activities

The evaluation consisted of a series of observations and data collection instruments, which were created in collaboration with Digital Pathways staff. These instruments were designed to meld with the curriculum and student activities as much as possible, such as director's statements (discussed later) that mirror similar pieces by media professionals. Evaluators observed and took notes at the Rough Cut Reviews and final class and public screenings. In addition to these observations, evaluators analyzed students' Revisiting Your Story worksheets completed after the Rough Cut Reviews, and director's statements, and designed a rubric to evaluate the quality of students' final products. Complete details about the technical quality of students' pieces, including an analytic rubric used to rate story and production elements, can be found in the final evaluation report (Rockman *et al*, 2007).

To provide guidance for the types of information students should include in their director's statements, they were given the following prompts:

1   What led you to make this piece?
2   What inspired you to make this piece?
3   What was the message you wanted to communicate in your piece?
4   How did your artistic decisions help to support your message?

The advanced video students were asked several additional questions about collaboration:

1   What was your role(s) in the collaboration? What were the role(s) of the other team members? (Did everyone do everything, did you split up jobs, did you take turns being the driver? Who did what?)
2   What was helpful about collaborating?
3   What perspectives did you bring to the project?
4   What perspectives did the other team members bring to the project?
5   What was challenging about collaboration?
6   What did you do to work out the challenges?

These director's statements provided some of the richest data collected during the evaluation and offered insights into students' production processes, problem solving, and growth as media creators and individuals.

To add a final layer to the evaluation of the students' work, ushers distributed surveys to audience members during the public screenings of students' video pieces. These surveys asked respondents about their impressions of the pieces and the Digital Pathways program in general. There was an estimated return rate of about 25% per screening.

For the follow-up evaluation with program graduates, telephone interviews were conducted with former students regarding their experiences with the Digital Pathways program and its impact on them. Students were asked about their current work/educational status, their future goals, and their perceived impact of the program. Although these data come exclusively from self-reports, these interviews allowed us to revisit themes from the program evaluation and explore Digital Pathway's potential for lasting impact.

Evaluation Findings

Though the evaluation encompassed all students in cohorts two and three, in this section we present two case studies that offer an in-depth review of the process a few students engaged in as they progressed through the beginning and advanced video classes and produced their final pieces.

When the students set out to make videos, they had multiple things to consider. What role would each take in the process and how would work be divided? What story would they choose to tell and how would it connect to their communities and their own voices? How would they convey their story and make it compelling for others? What format would they choose? What techniques and devices would they employ? Each story below highlights aspects of this process and the different struggles, decisions, and outcomes of two pairs of youth producers. In particular, we focus on the ways in which students were able to collaborate with one another to solve production problems and create inspiring, socially relevant messages in original ways.

After the case study descriptions, we discuss the twenty-first-century skills development observed in these cases and among the students as a whole during their participation in the beginning and advanced video classes. We then consider the lasting influence of Digital Pathways as voiced by program graduates.

Telling an Inspiring Story: The Case of Jake and Cindy

A bad case of senioritis was Cindy and Jake's unlikely catalyst for a documentary that inspired the producers and audiences alike. Skipping class one day, Jake came across a man in his high school courtyard and, in search of an idea for his next BAVC project, Jake asked the man whether he had any stories that would inspire him. The man, who turned out to be a former teacher at Oakland Tech High School, told Jake about a group of remarkable students he'd advised in the late 1970s. Calling themselves the Apollos, the students successfully lobbied the California state legislature to make Martin Luther King Jr.'s birthday a state holiday.

When Jake relayed this story to his production partner, Cindy, she unsuccessfully searched the Internet for information, later recalling "You'd think something this important would be documented online ... But I guess not" (Berton, 2008). Jake and Cindy explained in their directors' statements that they had wanted "to increase youth involvement in social issues" and found the Apollos to be a powerful example. Through the Apollos' story, Jake and Cindy could demonstrate how a group of high school students from an urban and traditionally minority, low-income area took on an important social issue, made their voices heard, and effected real change. They knew that they wanted to tell this story—but how?

Cindy and Jake ultimately produced a six-minute documentary chronicling the Apollos's efforts as told by one of the original students and their faculty advisor. The interviews were interspersed with archival materials that included shots of still photographs and newspaper clippings documenting the Apollos's journey. This material was framed by a voiceover of segments from Dr. King's speeches. Adding one more voice, the piece opened with a shot of Jake explaining how he had learned about the Apollos. He reappeared later in the documentary to explain how the students "decided to make a law because they believed in something" and how their story should not be forgotten.

Audiences who viewed the film were impressed with the story and the way it was told. At the final in-class presentation, one of the invited guests, an instructor for another of the BAVC's youth media programs, said the documentary looked like it had come from PBS. Another BAVC media arts instructor commented on the rhythm and pacing of the piece, noting that the editing was very good. She said that Jake and Cindy had shown how students could make a difference. Fellow Digital Pathways students appreciated Jake's putting himself into the piece, as one stated, "having you in it completed the whole movie." At the public screening for family and friends, audience survey comments included "story is fantastic, well paced footage"; "I loved the subject; part of history not known"; "taught me something new"; and "clean, powerful, inspiring." Jake later observed of his experience with the film, "I got to see how our work can impact other people ... which was cool because their work [the Apollos] had an impact on us" (Berton, 2008).

Jake and Cindy created a final product that effectively conveyed a compelling story. The piece they ultimately created resulted from their unique abilities and experiences and the ways they combined them. We can trace the development of some of the skills and abilities demonstrated in *The Apollos* in the two producers' earlier work in their beginning video class.

Jake's beginning video piece, *Basketbol*, presented basketball as "a game that connects the local to the global and translates across cultures and languages" (director's statement). At the final class presentation, Jake explained that he had revised his piece significantly after the Rough Cut Review, keeping the story but improving its technical quality. Though Jake was a good story teller, editing was admittedly not his strong suit. The version of *Basketbol* he showed at the review offered a "jumbled mix of shots" that he worked to fix and clean for the final product.

Though Jake edited his first piece to clean up shots and improve pacing, Cindy's beginning video piece relied on strong editing skills to help her pull together a story. In her beginning video director's statement, Cindy observed, "usually when I make a video, I come up with a loose theme, shoot lots of footage and see if it comes together in the editing stage." Cindy's final piece, *Lovebirds: The Story of Rose and James Jones*, evidences this process. Through a voiceover of interview excerpts, Cindy's grandparents describe some of their history and how they met.

However, the strength of the piece lies in the visual imagery and editing. Cindy invites the audience into her grandparents' lives through a collage of still images of objects in their home.

Thus, each of *The Apollos* producers brought individual strengths and weaknesses to their collaboration. When Jake and Cindy came together to work on their advanced video project, they had to recognize and play on their own and each other's strengths in positive ways. Cindy described the collaboration in this way:

> The collaboration with Jake worked out nicely because we were able to use both of our strengths to make the documentary. Jake used his gift for storytelling to create a basic structure and storyline for the video. I took his idea, and edited it to make more complete. If it weren't for Jake, I would have been left without a story, and without me he wouldn't have had the technical support necessary to complete the documentary. During our collaboration Jake and I worked very well together, and without each of us the film wouldn't have been completed (director's statement).

Jake made similar role delineations in his statement about the collaboration, but he also noted situations wherein the two producers shared the same role:

> My role in the collaboration of *The Apollos* was primarily focused on vision and executing expressing that vision. Cindy's role was to formulate a coherent but beautiful story out of many lengthy interviews. We both had an equal part in the development of the story and how the story was being presented. We molded our good qualities as filmmakers and produced a very balanced piece. We both brought different ideas to the table and sifted through the ones that didn't emphasize our point 'till we had a few powerful snippets. Other than that the whole process was very positive on both ends due to the compatibility in personalities between us both (director's statement).

Overall, Cindy and Jake were able to complement each other's skill sets as they made mutual decisions about the content and style of their documentary. The end result of their pairing was praised for the thoughtfulness of its message, the professionalism of its composition, and the potential of its impact on audiences.

Merging Artistic Styles: The case of Simone and Henry

The second case, the creation of a piece on drug use entitled *Use, Misuse and Abuse*, brought together two students with diverse styles, perspectives, and experiences. Simone, an eighth-grader, was the youngest student in her class whereas Henry was a high school junior—an enormous age gap by adolescent standards. During their collaboration, the younger and less assertive Simone had to learn how to express her opinions to the older and more dominant Henry. Moreover, the students' artistic styles were quite different. Simone chose to use animation and drawings to tell serious stories in a humorous way. Henry leaned toward a traditional documentary style of "talking heads" and b-roll video footage to inform audiences about lesser-known social issues. The students clearly demonstrated these styles in their individual, beginning video pieces.

Both Simone's and Henry's initial pieces conveyed socially important messages, albeit in very different ways. Simone described her piece, *String Bean Loser*, in the following way: "If you think you can pick on a shy 7th grade girl and get away with it, think again. With humor, pathos and integrity, Simone guides us through the heartache of being teased and the sweet taste of revenge" (director's statement). Her three-minute video described an experience she had had the previous year when her teacher called her "String Bean" because of her thin, tall frame. She ultimately spoke up, told administrators about what happened, and received an apology from the teacher. Simone explained in her director's statement that this video was part of a series of vignettes that she wanted to make about the challenges of being a seventh-grader and how to make the "right" choices. In this piece, she "wanted people to know that if someone says or does something that makes you feel bad, you should not be afraid to speak up for yourself" (director's statement).

Demonstrating her unique style, Simone's video piece consisted entirely of cartoon-style line art sketches that often featured thought or word balloons expressing the character's feelings (Figure 2.1). These illustrations were connected with a voiceover narrative.

Simone originally intended to create a piece that combined live action with illustrations but ended up cutting the live sequences to keep the piece within the assignment's time limit. She was pleased with the end result: "As this was my first animation, it was interesting to see how drawings and stories can take on a life of their own in video" (director's statement). The audience at the final class presentation was also impressed, complimenting the quality of Simone's narrative and the honesty of her emotions.

Henry's beginning video piece also tackled a subject of personal and social importance. His video considered how different audiences perceive

Figure 2.1 Screen shot from *String Bean Loser*

street art, particularly graffiti. In his director's statement, he explained, "With media, I want to raise awareness about local issues in local communities. I made this video to clear up the negative misconceptions people have about graffiti. I also wanted to acknowledge the existence of graffiti as an accepted form of street art."

Henry combined commentary about the illegal nature of graffiti with an interview from a street artist to contrast the idea of graffiti as a destructive act with opinions that street art is a constructive form of personal expression. This contrast was further enhanced with images of graffiti-tagged buildings and framed street art displayed at a gallery opening. Henry concluded his piece by asking "Now that we've perceived the work of graffiti artists from a more comprehensible perspective, does that make it more acceptable to be seen on the street in appropriate locations?" and closing with a black screen. In an earlier version of the piece, Henry had placed the words "you decide" into the screen but removed them after suggestions that he let the art speak for itself.

Though both Simone and Henry created pieces that represented strong voices and perspectives, they approached their beginning video projects in quite different ways. The primary challenge for their advanced video project was how to respect each other's ideas and styles. Their chosen topic, teenage drug use, which they later refined to focus on the abuse of commonly available medicines, provided an initial point of cohesion. In the director's statement, Henry explains their message as follows:

> We want to change how parents and teens look at prescription drugs. We want parents to worry more about the easy access to pills in their own homes and not as much about the illegal drugs (and alcohol)

that are usually a lot harder to find and obtain than prescription and over-the-counter drugs in the house. Parents need to understand that their child could be taking pills when their gone or when they lest expect it. We want teens to understand that they should only take pharmaceuticals for medicinal purposes, under the supervision of their parents and/or doctors. We want their perception on this issue to be bolstered through parental and teenage insight that explain why they need to be careful around pharmaceuticals.

Their documentary described the types of prescription and over-the-counter drugs abused by adolescents, the reasons why teenagers abuse them, and the consequences of misuse. Facts about the accessibility of household drugs were reinforced with personal observations about the risks of prescription drug abuse from a teenager and a parent of a teenager.

To tell this story, the two producers combined the straightforward format of interviews and voiceover narrative preferred by Henry with Simone's technique of cartoon-style drawings and humor. The decision to use drawings emerged from several fronts. Simone enjoyed drawing and had already seen its value for telling stories. That experience proved fortuitous when Simone and Henry had trouble taping desired scenes using live action reenactments. Simone "drew parts of the movie where it helped the story and would have been difficult to shoot the scene" (director's statement).

At a public screening of the videos, Simone explained that she was the youngest student in her video class and that at first she found working with a partner to be difficult. As her *String Bean Loser* piece demonstrated, however, Simone was not one to give up her voice. Though Henry had a clear vision for the story and how he wanted to tell it, Simone stood up for her ideas. She insisted, for example, that though it was okay to have an important and educational message, the video should not take itself too seriously. As a result, her animations not only advanced the narrative but added some humor to an otherwise dark subject matter.

Throughout the piece, Simone's drawings dramatized the inner struggles of drug users (Figures 2.2 and 2.3.).

People who viewed multiple versions of the piece felt the animations were extremely effective. At the Rough Cut Review, most of the drawings had not yet been completed. The rough cut contained interviews, b-roll (e.g., a live image of a teen rummaging through a medicine cabinet), and most or all of the voiceover that was going to be used. At the screening of the final cut, a peer teacher said that the added drawings really clarified the relationships between the interviews and script and highlighted the story's multiple layers.

Figure 2.2 Screen shot from *Use, Misuse and Abuse*

Figure 2.3 Screen shot from *Use, Misuse and Abuse*

When viewing the final video piece, one can see the distinct styles and perspectives of Henry and Simone. Still, audiences singled out *Use, Misuse and Abuse* for the quality of its subject matter and animation and the choice of its interview subjects. Despite initial struggles to communicate and to respect one another's perspectives, the youth producers succeeded in telling their story with a style that was uniquely their own.

The cases of Jake and Cindy, and Simone and Henry provide two snapshots of what it was like to participate in Digital Pathways. Though students' pieces were all unique, their underlying process was common to everyone. Students moved from short individual videos to longer collaborative pieces. As these cases show, students' advanced pieces capitalized on the skills they had developed in their beginning class. The process also presented opportunities to revisit skills they had begun to master and challenged them to learn new skills related to advanced storytelling and collaboration.

Demonstration of Twenty-First-Century Skills in Digital Pathways Activities

Both of the cases discussed earlier illustrate how the Digital Pathways program helped students develop technical, critical, and interpersonal skills as they created video pieces, both individually and in collaboration. Similar stories of learning and growth can be found among the experiences of these four students' classmates. This section examines multiple categories of twenty-first-century skills development highlighted in the case studies and seen in the Digital Pathways video track evaluation as a whole.

The evaluation of Digital Pathways students revealed a full array of twenty-first-century skills acquisition, the most obvious of these being in the area of information and media literacy (Partnership for Twenty-First-Century Skills, 2003). This area includes both technical and production skills and critical media literacy skills. Clearly, students needed technical production skills to put together a finished piece. In most cases, students were so technically proficient that it was only the small, unintended discrepancies—an unflattering camera angle, an underlit scene, erratic audio levels—that betrayed the fact that they were still novices. Students also learned how to analyze media critically, a skill demonstrated frequently during the Rough Cut Reviews' peer feedback sessions and reiterated in the interviews of program graduates (see Lasting Impact section.).

A second group of twenty-first-century skills, thinking, and problem solving can be broken down into critical thinking and systems thinking; problem identification, formulation and solution; and creativity and intellectual curiosity (Partnership for Twenty-First-Century Skills, 2003). The very nature of the Digital Pathways assignments ensured that students would encounter many problems to solve and receive considerable leeway to demonstrate creativity in the process. As the case studies demonstrated, each solution was unique to the group that encountered the problem. Of all of the students in Digital Pathways, only Simone experimented with animation. Her solution of drawing scenes (in place of reenactments) for *Use, Misuse and Abuse* was, therefore, different from what anyone else in her class would have done in the same situation. Likewise, Cindy used newspaper articles about the Apollos in a way that none of her peers might have considered. Cindy's first piece celebrated her grandparents' long marriage by displaying images of their home. She used the same technique of still images and panning shots to document the public recognition of the Apollos's accomplishments.

Sometimes students discovered problems while they were working individually; other issues came to light from peer and adult feedback. The Rough Cut Review sessions gave students the opportunity to show a draft of their piece to an audience of peers, peer teaching assistants, instructors, and adult media professionals. After the session, students completed a worksheet that summarized (1) the feedback they had received on their message and the technical, creative elements, (2) their reactions to that feedback, and (3) the changes they were going to make in response. Students often reported fixing the visuals, adjusting the sound, or editing shots after their Rough Cut Reviews. Cindy decided after her review that she would end her beginning video piece with a shot of her grandparents. Until that time, she had planned to tell her grandparents' story only through inanimate objects; however, the audience wanted to see the people behind the voices and household items. Of course, students also had the option of ignoring feedback if it contradicted their intended message or style.

Students spent a great deal of time bringing their pieces together in the editing room. It was here that students' creativity and problem-solving skills were frequently put to the test. It was in the editing stage that a mix of shots became a story or that voiceovers and b-roll footage merged into a single narrative. One student observed, "I always feel that in the middle of editing, I hate my movie, but after it, I love it. And I hope the viewers do too."

A third category of twenty-first-century skills—interpersonal and self-directional skills—includes "Demonstrating teamwork and leadership; adapting to varied roles and responsibilities; working productively with others; exercising empathy; respecting diverse perspectives" (Partnership for Twenty-First-Century Skills, 2003, p. 9). The case studies illustrated the role of collaboration in two different productions. For Jake and Cindy, collaboration helped tell a compelling story. With Simone and

Henry, the merger of artistic styles led to a wholly unique message. These experiences were reflective of the students as a whole.

Evidenced throughout the discussion of the two case studies, students' director's statements were rich with details about how different groups shared ideas, resolved conflicts, and ultimately made videos that reflected all members' voices. One student observed:

> What was most challenging in working with others was when there were points of disagreement. We each have distinctly different styles, and as such, we were unable to concur on some points. But because there was some give and take in the decision-making, as all groups must have to be able to function, our film became a fusion of all of us, as it should be.

In spite of the challenges, students found lots of advantages in working as a team: "Working in a group really gave me the opportunity to bounce my ideas off of someone to get a better understanding of the direction I wanted to take the piece" and "Collaborating in groups was helpful as we would have more ideas to pursue. It also helped as we would give each other feedback."

Development of interpersonal and self-directional skills was seen not only within students' collaborations. Students also demonstrated respect for diverse perspectives by telling stories that were heretofore forgotten or unknown, sharing different ways to think about the world, and communicating socially relevant messages that pushed boundaries. In his first piece, Henry challenged conventional wisdom about the destructive nature of street art. In his second, he and Simone asked people to reconsider whether alcohol and marijuana were really the greatest drug threats to teenagers. Simone's *String Bean Loser* and Cindy and Jake's *The Apollos* showed how traditionally disenfranchised young people stood up for their beliefs, influenced people in power, and ultimately improved the world around them.

Digital Pathways students used media creatively as a force for change and described the desired impact of their pieces in their director's statements:

- Turn on the news channels and you'll understand why we made this film. We made this film to make people realize how missing people are portrayed on the news and emphasize how minorities are never represented when it comes to missing people. We personally feel that many of the major news corporations, (CNN, FOX NEWS, etc.) aren't telling you the whole story. We both decided to work on this film to get people aware of this situation. What really inspired us, or what really sparked the fire, was the massive coverage on the Laci Peterson case frenzy which can be seen still every once in a while in the news.

- I made this piece to show that anyone (immigrant) can make it in the U.S. ... I always was attracted to the stories that my family members would tell about there experiences. ... This message is aimed towards all people because we all at one point came immigrant ancestors.
- The idea behind the Apollos came from us wanting to increase youth involvement in social issues, so we decided to use a powerful example. ... Hopefully today's youth will learn from the Apollos and flex that metaphoric bicep in today's adult run society. We want youth around the world to know they too are world citizens and have a voice, USE IT.

In sum, students' video creation experiences required the application of multiple twenty-first-century skills. This skill development was not a secondary consequence of digital media production but rather an essential part of the process required for the creation of the final products. Though individual students may have been more competent at certain skills than others, they needed to develop each of the twenty-first-century skills to some degree to be able to create their pieces and communicate their messages to targeted audiences.

Lasting Impact: The Graduate Interviews

Interviews with Digital Pathways program graduates demonstrated how participants retained and transferred the twenty-first-century skills they had learned to other areas of their lives. In the interviews, students were asked about their current academic and/or career activities, whether Digital Pathways had changed their perceptions of media, and whether they applied what they had learned in Digital Pathways to other situations. Though these data are based on students' informal self-reports, they offer highly encouraging indicators of the program's potential for lasting impact in the areas of media making, media literacy, and career preparation.

Sixty-two of the students who completed BAVC's Digital Pathways program (either digital arts or video) participated in follow-up interviews. Of those who were in college at the time of their interviews and had declared a major, half were engaged in a field related to media or creative arts (e.g., film, audio, graphic design, communication). Moreover, almost two-thirds of the students (38) said they were working on video or design projects, including videos for school, family, or private clients; music productions for schools or friends' groups; and Web sites for private clients and community organizations. Students identified several differences between their current projects and the ones they had done for Digital Pathways, such as more limited access to technology, more production-oriented, and different topics (fiction vs. documentary) or media formats (e.g., a digital arts graduate now working in video, a video graduate working with audio).

Graduates reported that Digital Pathways had a significant impact on their area of study or employment and their perceptions of media and technology. Eighty percent of respondents said that Digital Pathways influenced their decisions about their primary area of study or employment. Graduates talked about Digital Pathways empowering them with interests, skills, and career opportunities that they did not realize they had:

- Digital Pathways opened up a new option to me, an option that I would like to pursue. After doing the program, I realized how much you can do. That had a huge impact on me.
- I got job experience, new friends and video experience. Digital Pathways was a first step for me for something outside of anything I had done before ... I was stepping outside of my element and world and trying something new. This makes me truly want to seek out new opportunities and experiences.
- It did influence what I want to do. I want to take production and film analysis classes. Before I would have never thought of that as something I'm interested in. Now I see, especially through taking Chicano classes, I'm interested in art that raises awareness.
- Reading and math were nothing to look forward to, but video and audio really caught my attention. After BAVC I realized I wanted to pursue a career in it. Realizing this gave me reasons to go see the counselors and ask them about classes I didn't even know they had in college. They told me about the audio classes at City College ... My goal is to do audio engineering and also video.

Other graduates said that Digital Pathways helped them stick with interests they already had in media making:

- I wasn't sure about majoring in film, I was flirting with it, but I made a definite decision to make film afterwards—it's really what I want to do.
- Before it was just a hobby, I had done it as an elective at school. I liked it, but wasn't taking it that seriously. Digital Pathways made me think about how I could use the skills I learned for a career for the future.

- I took Digital Pathways because I wanted to make a portfolio. Digital Pathways influenced me to stay in that field of study. It increased my media literacy and boosted my art creativity to produce more. Real artists are constantly making stuff.
- I already had the idea to study film, that is what brought me to Digital Pathways ... but it was a vague notion. From my Digital Pathways experience, I got confidence that film is a path for me and what will make me happy in life (for now).

One goal of the Digital Pathways program was to give traditionally underrepresented youths a sense of themselves as the creators of media messages with unique voices, rather than just as consumers. Not only were most graduates working on media-related projects; many explicitly identified themselves as media-makers:

- I think that I can have a part in the media and that I can make it, rather than just watch it or read it.
- You have influence. I learned pre-production, which is essential. That's where you get the idea and structure for how you will do everything. You get a good idea and you have to take the right stance from the beginning. You need to get the message out to whomever you want, and make it powerful. It needs to have a psychological effect.
- I used to think media was just news, but now media is a vehicle to put your own voice out there for other people to see what you think.
- I think with media, the stories we tell can impact a lot of people, and educate people about your community and your ideas.
- My experience of making Tent City changed my perspective of how you can use media to change the world. I see media as a way to affect community and bring awareness to certain things. Like journalism, I was using my camera to educate and report to people what is going on in the world and things that are important.

Students also reported sustained application of critical media literacy skills. Almost all students (92 percent) said that since Digital Pathways, they thought about media differently. They became better able to analyze media, both in terms of the production elements used and the implicit or explicit messages being conveyed:

- I notice a lot of things when I watch a movie. If a position isn't right, if it's not consistent, I notice. I don't think about just the plot, I think about the storyboarding and the production. I know what it's like to produce a video, for a director to direct the actors. I know how to do the setup, the camerawork, I know the different kinds of angles.

- I know that all media has an intent. Everything I see now is designed for a certain audience. The design is targeted that way. When I watch movies, I understand the hard work it takes to make a simple 30-second PSA.
- I feel like what's in the media is not the whole truth. Digital Pathways showed me how much work you have to put into it in order to get a story or make a website that will attract people. I understand that people might not always be that interested if they tell the whole story all at once.
- I used to be suckered in. Now I analyze every ad that's on media today, like why is that naked woman being used to sell a car? I look at what they're trying to do. I talk about Disney shows and what messages they're trying to send to kids. I analyze what they're wearing. My girlfriend thinks it's annoying, but I like it.

Almost all graduates (89 percent) said they had been able to apply some or a great deal of what they had learned from Digital Pathways. When probed for examples, 52 graduates identified 64 separate applications. Evaluators analyzed the graduates' responses for evidence of twenty-first-century skills learning and application.

Nearly two-thirds (62.5 percent) of the skills graduates mentioned were information and communication skills, such as analyzing different forms of media or creating multimedia communication. Graduates talked about directly applying skills they had learned in Digital Pathways to their own media projects. Examples included the following:

- I shot a wedding, I shot a couple of basketball games. Before Digital Pathways, I didn't know about getting the best picture and focus, white balancing, getting the best color. Because of what I learned, I was able to get a better picture. I learned terms, how to focus, the rule of thirds. I know how to shoot a better picture.
- I incorporate the stuff I learned and in class and in the internship for school, like when I was designing a website, I knew about colors, what's original and what isn't, creativity, and having interest in what you're actually doing. In my BAVC internship, it gave me an edge because what my internship supervisor wanted us to do was mostly what I was doing in Digital Pathways. He went through the same steps and process that I did when I was learning web design.

The next most common set of skills mentioned were interpersonal and self-directional skills, with 29.7 percent of responses fitting this category. Graduates described how Digital Pathways taught them to work in groups, organize busy schedules and persist in difficult situations:

- In Digital Pathways I was constantly working with people, meeting with people from different backgrounds, working with them.
- When I was in a group in my civics class, I took what I learned from handling tense situations, and was a mediator. Before Digital Pathways I did not know I was good at this, and it turns out I am.
- In some of the programs I'm working with now, at times I feel pessimistic, and feel that the program won't work out. Digital Pathways taught me to push myself. I try to think positively and encourage myself to stay focused and put hard work into what I'm doing. It helped open more doors for me and helped make great work come out of something I wasn't sure about.

The remaining applications of twenty-first-century skills (7.8 percent) were either explicit mentions of thinking and problem-solving skills or general comments about applying everything learned. In two instances, graduates mentioned being able to help friends with technology problems (e.g., "Everybody comes to me for help with projects. A lot of classes help with a video presentation. I either film or help edit their projects").

Recall that Digital Pathways had multiple goals: to teach practical digital media production skills, to encourage further educational and career opportunities in media and technology, and ultimately to diversify the media and technology field. The previous findings provide evidence of how the program has met its short- and long-term goals. One graduate's story in particular represented the total impact of Digital Pathways on a student's personal and professional development.

In Justin's interview for the Digital Pathways program, he said, "I always thought my life should be a movie." Once admitted to the program, Justin's first video explored stereotypes about race and ethnicity that had personal relevance. Beyond his productions, he said that Digital Pathways became his "safe space," the one place in the city where he did not have to look over his shoulder. After graduating from Digital Pathways, Justin attended an out-of-state college. Still, he returned to BAVC during every school vacation to visit with staff and use the resources for the films he was currently making. Here is how Justin described his post–Digital Pathways media making:

> I am making short films and directing music videos. I've been making the films about things in my environment that will make a positive change. I've been doing them on my own. I've liked music my whole life. Joining BAVC gave me a new love for film. I've been able to incorporate two things that I love. I'm also working on a documentary called Bigger Than the Block, showing youth that they can make it. We interview artists and entrepreneurs who are very successful and

hopefully influence these people to not stand on the corner selling drugs, but to have a goal in life ...

When asked what he got out of Digital Pathways, Justin responded:

I got a life-changing experience. I got a purpose. I want to do something in life besides a pencil-pusher 9 to 5 type of job. With film you're interacting with your job, so it makes it a lot more fun. ... It's a great opportunity. Being in the program opens a lot of doors for you. I don't see what I'd be doing with myself right now if I hadn't attended. ... I wouldn't change it for anything.

Discussion

We introduced this evaluation by stating that BAVC worked, through its Digital Pathways program, to provide students with opportunities to develop critical media literacy and twenty-first-century skills in the context of practical digital media production education. In reality, these skills sets have become increasingly interconnected and interdependent. The idea behind twenty-first-century skills is not that, for instance, collaboration is a new skill for the new century. Rather, organizations such as The Partnership for Twenty-First-Century Skills have delineated the types of skills and abilities required to work and live in an environment of new digital technologies. To engage in activities using those technologies, young people must be able to apply those skills.

If they had not learned to work together, solve problems, and respect one another's ideas, neither Cindy and Jake nor Henry and Simone would have been able to create successful video projects. Yet, students were not simply expected to master these skills on their own. The Digital Pathways program curriculum and instructors were committed to helping students practice the various skills. Though students were asked to collaborate on the advanced video projects, this task came only after they had the opportunity to develop their own technical skills and creative voices through individual projects in the beginning classes. Furthermore, students were given multiple opportunities to reflect on both their process and products and to incorporate feedback from their peers, instructors, and media professionals. These reflection opportunities helped students develop both technical and critical media skills.

Part of the students' reflection process evolved from our approach to the evaluation. Rather than measuring twenty-first-century skills development through an external survey, our evaluation captured evidence of these skills by looking at the artifacts—from rough cuts to worksheets to question-

and-answer sessions—that students created throughout the program. Further, the two data collection instruments we added to the curriculum, the director's statements and a video rubric, were designed to be a logical extension of the students' existing work. This "embedded evaluation" approach measured twenty-first-century skills in a way that was valuable not only to the evaluators but also to the Digital Pathways staff. Indeed, the instructors and students used the director's statements and video rubrics as tools to monitor and improve student learning after the evaluation ended.

Overall, the evaluation indicated growth in student achievement from beginning to advanced classes and lasting influence on the graduates, suggesting that the Digital Pathways model of classes and internships is effective for preparing students for the new media and technology environment. Building on what they learned through the process of this evaluation, BAVC continues to train students through its Digital Pathways program, currently offering audio and video production tracks. Recently, they added two advanced digital pathways tracks in audio production and 3-D animation and gaming. The advanced program will give students who have graduated from Digital Pathways an opportunity to take their artistic visions "to the next level" and gain a deeper exposure to media design and technology. As media consumers, we can all look forward to the creative expressions of new ideas that these students are sure to generate.

References

Berton, J. (2008, July). Student film tells of drive for King holiday. *San Francisco Chronicle*, p. E-1.

Center for Media Literacy. (2009). *Promotional materials*. Retrieved January 3, 2009, from the World Wide Web: http://www.medialit.org/reading_room/article540.html.

Jenkins, H. (2006). *Confronting the challenges of participatory culture: Media education for the twenty-first-century (Part One)*. The John D. and Catherine T. MacArthur Foundation. Retrieved November 5, 2008, from http://digitallearning.macfound.org/site/apps/nlnet/content2.aspx?c=enJLKQNlFiG&b=2108773&content_id={CD911571-0240-4714-A93B-1D0C07C7B6C1}&notoc=1.

Lenhart, A., Madden, M., Macgill, A. R., & Smith, A. (2007). *Teens and social media: The use of social media gains a greater foothold in teen life as they embrace the conversational nature of interactive online media*. Pew Internet and American Life Project. Retrieved November 5, 2008, from http://www.pewinternet.org/PPF/r/230/report_display.asp.

Partnership for Twenty-First-Century Skills. (2003). *Learning for the twenty-first-century*. Report downloaded November 30, 2005, from http://www.21stcenturyskills.org/images/stories/otherdocs/P21_Report.pdf

Rockman *et al* (2007). *Findings from the evaluation of the Bay Area Video Coalition's YouthLink Program*. San Francisco, CA: Rockman *et al*.

Part II

Views from the K-12 Classroom

Media Literacy in Formal Education

Chapter 3

Voices from the Trenches

Elementary School Teachers Speak about Implementing Media Literacy

Jeff Share

At the beginning of the twenty-first century, the U.S. Department of Education and the National Endowment for the Arts funded 17 demonstration projects across the country to integrate media literacy with the arts. Based at an elementary school in downtown Los Angeles, Project SMARTArt (Students using Media, Art, Reading, and Technology) was one of the largest grant recipients. For three years, students from kindergarten through fifth grade worked with teachers and artists to analyze media and create their own alternative representations of everything from violence, to advertising, to their community. Students produced animation, performed original plays, painted, wrote, photographed, and used numerous types of media to analyze and communicate, read and write their world. (A case study of this project can be accessed at the Center for Media Literacy's Web site at: http://www.medialit.org/reading_room/article659.html.) In 2006, approximately two years after the grant ended, 14 SMARTArt teachers were interviewed about their past and present experiences learning about and teaching media literacy. The ways and degrees to which these teachers are currently using what they learned from the grant vary across the board. All the teachers spoke about the importance of media literacy while also admitting to a sharp decrease in implementation since the grant ended.

These interviews provide an opportunity to hear the voices of teachers in the trenches, the ones who know schooling best from their first-hand experiences, discuss their challenges and successes implementing media literacy in their classrooms. All the names have been changed to pseudonyms to provide anonymity. This chapter is divided into topics that emerged from the interviews. The first explores various types of media pedagogy as distinguished by Douglas Kellner (1995). Next, the teachers share their common beliefs about the importance of media literacy. The following topic deals with examples about how teachers integrated media literacy into their curriculum and confronted issues of social justice. This is continued by an unanticipated finding that suggests media education holds considerable potential for special education. The teachers then discuss the obstacles they face now that the grant is over and the school's test scores have dropped. Finally, the teachers share their opinions about what they think is necessary for media literacy to flourish in an elementary school.

Different Types of Media Education

Kellner divides media pedagogy into four separate approaches: protectionist, media literacy movement, arts education, and critical media literacy (1995, p. 336). Even though these differences are less distinct in the lower grades, they are general tendencies that reflect various perspectives about media and education. Kellner's four categories can be seen as cumulative, like a pyramid, building on one another rather than just an assortment of separate ideas. In this pyramid analogy, critical media literacy is at the top as it incorporates ideas from the other three approaches. The approach with the least to offer the pyramid is the protectionist because it is based on a negative view of the media and a limited view of the audience's potential to negotiate alternative readings. However, it can contribute positively to spreading awareness of media as influential and worthy of analysis and critique. The art education approach offers a useful base that can open education to be more experiential, multimodal, creative, fun, and expressive. The media literacy movement pedagogy expands the notions of print literacy to include more types of media but with little consideration of ideology and social justice. The integration of the media literacy movement core concepts with arts education helps push arts education to be more inquiry-based and thus deepen the potential for critical thinking. The final layer, critical media literacy, incorporates the arts, multiple literacies, and cultural studies to provide a problem-posing pedagogy that addresses issues of power and social justice that can be individually and socially empowering and transformative (Kellner & Share, 2007).

The majority of the 14 teachers interviewed tend to embody a media literacy movement perspective that aims to empower students to analyze and create media as a way of developing cognitive critical thinking skills. Though this was the most common approach, aspects of three of the four types of media education could be found in the interviews. Protectionist fears of the negative effects of violence on TV and in video games were voiced once or twice, yet none of the teachers promoted a negative attitude toward media or partook in media bashing. The absence of the protectionist approach to media literacy is notable. Some teachers viewed media literacy similar to art education; a fun experiential tool useful for creative expression and livening up other subjects.

However, most of the interviews reflect a solid media literacy perspective, engaging a framework of *conceptual understandings* of media education (Buckingham, 2003). Various people and organizations across the globe have generated and continue to create different lists of media literacy concepts that vary in numbers and wording but, for the most, they tend to coincide with at least five basic elements:

1 Recognition of the construction of media and communication as a social process as opposed to accepting texts as isolated neutral or transparent conveyors of information
2 Some type of textual analysis that explores the languages, genres, aesthetics, codes, and conventions of the text
3 Exploration of the role audiences play in actively negotiating meanings
4 Problematizing the process of representation to uncover and engage issues of ideology, power, and pleasure
5 Examination of the production, institutions, and political economy that motivate and structure the media industries as corporate profit-seeking businesses.

The interviews also reveal a desire to expand print literacy to be more inclusive of other forms of communication such as photography, music, animation, and the like. Only a handful of teachers explicitly engaged in critical media literacy by addressing issues of power, inequality, and social justice.

Teaching media literacy can be a major paradigm shift for many teachers because it requires movement from a psychological model of education to a sociological one (Luke & Freebody, 1997). This means less focus on individual cognitive development and more incorporation of the social contexts of the student and the content being taught. Media literacy aims to expand the type of tools students and teachers use to read and write and expand the content of what is acceptable to study inside the classroom to include popular culture, media, and technology. Therefore, encouraging teachers to broaden their definition of literacy can be the first stride in this movement toward a more sociological model.

A next step should be to deepen critical thinking in relation to social and cultural contexts and, for this, one can benefit greatly from engagement with cultural studies concepts, such as textual analysis using semiotics and visual literacy, audience theory and the importance of different readings versus dominant readings, and the politics of representation with its focus on ideology and issues of bias as they conflict with assumptions of objectivity (Durham & Kellner, 2002). Cultural studies also provides a critique of the political economy, the institutional influences, and the commercial purposes of entertainment and media, which are often absent from teaching that involves mass media (i.e., journalism, music, documentaries). These ideas emerge from an overarching understanding that all media and information are socially constructed.

The movement to critical media literacy is yet another step up the pyramid that entails a progressive mindset in which social justice and equality trump property rights and consumerism. This pedagogy encourages empathy and an openness to explore the hierarchical relationships of power in communication that benefit and disadvantage individuals and groups. It also involves the process of critical inquiry to unveil the way social systems function in perpetuating themselves and reproducing the status quo. Critical media literacy is transformative pedagogy that aims to empower students to challenge the problems and systems they encounter, thus connecting themselves in what Robert Ferguson calls *critical solidarity* with the world around them. Ferguson suggests that our relationships with media are not autonomous; rather, they depend on taking positions related to social contexts. As we are always taking sides, Ferguson calls for critical solidarity as "a means by which we acknowledge the social dimensions of our thinking and analysis. It is also a means through which we may develop our skills of analysis and relative autonomy" (2001, p. 42). Critical solidarity means teaching students to interpret information and communication within humanistic, social, historical, political, and economic contexts for them to understand the interrelationships and consequences of their actions and lifestyles. It also means joining in solidarity with the disempowered in a collective struggle for a more just world.

The Importance of Media Literacy

The most common sentiment from all 14 SMARTArt teachers interviewed was a belief in the importance of media literacy for various reasons, yet most commented on the need for students to think critically about media because it surrounds them all the time. Second-grade teacher, Ms. Vargas, stated that when you learn media literacy,

> you're able to dissect back from that [message you receive] and know what was involved in the creation of that message. Just being able to have higher level thinking skills about what that message is, whether it's advertisement or news media or newspapers, anything that carries a message, you are able to step away from just reacting to it, you take into account what your reaction is, but you step away from it and you look at it analytically and see what was involved in constructing it and

what was the reason for it and who the target audience was and what [was] the objective; you're able to think about that message critically.

In her description of media literacy, Ms. Vargas expresses a critical perspective of media that moves away from censorship and protection toward empowerment and analysis. She stated,

> I think because media is just such a part of our society, you can totally get swallowed in that whole world if you don't stop, step back and say, "OK, there's a reason why they're doing that and I have to be aware so I can make a more educated choice." The whole concept of stepping out of that box and looking at the overall picture—if anything, that's what I've taken away from media literacy training.

Special education teacher Ms. Hendrix also believes that media literacy is important to help students and teachers start "thinking out of the box." She suggested that everyone should be "more self-reflective in one's interpretation of media. Opening up more dialogue to access that, from not only the kids, but ourselves." Ms. Hendrix's comments align with bell hooks's ideas "that teachers must be actively committed to a process of self-actualization that promotes their own wellbeing if they are to teach in a manner that empowers students" (hooks, 1994, p. 15). Awareness and engagement with media are now necessary elements of twenty-first-century self-actualization. Accompanying this awareness is the teaching of metacognitive skills in thinking about thinking. Special education teacher Mr. Shaw values media literacy

> because it teaches kids how to think critically for themselves and apply the essential questions to everything in life. Who sent the message? Why did they send it? Who is this targeted to? Are there any biases? It teaches them how to think and I think, isn't that what we're in business to do, to teach kids how to think for themselves.

He connects media literacy with social justice through teaching empathy. He said,

> I think when you teach a person to think for themselves and think outside of the social box that they may live in, in terms of their family unit, in terms of their cultural unit, in terms of how they were brought up, I think if you teach them how to question what has been presented to them in their life, they will be able to see things from an empathetic point of view and step into other people's shoes.

The connection of critical thinking with empathy that Mr. Shaw mentions is essential for critical media literacy and the goal of critical solidarity (Ferguson, 2001).

Teaching students that all media are constructed is a challenge for third-grade teacher Mr. Gomez, who stated that often students don't realize media messages are constructed by people for particular purposes. Mr. Gomez commented that it is important for students to know, "there is always a different viewpoint to something. What you think is fact is actually someone else's version of the facts." He said that students should learn to apply this concept "to a lot of things, even textbooks" as often people "think it's fact, just because it's in a textbook." Mr. Gomez stated,

> I remember we went to a workshop at the Center [for Media Literacy] somewhere and they were showing how news clips or media is a reflection of the person reporting the news. Also, how music and camera angles can change the effect it has on a person. You add scary music, then you feel scared and creeped-out. Where if you remove it, it doesn't have as much effect on you … the information is someone else's viewpoint and it's affecting you, they're controlling you in a funny … subtle or indiscreet way, they are controlling you. Controlling what you know, so you have to be critical of what information you're receiving, don't just take it for fact.

A wonderful example of fourth-grade students internalizing a media literacy frame of mind is told by Mr. Ruiz. He explains,

> I know that group of kids got it because near the end, we received a big pack in the mail. There was a big pack of free book covers, something like *Madagascar*, some movie for kids … we had talked about billboards and advertising and how much it costs, and one of the kids said to me, "Well, are they giving us anything else for advertising?" I said, "No, they just think that by giving you a free book cover, it's …" "But we're doing free advertising for them." I said, "Exactly!" So he came to that conclusion and then I said, "Find a solution, what can you do?" "But, it's good paper," they said and it really is. They came to the conclusion of flipping it over and drawing their own. So the advertising went inside and they drew their own, it was really neat.

Mr. Ruiz used this example to demonstrate how his media literacy lessons had led to the goal of media education that Len Masterman (1994) calls *critical autonomy*, the ability and desire to think critically without prompting by the teacher. Mr. Ruiz's students had recognized that they were being used by advertisers to promote a movie for free through the mere donation of book covers. The students not only perceived the manipulation but they counteracted it by appropriating the material for their own purposes. Mr. Ruiz said that this example was just one of many where he was able to see his students developing their critical consciousness. Mr. Ruiz stated, "We talked about the advertising around here and we get alcohol advertising so much more here than in other higher affluent communities. They were becoming much more aware sooner than I expected or sooner than the other kids around."

Integrating Media Literacy Across the Curriculum

In elementary school, there are basically two options for teaching media literacy; one is as a separate subject in addition to the mandated curriculum, and the other option is to integrate it with subjects that the teacher is already required to cover. As time is limited and the expectations of what to teach are great, most SMARTArt teachers tried to integrate media literacy concepts and questions into their curriculum in many different ways. Mr. Baker told about how he uses the chart from the Center for Media Literacy with the key questions: (1) Who created this message? (2) What creative techniques are used to attract my attention? (3) How might different people understand this message differently? (4) What values, lifestyles and points of view are represented in, or omitted from, this message? (5) Why is this message being sent? Mr. Baker said,

> I have my chart with the questions to reference them. The primary way that I reference them is, especially at the end of each story that we read in Open Court, I review those questions and I ask the kids to address those questions for that story that we've read.

During the SMARTArt professional development, some specific media literacy lessons were taught, yet the emphasis of the training focused more on integrating media literacy rather than teaching it as a separate subject. This is probably easiest in elementary school, where all subjects are taught by the same teacher, and curriculum integration is often encouraged. During the grant, Ms. Hernandez integrated media literacy throughout her curriculum and into her students' homes. For homework, she still has her students do the equivalent of a book report for a television show. She said that they "have to sit with their parent and watch a show. Not only watch it and just be passive, but actually go into it and say, who are the characters, what was the problem, what was the solution within the show?" Since the grant ended, Ms. Hernandez no longer does many of her media literacy lessons, yet this homework assignment continues. Ms. Hernandez remarked,

> I still do it because it's such a good way for them to see that people use media, but they also use stories and the storyboard and the story element to create a show. They enjoy it and television is just so much part of their lives. So, I figured why not go and tell the parents, this is a good way for you to analyze the shows that your kids are watching and make sure that they're watching something that's good for them instead of something that's not going to be any benefit to them. The parents enjoy that homework a lot, so I still do it.

Ms. Martin commented on how teaching media literacy has become a natural part of her teaching and she now incorporates it incidentally. Ms. Martin spoke about the challenge,

> My biggest concern, and probably the concern of almost every teacher, was how do I fit this into what I already have to do, because there's so much to do. I think what was eased [during the grant] was that there was no pressure. It's not that you have to do everything. It's that you learn all these things and that it was okay for them to become sort of integrated into the program; to just happen naturally. And it did, and I was in it for three years, a full three years, and it has become a part of my natural planning and decisions and that's been really good ... I'll notice we can talk about symbols, we can use newspaper images, we can use imagination, we talk about how these images are created when we were looking at magazine images. So definitely, all these things are being used, just not as systematic as it used to be, but it's there. It's in my head, and so I'm using it. That's good and the kids are getting it. It's probably easier. And I think that's how we need to do things anyway. It just kind of is integrated and it just kind of happens naturally. When I'm planning, I can say, oh I can do media literacy here, we can talk about one of the media questions. It happens, it's just not as structured as it was before.

Though Ms. Martin's natural incorporation of media literacy concepts and questions into her teaching lacks a structured approach, its profound understanding allows for a more dynamic application that can be applied to any educational program or fad that too often comes and goes.

Mr. Ruiz told about a lesson where he combined popular culture and media literacy with a math lesson. He said,

Just last week I received my renewal for *Time* magazine and ... it didn't give me a total of how much the subscription was, but I know there was a [subscription card] you get 58 issues for 63 cents, but it didn't tell me the total and it bothered me because I needed to see a total so I used that for example. I brought *Time* magazine in and had the kids try to figure out and I decided to go through some magazines and cut out the subscription ads and realized that was a way that I can use it in Math and we ended up doing a little project where they each got one. I was able to steal some from a store magazine rack, enough to make their own little poster and talk about it, and that the intention was to really lure you in to getting the magazine. Off the rack it's $3.95 but for you, 52 cents, you get 37 of them, but it didn't give you a total.

This is an excellent example of a real-world connection to math and media literacy concepts. Mr. Ruiz brought into the classroom an experience from his personal life that involved popular media and a math problem for his students to wrestle with authentic applications for abstract concepts.

Social Justice and Critical Media Literacy

Ms. Vargas felt that media literacy is good for building interdisciplinary bridges with social studies. She stated,

A lot of present problems could have been prevented if we would have learned from our mistakes in the past. So maybe looking at history, looking at different periods and using media literacy as that bridge between, yes, this is an event in history, let's say the Civil Rights Movement, and then having media literacy be that bridge to what's going on presently and using the messages that we see today, that we receive today, what's a part of our society, our environment, our immediate neighborhood, where do we see, maybe not the exact same thing, but the essence of it, how it does still exist today. Right off the bat, I'm thinking always looking at social studies, history, the social sciences for that.

Although Mr. Ruiz is not able to teach a lot about social justice these days, he believes that using media literacy can be a great way to expose his students to issues of social injustice. He commented,

Just last week during ML King, the kids were learning that it wasn't just ... a black issue. I asked the kids, here's a picture of a water fountain, Colored Only and Whites Only, where would you drink? All the kids think they were able to drink from the White Fountain, just because they're not black. Defining what colored means and I found some old, old newspapers that have copies of older newspapers during the time of the boycott and Rosa Parks, and the kids were able to make that connection, that they're colored. When they mean colored, they don't mean the Blacks, because they think they could walk through that front door, they think they'd be able to drink out of the White Only fountain, so, very little social justice but I think through media literacy it would be a great way; easier and more fun. I mean the kids would just enjoy it. You can integrate so much, you can integrate art and take care of a couple of standards, couple of subjects all in one.

Ms. Rogers mentioned that the media literacy training has helped her teach more critically as she now moves beyond the textbook. She stated, "I think I present more of both sides of things, like Columbus Day, when we're doing why we have Columbus Day. So it's like I read the story, but then I also tell them about other people's opinion." Presenting various perspectives and analyzing messages for bias teaches textual analysis and issues of ideology. This is often difficult for critical educators because recognizing difference is not the same as valuing all ideas, especially when some are discriminatory or harmful. Ms. Rogers spoke about one student who told the class that his father doesn't like black people. Ms. Rogers said,

It's amazing. You know some of the values the kids are taught at home and then sometimes they're not correct, I mean ... they're prejudicial and the kids haven't seen the other side. So, when you present them with the other side, it kind of opens up the conversation. I don't know what they say to their parents when they come back, but it's good to do that.

When teaching critical media literacy, primary sources can be a powerful tool for helping students empathize with the victims of injustice. First person accounts of injustice have a power and authenticity that can help students understand issues at a deeper and more empathetic level. Third-grade teacher Mr. Baker told about an experience he had using primary sources:

I went to Manzanar[1] last summer and they had a packet. The main aspect of it was diaries, short diaries of individuals who were at Manzanar ... We discussed what happened and some of the reasons behind the internment. And then I asked them some questions about them, some probing questions: Why do you think this happened? How do you think the people FELT who were there? You know, got them to start thinking a little bit. That was kind of OK. Until I had the kids actually open up and start *reading* what these people had written. Primary sources, and it was like three or four, five minutes into the work and suddenly I could FEEL, this undercurrent in the classroom and I heard one of the kids say, "Is this what this person really said?" I said, "YESSS." And suddenly everybody understood it from a different level, what we were talking about and then we were able to have a discussion, you know: Well how does that compare to what's happening now? What do you think we would find in somebody's diary from Abu Ghraib? You know real heavy duty questions for fourth-graders ... I also had *Teaching Tolerance* from ... the Southern Poverty Law Project and we're going to be doing some things with that and we'll be discussing them and obviously using the media literacy probing questions to get them to think about it some more.

Many teachers don't teach social justice issues in their class because they don't know how to go about it. This teacher offers a powerful example of how primary sources can be an excellent tool to help students develop deeper understandings of social justice issues and more empathy for the victims of discrimination and injustice. Primary sources that provide perspectives from people who have experienced marginalization or oppression offer perspectives that can shed light on injustice and illuminate systems of oppression.

Another strategy for teaching critical media literacy is using a Freirean problem-posing pedagogy (Freire, 1970). Mr. Baker did this when he posed the problem of Japanese internment to his students and then connected it to questions about current-day situations of social injustice. Mr. Harvey demonstrated this when he took his students on walking field trips around their neighborhood. He explained that while on the walking field trips,

> I wanted them to focus on their community. What did they see out there as problems? They came up with people throwing trash around, it's dirty, there's a lot of noise. Then I had them try to come up with solutions. What would you do to help or address some of these problems?

Though this was an excellent beginning for critical media literacy, unfortunately he ended the activity with the discussion, and the students never had the opportunity to actually tackle some of the problems that they encountered. Critical media literacy can be an opportunity for real action in which students become agents of change through creating alternative media, writing letters, photographing situations, circulating petitions, or any type of action they believe will, in some way, counteract the problem they want to solve. Some of the actions that SMARTArt teachers mentioned taking include creating tee shirts with messages about environmental issues, making animations to counteract problems of violence, drawing posters that offer different perspectives on urban wildlife, and producing a PowerPoint presentation to educate others about recycling and convince them not to pollute. Through taking action, as small as it may be, students have an opportunity to feel a sense of agency in the face of situations that can too often overwhelm them into apathy and depression.

Especially Special Education

During interviews with the four special education teachers, they often mentioned problems related to the marginalization of special education within the public school. Their unique perspective brings awareness of the value media literacy can offer to students with special needs. They commented on how often their students are forgotten or assumptions are made about what they cannot do. These interviews and the experiences during three years of the grant make a strong argument that students in special education can benefit greatly from media literacy for many reasons.

As media pedagogy is multimodal and experiential, it helps overcome some of the limitations of a print-based literacy and lowers the affective filters (Krashen, 1995) that create invisible barriers for children acquiring a new language or with special needs, be they physical, mental, or social. Mr. Shaw offered an example whereby lowering his students' affective filters gave them more of a level playing field than they usually had when mixing with regular education students. He said about his former students,

> they become just normal kids without having to think about the burden of being understood when they speak ... [Sandy] had a really tough time speaking and communicating just basic needs, like having to go to the bathroom, being hungry, so when he was able to be that tiger when [the drama teacher] came in, he wasn't a kid with special needs anymore, he became a tiger ... And they interacted with their general ed peers, you could really see the confidence level, especially [Sandy], increase because he was more talkative, he understood that he could be something else.

Mr. Shaw also spoke about media literacy activities with music:

> I also saw that again when they were playing the instruments with [the music teacher]. They didn't have to talk, they didn't have to communicate any needs. All they did was pound on those instruments and again, it takes all of the affective filters and it diminishes them to a point where everybody is the same; extremely powerful.

Ms. Hendrix commented on the ability of media literacy to help her students improve their critical thinking skills. She stated,

> The kids I had at that time, many of them had significant speech/language impairments and learning disabilities. They definitely started to demonstrate an increased level of critical thinking and expression. Definitely with some of the activities ... they started making really great connections and they were definitely better critical thinkers.

For example, Ms. Hendrix mentioned,

> one activity was when the elections were coming up and there was all the campaigning going on. What I would have the kids do when we went to the computer lab was to find the latest photographs of the election and the kids had to express their impressions of why they're going to vote for who. Why they would vote for Kerry or why they would vote for Bush, based on the images they were looking at and the captions that they could read. I abstained from reading too much to them because I really wanted them to focus just on the images and we built this kind of portfolio or this album of images and we kept pictures of Bush and Kerry. It was amazing how, from week to week, their perceptions of these individuals would change, based on the images that they were looking at. For example, students would express perceptions such as, "Bush was a good guy cause he was with the animals in that other picture, but this week, he's with some military," you know like some person in the army or something. So that was really amazing, I thought. It's how they started to look. Or I was able to pose questions to them about what does what or where somebody is, the setting that they're in, or who they're with or what they're doing, why does that make you think a certain way about a person? They would definitely get very, very excited about voting for one or the other and then when they started to see how they were changing their minds, that was pretty neat because they were questioning ... I think (hope) it had some lasting impressions for

some of them. To witness their oral skills and critical thinking skills increase was exciting.

Another special education teacher, Ms. Smith, also felt that media literacy was a wonderful way to integrate students.

> I think it's great because it's multi-level. You can do it with a variety of ages and it's just multi-abilities. Not everybody has to be reading at the same level to do a lot of these activities. So, I think it provides a lot of great mainstreaming activities, mixing activities.

Though many of these benefits could also apply to art education without any of the media literacy layers, Ms. Smith also spoke about other values of media literacy for her special education students, such as exploring the politics of representation and how her students see themselves being represented. Ms. Smith explained that she and her students talk "extensively about how we communicate with others and I think because we are dealing with a disabled population, we talk about self-image and how you want others to perceive you." Ms. Smith analyzed with her students the fact that people with disabilities are often underrepresented or misrepresented in the mainstream media. While her students were investigating the scarcity of images of senior citizens in mainstream media, they also noticed "the fact that they [children with physical disabilities] were in magazines that were focusing on equipment," commented Ms. Smith. By teaching students about the social construction of media images, they become better prepared to question these types of inequalities as choices made by individuals for specific reasons. Being able to reject the "common sense" notion that media is neutral or natural allows students the framework to position their own identities on their own terms and reject discriminatory representations of themselves and others.

The importance of media literacy can also be seen in Ms. Smith's comments about her new attitude with media tools. Ms. Smith said,

> I think empowering them with tools, I'm thinking back then [during the grant] when, like now, I don't think twice about handing a kid a camera, where before I did. That's something that changed me a lot, it's giving them more opportunities to do things and I really think that was a big thing. I was thinking, are they going to be able to, do they know what, talking about the video camera too, it's more use of the equipment, the tripod. I'm thinking I still have the tripod here, it really empowered them, those are like an adult toy. You know, a lot of parents say, No, you don't touch that. On top of that, using a

wheelchair and being able to use something like that, why shouldn't they? I think that was really something that I feel made an impact on me, made me think differently.

New Obstacles

Since the grant ended in July 2004, many changes have occurred at Leo Politi Elementary School. The standardized test scores dropped in language arts, thereby lowering the school's academic performance index (API) score to the lowest level, API-1. Once this occurred, a new administration replaced the previous, and the district placed the school on a Watch List. The new administration, which began this school year, created a focus on just three core academic subjects that are tested with standardized assessment (language arts, math, and English language development). They call this focus the Daily Three, and it is accompanied by a schedule for what and when all teachers are expected to teach every day. The administration required lesson plans to be submitted in advance, they closed the computer lab, and have been writing up teachers for being out of compliance. According to the teachers interviewed, many of the new changes have made teaching media literacy much more difficult. In an interview with the new principal, he rejected this comment by the teachers as merely an excuse. It is interesting to note the new principal's resistance to consider how these changes could have such consequences. The principal's comment echoes the current neoliberal agenda and the emphasis of national policies such as No Child Left Behind (NCLB) on accountability without support. The mandated schedule for when each subject must be taught aims for consistency and standardization throughout the school and across the district. NCLB encourages this push for efficiency and standardization, much along a business model. Though a business model might function well for corporations aiming to maximize profits, standardizing children is not the best way to encourage participative democracy nor creative innovation.

Among the obstacles that the teachers mentioned, the biggest was the lack of time to teach everything they are expected to teach. This was also a problem during the grant, yet all the teachers agreed that it is even more difficult now. Most of the teachers felt intimidated to not rock the boat by an atmosphere of fear that was not present during the grant. Since the API level dropped, the school has received many more observations by district personnel than previously. These unannounced visitations of as many as six people at one time have had an intimidating effect on many teachers. Although none of the teachers interviewed mentioned being written up themselves, many spoke about the fear of being written up for not being on schedule or for doing something different, such as media literacy. Principal Sullivan said that he has already written up between 6 and 10 teachers and some several times. Even assuming that only incompetent teachers are being punished for bad teaching, the interviews reflect an atmosphere of fear in which many first-rate teachers feel intimidated. The principal insisted that he is open and could give some "wiggle room," but as no teacher has approached him about teaching media literacy, he assumes that media literacy is something they really don't want to teach. Based on the comments from the interviews, it seems more probable that the structure of rigid schedules, scripted curriculum, and consequences for those who do not do as told are keeping teachers from doing many things they would like to do. The teachers also emphasized the importance of support that encourages innovation, which is the opposite of this climate of fear. Yet, in spite of this difference of opinion, none of the teachers interviewed blamed the new administration for these changes; most see it as consequences of NCLB and their school district's policies.

The other obstacle that several teachers mentioned is the closing of the computer lab. This is related to the school's focus on the Daily Three and the desire for constant accountability. The administrators claim to have closed the lab because of lack of a plan for how to use it and because they believe most of the computers are "obsolete." Mr. Harvey, who used to work in the lab, counters that the computers are old but not obsolete. He agrees that the computer lab was not being used systematically because there was no teacher running it, something he said is all too common throughout the district. However, instead of hiring someone skilled to run the lab, the administration took the easiest action, thereby removing one more tool from the teachers' and students' limited chest of resources. This is almost ironic as the administration is claiming to give top priority to literacy taught during the Daily Three, yet information technologies are not seen as part of that literacy.

Recommendations for Making Media Literacy Flourish

The previous tendencies that were culled from the interviews reflect the teachers' beliefs in the importance of media literacy, different approaches to media literacy, and reasons why many are not teaching media literacy now. In the final section of this chapter, the teachers discuss what they believe would help make media literacy not only a seed of change that could grow but a plant that could flourish.

The need for support from top to bottom was voiced by almost all the teachers. Many wished for the possibility of having once again the support they had during the grant, though most wanted even more support from within, rather than just from outside the school. Ms. Martin said, "When we were part of the media literacy training, it helped to be with other people and to have all this training because you were in the middle of it. When you leave it, it's so hard to get back into it."

The most common suggestion from the teachers was for more time and support for them to collaborate on planning and teaching media literacy. While reflecting on her experience during two years of the grant, Ms. Vargas said,

> I just wish I would have had more time to plan and maybe even plan collaboratively with other media literacy teachers. Even though we weren't all on the same grade-level, some of the concepts, hearing from different grade-levels how they're going to teach a certain concept, all I would have to do is modify it for my students.

Mr. Gomez suggested the ideal would be weekly meetings

> to discuss what activities we had done related to media literacy. Then you get to share with each other and the other person reminds you, gives examples of what you can do, and at the same time, it helps you review what needs to be done and just keep going like that. That's what I would imagine. I do know when teachers come together and they share their ideas, other teachers say, oh that's true and they think of other things, it sparks creativity.

The power of collaboration and the importance of using language as a tool for collective problem solving can benefit teachers and students. Neil Mercer (2007) uses an example of three people working on a crossword puzzle to demonstrate how using language to collaborate can solve problems that none would be capable of solving alone. Mercer writes, "Information is shared, but more than that is achieved. Using the tool of language, the three people together transform the given information into new understanding. As a result of their combined intellectual efforts, they solve the problem" (p. 2).

Along with time to collaborate, several teachers mentioned the value of having a media literacy coach. Mr. Gomez sees much benefit in having someone

> going around saying, do you need help with something, you know, support. A teacher may say, "well I'm having a little trouble with this." "Well, let me see what you do. Maybe we can tweak it this way," stuff like that …That's where the ideas about different viewpoints of the animals and all that came about.

Ms. Vargas also felt that a media literacy coach is very important to provide feedback. She said, "now that I'm a [Open Court literacy] coach, I think about how I've seen teachers, their practices improving, maybe their pacing improving because I was there to help and give feedback." She spoke about the value of having a media literacy coach to observe lessons and provide feedback about "if my questioning was on target, or if I would have added this question, it really would have gotten me to where I wanted the children to be."

The need for ongoing support was echoed by many teachers. Mr. Harvey stated that just the learning process alone requires lots of time. He said, "it took at least two years, the third year, we were just starting to roll; we started to internalize it. When you internalize it, then you can look for places." Like Mr. Harvey, Ms. Vargas also mentioned feeling overwhelmed by the difficulty of trying to learn media literacy and then also trying to teach it at the same time. She said that she wishes she had more time

> for myself to really let it absorb so that then I can, in turn, give it to the kids. But, I think for me that was one of the most important media literacy moments, just like being conscious of my own learning. I just wish that I would have gotten to the point where I was handing it off to the kids a little faster.

At the end of the first year of the grant, several teachers worked together and created introductory media literacy lessons and two lists of vocabulary words, one for lower grades and one for upper elementary. (These lessons and vocabulary lists can be found online at: http://www.medialit.org/reading_room/casestudy/lessonsactivities.htm)   This, combined with the Center for Media Literacy's five core concepts and key questions, were the primary tools and framework for SMARTArt teachers. Ms. Vargas commented on the importance of having a common language and framework. She stated,

> I think the first thing is just getting all the teachers on the same page as to the terminology and the core concepts of media literacy, just the language that's involved in the curriculum of media literacy, like sexy kind of advertisements and the whole gamut.

She stressed the importance of this because, "if teachers are really comfortable with language and comfortable talking about media literacy, then they'll be more comfortable to just embed that." Mr. Gomez liked the idea of having a packet of specific media literacy lessons like the introductory lessons the first year teachers created. He stated, "I remember that it was something to start off with. That would be good for teachers who want to introduce something to the students. I don't think it'll replace, but it helped jump start some kind of media literacy."

Ms. Jones suggested that the best way to integrate media literacy into the elementary school curriculum is doing it "their way" and scaffolding the concepts by grade level. By that she meant:

> [you need a] reason for it. So, it would be fine if we weren't presented all the facts at the same time. Maybe starting in kindergarten where they're concentrating on some of the basic facts, like color and maybe emotions they can understand and become more sophisticated. After, those in first grade could pick-up and add to that. I think that would help students pick it up faster if they had a background instead of all at once.

Ms. Jones offered these ideas as a constructivist vision for teaching media literacy systematically across all grade levels. She also asserted the need for teachers to be part of this process:

> It would be nice if teachers could have something to say about that and I know we started putting lesson plans in folders which students lost or disappeared, but if a few on grade level decided among yourselves to be responsible for creating a couple of lessons and you held on to them at grade level, I think that would work. Put some of the goals that they keep saying, they have to be able to write paragraphs, they have to be able to do this and that, I think they could do that over, by looking through some of the curriculum guides that they already have, some of the standards we have to meet.

A previous teaching method at the Los Angeles Unified School District involved teaching content connected through thematic units. Now with scripted skills-based programs like OCR, lessons might be thematically grouped, but teachers are not encouraged to design units around themes. Ms. Jones commented that even though it is "not in fashion right now," thematic teaching might be an easier way to teach media literacy. She said, "I think one way to get away with that is in the primary grades, where you can push your specific ideas so they can really be mastering something in media literacy that goes with their theme." Mr. Shaw said,

> I guess the best way is to start with a theme and that theme can then harbor within or engender, expand upon the critical questions, the essential questions. Without a theme, you lose focus and the questions become entities that are disconnected. There needs to be a focal point.

I think that thematic based teaching is the way those questions need to be brought into the elementary school.

He suggested beginning by explicitly teaching media literacy vocabulary and the key questions. "Then I would take a theme and I would say, now we're going to apply this in a concrete way, and apply the questions to a theme, throughout that unit."

Often, thematic teaching is done through projects, sometimes referred to as *project-based learning*. This is another strategy that was mentioned for teaching media literacy and making learning more experiential. Many best practices for teaching (Zemelman, Daniels & Hyde, 1993) include both thematic and project-based pedagogies. Ms. Jones told about a project her fourth-grade students undertook that flowed naturally from an OCR story and addressed a real problem that her students recognized and wanted to solve. After reading about middle-school boys who started their own business, Ms. Jones had her students create their own products that they could sell. This assignment required that students plan everything from focus groups for assessing needs to advertising campaigns for selling their products. Working in groups, they discussed media literacy concepts and explored issues of gender and target audience. When Ms. Jones's students encountered a real problem that existed at their school, they focused their project to solve it. They discussed the fact that many students are dropped off at school at 6:00 AM and are not picked up until 6:00 PM, when their parents finish working. Waiting for two hours before school was boring, and Ms. Jones's students decided to create board games that would be academic and fun for the students who have to arrive early and have nothing to do. The process of making real products that had value to others taught her students many lessons and gave them a strong sense of pride. Ms. Jones said the games were such a success that other students also began making their own board games; "it had a little life of its own."

For Project SMARTArt, many different media projects were created, from plays to posters and from newspapers to animation. The notion that media literacy should involve production and analysis has become a widely accepted tenet of media literacy movement proponents in the United States. The benefits of media production are numerous, especially when creating media is part of project-based learning. All the interviewed teachers agreed that production can improve learning for many reasons, from being more motivating to making learning more intrinsic. Ms. Hernandez asserted that when students do something and not just talk about it, "the benefit is that they'll take it with them for the rest of their lives." Ms. Ramirez commented that when learning is hands on, "I think they solidify their learning much quicker and are able to express themselves a lot clearer." Ms. Martin spoke about an activity wherein her students photographed adults on campus for a newspaper they created. She said, "They started to notice things when we looked at newspapers because they had done it themselves. And I think critically, they were able to look at media in a way they hadn't looked at it before."

Mr. Baker said that when children create,

> they learn so much deeper ... because it's a multi-modality, they're using different parts of their brain, different aspects of their personality, different aspects of things they have learned. To be able to express something using different media, they are using different parts of their brain and they're trying things together.

Mr. Gomez commented on the value of production as a means of authentic assessment. He said,

> If they're able to do that project, then they're starting to internalize what they're learning, hopefully, and if they get it, they'll produce a product that reflects the learning. So if they get the idea, of any concept you're trying to teach, and they're able to produce a product that reflects what you're trying to teach them, then it's proof that they understand it.

Production offers the benefit of letting children have first-hand experiences, and experiential education is something that Mr. Shaw recommends to his students. He said, "I always tell the kids I work with, in order to learn a concept, three things need to occur: you need to see it, you need to say it or hear it, and you need to do it. So, that was the doing part." This recommendation is similar to Fredric Jones's *Positive Classroom Discipline*. Jones insists that students need to be doing more and listening passively less (Charles, 2002, p. 57).

Ms. Vargas is one of two SMARTArt teachers who have left the classroom to train other teachers as a literacy coach. Her advice for teaching teachers about media literacy follows an experiential model whereby teachers learn through doing. She stated,

> I go through that learning experience and then think about what was it in the presenter's strategies or methods of presenting this to me that helped me understand it and how I can thereby replicate that with my own kids at an appropriate level so that they can feel successful learning it the way I just did at the end of this PD [professional development]. It's a different kind of PD, it's not like I'm presenting a concept and let's plan it, it's like I'm making you go through the

experience so that then you can replicate it with your own students. I think that would be valuable.

This type of hands-on learning is part of the pedagogy that was promoted in the SMARTArt trainings and follows an experiential process that is useful for children and for teachers (Dewey, 1916/1997).

Conclusion

These interviews provided the opportunity to investigate some of the impact of a three-year federal grant to teach media literacy and the arts at an inner-city elementary school and the current obstacles that some public school teachers face. Through listening to teachers who have been trained in media literacy and have had experience teaching it in elementary school, many lessons can be learned about the intersection of theory and practice. In spite of the obstacles and lack of support, all the teachers interviewed are strong proponents of media literacy for young children. They have also brought to light a seldom researched topic, that of the added importance media literacy holds for special education students.

The inclusion of special education classes in Project SMARTArt and four of those teachers in this data sample was very fortunate because it has illuminated the considerable potential that media literacy holds for special education students. These teachers reflected on the marginalization of special education that often occurs in public education and the importance of making media education available to their students and to general education students. These four teachers spoke about the benefits media literacy offers their kids through lowering the affective filters and increasing the avenues for students with all sorts of needs and abilities to participate at different levels and in different ways. The value of having students with special needs address issues of representation was also highlighted because they are often misrepresented or underrepresented in the media. Issues of representation are so intimately linked with self-image and identity that exploring these concerns with special education students holds great potential for them personally and academically.

As most of the writing on media literacy focuses on middle-school and high-school students, these teachers' ideas and experiences can be helpful to anyone interested in learning what media literacy can look like at the elementary school level. The fact that most of the interviewed teachers are now teaching very little media literacy is a significant finding. This lack of continuity by the majority of the teachers suggests that media literacy needs consistent support and must be integrated into the curriculum in a systematic manner. The fact that much more media literacy was being taught while the school was receiving the federal grant demonstrates the importance of having a mandate to teach it and the funding to support it. Of all the suggestions the teachers offered, the comment recurring most often was about the need for ongoing support. This is a process that requires trained teachers who understand cultural studies concepts and an educational system that can support the teachers to collaborate with one another and implement media literacy education through progressive pedagogy that is thematic, project-based, experiential, and critical.

Note

1 Manzanar is one of the internment camps that the U.S. government used to lock up Japanese Americans during World War II

References

Buckingham, D. (2003). *Media education: Literacy, learning and contemporary culture*. Cambridge: Polity.

Charles, C. M. (2002). *Building classroom discipline* (7th ed.). Boston, MA: Allyn & Bacon.

Dewey, J. (1916/1997). *Democracy and education*. New York: Free Press.

Durham, M. G., & Kellner, D. (Eds.). (2002). *Media and cultural studies: KeyWorks*. Malden, MA: Blackwell Publishers.

Ferguson, R. (2001). Media education and the development of critical solidarity. In *Media Education Journal*. Glasgow: Association for Media Education in Scotland (vol. 30, pp. 37–43).

Freire, P. (1970). *Pedagogy of the oppressed*. New York: Seabury Press.

hooks, b. (1994). *Teaching to transgress*. New York: Routledge.

Kellner, D. (1995). *Media culture: Cultural studies, identity and politics between the modern and the postmodern*. New York: Routledge.

Kellner, D., & Share, J. (2007). Critical media literacy, democracy, and the reconstruction of education. In D. Macedo & S. R. Steinberg (Eds.), *Media literacy: A reader* (pp. 3–23). New York: Peter Lang.

Krashen, S. (1995). Bilingual education and second language acquisition theory. In D. Durkin (Ed.), *Language issues: Readings for teachers* (pp. 90–116). White Plains, NY: Longman.

Luke, A., & Freebody, P. (1997). Shaping the social practices of reading. In S. Muspratt, A. Luke, & P. Freebody (Eds.), *Constructing critical literacies: Teaching and learning textual practice* (pp. 185–225). Sydney: Allen & Unwin, and Cresskill, NJ: Hampton Press.

Masterman, L. (1994). A rationale for media education (Part I). In L. Masterman & F. Mariet (Eds.), *Media education in 1990s Europe* (pp. 5–87). Strasbourg: Council of Europe.

Mercer, N. (2007). *Words and minds: How we use language to think together*. London: Routledge.

Zemelman, S., Daniels, H., & Hyde, A. (1993). *Best practice: New standards for teaching and learning in America's schools*. Portsmouth, NH: Heinemann.

Chapter 4

Thinking Inside the Classroom
Notes from the Field

Allison Butler

Introduction

Small, theme-based schools are the current face of urban education, and their relative value warrants examination. As media education positions itself within the context of school reform, this chapter produces knowledge from the intersection of practice and theory, examining the small, theme-based-school trend and reports directly from the field via young people's stories of their experiences inside the classroom. What does the integration of alternative curricula into schools, such as media studies, look like? How is media education defined, understood, and articulated by those most directly and immediately impacted by it—the students? Through participant observation over two years and interviews with 21 students over five months in a small, New York City, media-themed public school, I strove to answer these questions to better conceptualize the integration of media education today and to understand how students articulate their learning of the media as part of their high school training.

Assumptions about the student as consumer shape contemporary theories of school change. A holistic approach to understanding twenty-first-century students acknowledges they are active producers of their educations. Too often studies of education, including studies on radical pedagogy and urban school reform, approach students from a distanced, and arbitrarily authoritative, environment. I use one small school and its students to examine how students themselves define and understand media education and how media education is integrated across the curriculum and into specific media classes. Specifically, I privilege young people's self-awareness and self-told stories about how they experience and make meaning from their education. I interrogate media education directly from the source and work to refine understandings of small-school, theme-based education from those directly involved in its unfolding. According to the New York City Department of Education, small, theme-based schools provide an intimate environment for students and entry point to unfamiliar material (New York City Department of Education,

2008). The theme of any given school is meant to guide student learning and prepare them for college-level studies. In small schools with smaller classes, it is argued, students develop intimate relationships with teachers who follow specific students' progress throughout their school tenure. Because the majority of kids funneled into the small schools generally come from disenfranchised backgrounds, the small school was promoted as a place of learning, stability, and regularity for young people.

Over the course of two years, I worked in curriculum, program, and theme development at a small, start-up New York City public school whose theme is media. Theme schools do not necessarily imply a focus on vocational education. In the case of the media-themed school, students are not expected to plot a career in the media industries at the start of high school but rather to learn how to deeply interrogate a particular concept in a rigorous academic setting. Theme schools that are part of the New York City public school system are not exempt from expected course completion, and there are no official training or professional development programs for teachers on how to incorporate the theme into their curricula. Furthermore, there is no teaching certification for nontraditional subject matter, which leaves schools the choice to hire nonlicensed teachers in the classroom, to offer no courses specific to their theme, or to have teachers untrained in the theme teaching classes. The schools started in this wave of reform sometimes hired untrained teachers and administrative staff who figured out the management of the school on the job. As such, themes often become diluted.

I was brought into the school because of my academic work in media education, and it was my goal to draw from the British media studies integration of media education into particular classes and across the curriculum (Bazalgette, 1992; Buckingham, 1990, 1991, 1993, 1998, 2003; Buckingham, Grahame, & Sefton-Greene, 1995; Buckingham & Sefton-Greene, 1994; Grahame, 1991; Moore, 1991) and American media education scholars whose critical analyses show the struggles educators face in implementing media education into community organizations and classrooms (Goodman, 2003; Tyner, 1998).

Media education does not have a formal place in United States classrooms. Since the 1970s, media education has had many jump-starts in a variety of pedagogical areas but has not laid claim to one particular trajectory and, without a coherent set of professional policies and foundations, it is difficult to define it as a field. Broadly speaking, media education combines analysis and production, and teaches critical autonomy and questions to interrogate the media industries and our role in them (Aufderheide, 1993; Bazalgette, 1992; Goodman, 2003; Grahame, 1991; Tyner, 1998). Media education is inherently cross-disciplinary; American education, however, is focused on high-stakes testing and operates ideologically as a hierarchical, adult-centered system that works to prepare young people for the workforce; hence, arts-based and alternative curricula reside in a precarious position (Aronowitz, 2004; Giroux, 2004; Goodman, 2003; Greene, 1988; Leistyna, 2004; Tyner, 1998). Despite changes in the organization and structure of New York City public schools, traditional standards still hold sway. Goodman (2003) observes that government and private agencies, not teachers or those involved in pedagogy, conduct the majority of school reforms. This indelibly alters the face of reform and the inclusion of alternative curricula.

Lincoln Square High School[1] (LSHS) is in a unique position to conceptualize integrated educational models as part of New York City's small, theme-based schools. To best conceptualize how young people understand the changes they experience in the name of bettering their education, I engaged in qualitative, quasi-ethnographic methods that interrogate data directly within the site of research (Fine, 1998; Fine & Sandstrom, 1988; Guba & Lincoln, 1998; Lindlof, 1995; Schwandt, 1998). Consistent with Fisherkeller's (2002) and Way's (1998) work with teenagers, I strove to learn as much about the participants as they were willing to share, and interrogated their stories against the social norms of larger society. In respect to feminist methodology, the oppressions and struggles faced by young people were challenged and mapped against systemic ideology (Gorelick, 1996). Because I knew the participants and shared in their school environment, I relied on that connection to contribute to the analysis of their stories (Fine, 1998; Heldke, 1998).

New to the department of education myself, in many ways, I attended school with the students; I worked in the school and participated in the students' school-day lives for two years. This is simultaneously heartwarming and heartbreaking: I got to know and become involved in the lives of amazing people. However, getting to know those students sometimes means entering a world of serious pain and suffering, and it is impossible to leave that knowledge "in the field." The work here is to translate the emotional experiences of both the students and myself into scholarly work that advances theory, paints a practical portrait of the changing face of education, and begins to carve inroads for future study. Over the course of my two years, I got to know nearly all the students by name, knew a significant number of family, academic, and personal stories of several of them, and am honored to be intimately involved in a small but valuable number of their lives. I met parents, grandparents, boyfriends, girlfriends, siblings; saw family pictures, report cards, awards, hospital records, prison sentences, sonograms; talked about pets, heartaches, politics, movies, music; shared dreams, fears, jokes, tears, subway rides, and ambulance trips. Because of my position, I got to know and work with students, faculty, and staff, which afforded me a unique perspective on both the daily operations of this particular school and the larger system of schooling. The bulk of the data analyzed here grows from student interviews and includes my observations and analyses of the function of the school.

Over the course of five months, I interviewed 21 students in both group and private interviews. The 11 male and 10 female students represented grades 9 to 12 and ages 14 to 17. I strove to interview as broad a cross-section as possible of ethnicity, age/grade, and academic motivation. I had conversations with incredibly motivated, highly functioning students and students in academic peril and with behavioral problems. I interviewed students with drug problems, prison records, experiences of homelessness and domestic shelters, sexual abuse, and drug dealers and straight-A students with long records of extracurricular activities. The interviews were audio-taped with the participants' permission; after each interview, I listened to and transcribed the material. I coded the interviews in multiple directions through Coffey and Atkinson's (1996) data complication guidelines and Lindlof's (1995) procedures for organization. In the initial reading of the transcripts, I looked for concrete information, such as their definitions of specific terms, declarative stories on their classroom, media and personal experiences, and construction of their individual stories. In further readings of the transcripts, I broke the conversations into broad categories as a method of organization.

I was interested in how the students spoke about their experiences and what, exactly, they experienced. The group interviews took on the tone and flavor of conversations; the students who participated in group interviews were friends with one another and had a rapport that began long before they entered our interview space. In the group interviews, I provided some basic guidelines and asked the questions, but tried to play a minor role. I was interested in how the conversations flowed between the participants and observed how they engaged with each other. I listened for and documented when they interrupted each other, how the conversations went down avenues that I had not introduced, and observed how they interacted with one another. In the private interviews, I began with or repeated the questions from the group interviews. The private interviews were distinct from the group interviews because there were no conversational interruptions, and I was able to follow through more directly on each individual's personal stories.

Though much of what I have found both matches and challenges theories on young people, media, and urban education, it is in no way intended to be an exhaustive look at these theories. Though I believe I worked through a healthy cross-section of LSHS's student body, these are qualitative data, and I do not intend to make generalizations about urban youth. It is my intention to paint a picture of LSHS's role in new school reform, as a small, theme-based school, through the articulation and perspective of its students. I share the participants' stories not with voyeuristic intent but rather to present the challenges and realities they face as part of their educations. To censor their experiences would present a simplistic, one-dimensional portrait that would not show how their education and their interpretation of it are both historically and socially specific.

Underserved urban youth are constructed as delinquent by larger systems that serve to maintain the ideological dominance of current models. Media education alone cannot alter the cultural capital of LSHS students. However, bringing to the surface and making explicit the social and political injustices young people experience may serve to illuminate their self-awareness and thereby give them a more complete set of tools with which to approach their future academic and professional endeavors. To most thoroughly problematize the experience of young people, they need to be a primary source of data; therefore, I begin inside the classroom. The rhetorical promotion of alterative education does not translate to the classroom experience and, ultimately I argue, disjointed efforts to include media education into a curriculum will fail unless there are transparent and rigorous support systems developed for teachers and students.

Understanding the Environment: Lincoln Square High School

Despite the lofty rhetoric associated with radical pedagogy, LSHS students are consistently and subtly reminded that they are destined to be less successful than their more privileged peers. Their demographic makeup, the geographic environment of their school, and the actual space in which their school is housed are constant reminders that, despite changes in language and organization, these young people are primed to replicate, not break out of, social and political inequalities.

LSHS operates in a space made familiar by scholars of urban education (Anderson & Summerfield, 2004; Anyon, 1997; Goldstein, 2004). The majority of LSHS students are of African or Latino descent, many are from immigrant families, are the only English speakers in their families, will be the first to graduate high school and the first to contemplate, let alone attend, college. The majority of LSHS students live at or below the poverty line in public housing projects in the South Bronx or the upper reaches of Manhattan. A small, but significant, number have been in and out of the shelter and foster care systems. Single mothers raise many students because of absent or imprisoned fathers. A significant number of students enter the ninth grade at Level 1, meaning they are functionally illiterate, operating below grade level. In the 2007–2008 school year, at least six male students were permanently or temporarily discharged from school while they were imprisoned, which, with a population just under 400, exceeds the national standard of 1 in 100 men in prison (Liptak, 2008; Western, 2006). Five girls were pregnant or gave birth during the school year and several more girls were suspected of handling unwanted or unplanned pregnancies on their own, without school help. In this aspect, LSHS again meets or exceeds national standards (Altman, 2008; Harris, 2007). In the 2007–2008 school year, LSHS had abysmally low attendance, with a daily average of 74 percent.

LSHS is located in a geographic area typical of New York City: as extreme wealth moves in, it pushes the extremely poor further to the edges. The school is located in a literal and figurative intersection between art, commerce, and urban blight, settled uncomfortably between Lincoln Center, a series of housing projects, the West Side Highway, and Columbus Circle.

LSHS is one of seven schools housed in a massive concrete building. The building used to be one large school but, owing to a variety of academic and personnel problems, it was shut down in 2005; since then, a series of small schools have moved in each new school year. As Goodman (2003) and Giroux (2004) each argue, schools take on the feel and look of prisons; LSHS is no exception. The building is a severe concrete and glass square, surrounded by an equally unforgiving outdoor plaza, part of which is enclosed by a wire mesh fence. Four floors are above street level, and there are two levels of basement classrooms. Each of the seven schools occupies a floor or series of hallways in the building. Roughly 3,000 students enter and exit through the same doors and share the cafeteria, gym, and auditorium spaces, though the students in each school are not allowed in any other school's space. All students must enter through scanning, where their bags are examined through x-rays, they must remove belts and any metal objects, their bodies are randomly scanned, and their belongings may be searched.

LSHS occupies the basement of the building, with no natural light and a vertical wale, reminiscent of prison bars, to the cement walls. The basement often leaks or floods, there are mice, and because of its location under and next to the building's ventilation system, one classroom may be insufferably hot whereas the one next door might be frigid. Classrooms are painted bright colors; however, with the neon lighting and lack of natural sunlight, these rooms are more garish than welcoming.

In any school, the singular individual with the most perceived power is the principal who occupies the unenviable middle-management position between unforgiving departments of education that deal primarily in statistics and test scores, parents, and the young people she or he is to guide, who enter school with outside life experiences that do not always blend seamlessly with the expectations of school. Students and their families have more collective power than a single principal, but this knowledge—and how to use it—are generally lost to families who have grown accustomed to, and accepted, the institutional authority of the principal. In many cases, ill-equipped parents—or parents whose self-perception is that they are ill-equipped to raise their children—rely on the principal as caregiver. Under the best of circumstances, the role of the principal is a difficult position to occupy: she or he is in the service of his or her students and their families and must also answer to city and state expectations. At LSHS, the principal is a key decision maker with a top-down, demoralizing management style.

In spite of its designation as a media theme school, at the end of the 2007–2008 school year, media studies were conspicuously absent from the curriculum. From 2004 to 2006, the specific "media" classes were piecemeal at best, taught by faculty with arts experience but no pedagogical training. The students took courses in color theory, aesthetics, dance, or poetry. In 2005–2006, there was a loosely organized video production course and a journalism class for a brief period. Both courses did not last the entire year and were not taught as skills-based or critical theory classes but rather were places for students to create videos or written texts without coherent goals or objectives.

In 2006–2007, there were two media courses: media literacy and video production. These courses, along with other elective courses, were made into a formal four-cycle, 10-week rotation of classes. Students moved through the courses throughout the year; every effort was made for every student to take media literacy or video production, though this did not always happen. In 2007–2008, the media literacy class was dropped. There was a video production course for three-quarters of the year until the teacher resigned. In my estimation, the only "official" media class was the video production course; however, there was no official scaffolding of skills in this class. The first graduating class of LSHS had little consistency or coherence in their media studies training.

The division between media/elective classes and core classes is palpable in multiple ways. The media/elective teachers are part-time; the core teachers' preparation period is "covered" by the media/elective classes. In urban schools, there is often high teacher turnover; in LSHS media/elective classes, there is often multiple teacher turnover within the school year.[2] Because there is no licensure for alternative curricula, and as a way to keep the budget down, the media/elective teachers are not hired as teachers but rather as community associates, a legitimately vague job title that allows for flexibility in job description and expectation. If students fail a certain number of core classes, they will be held back and forced to repeat the grade. If students fail their media/elective courses, they will be moved to the next grade and will make up the missing elective credits over the course of their time in high school.

In observations of the core classes and curricular scope and sequence, teachers intend to respect the media theme but do not have any formal training in media studies. Many of the teachers try to include media as part of their curricula through the use of technology rather than critical analysis of media texts within the function of the subject. Professional development workshops in media education integration were offered, but time was not allocated for these for the teachers to attend.

New York City Public Schools and School Reform

The New York City Public School system has more than 1,400 schools serving a little more than 1 million young people (New York City Department of Education, 2008). It is the largest school system in the United States, serving a diverse collection of young people, the majority of whom are of African and Latino descent, from lower working-class and impoverished economic backgrounds. In 2002, Mayor Bloomberg took over the New York City Board of Education in an effort to heal a fractured system. He replaced the Board with the Department of Education and began systematically closing large failing schools and replacing them with small, theme-based schools (Anonymous, 2002; Hartcollis, 2002).

Bloomberg and his appointees did not come from political or pedagogic backgrounds but rather from business and corporate environments (Goodnough, 2003; Hartcollis, 2002). For the most part, New York City's academically competitive high schools were not impacted by Bloomberg's changes; these highly functioning, successful schools have no pressing need for broad, systemic changes. Indeed, after the large, failing schools were liquidated, faculty and staff at schools that were *not* dismantled expressed a degree of pride in "survival" (Miller, 2008).

The latest wave of school reform in the United States is a reemergence of the primacy of standardized testing, especially through the No Child Left Behind (NCLB) parameters. NCLB is the lens through which scholars currently examine the continued failure of schools to teach young people of color from impoverished backgrounds. Aronowitz (2004) writes that standardized tests "are the antithesis of critical thought. Their precise objective is to evaluate the students' ability to imbibe and regurgitate information and to solve problems according to prescribed algorithms" (¶1.4). Carlson (2004) writes the NCLB agenda "includes steep and continuing cuts in financial support to urban schools, both at state and federal levels, and the reorganization of the urban school curriculum around high-stakes testing in ways that are spiking dropout rates among poor African-Americans [and] Latino/a ... youth" (¶1.1). No systematic change on any level in the school system will cause the destruction of public school education for youth of privilege. In turn, no systematic change seems able to embrace the intellectual rights of poor students of color. In the era of standardized testing, schools and students are explicitly taught how to take (and pass) tests, not how to critically think about or engage material (Aronowitz, 2004; Carlson, 2004; Miller, 2008).

Any successful school reform will have to make serious, drastic changes that will inevitably disrupt the status quo for broad sectors of the community. According to education scholars, these changes need to be made at the ground level, and those involved in radical change must contend with upsetting a large number of powerful people (Anyon, 1997; Greene, 1988). School reform is also driven by political considerations. In New York City, the massive overhaul of the public school system was widely perceived as a political maneuver on the part of Mayor Bloomberg as a way to curry favor among a constituency believed to be largely forgotten and further disenfranchised through the Giuliani administration. Ironically, the students were swiftly left out of the conversation and, inevitably, their educations have suffered in the name of reform.

Defining Media Education

Any student studying the media and participating in media education deserves a clear starting point. There are significant and important definitions of media education and, if these definitions are not brought into the classroom, students will not move beyond their own colloquial understandings. Drawing from Tyner (1998) and Moore (1991), it was my intention to integrate a critical democratic approach that privileges students' preexisting knowledge, teaches them to question ideas, encourages them to challenge authority figures and authoritative systems, and to be self-aware of how they know what they know. Students have a great deal of knowledge about, and experience with, the media; however, this knowledge is largely colloquial. They can be very critical of texts and demonstrate solid analyses, especially on positions of subjugation. However, they do not employ a formal vocabulary nor do they negotiate the differences between their opinions and critical inquiries and analyses. The presumption is that their teachers are trained in and aware of formal approaches to the study of media and critical approaches to analysis and production of texts.

In the 2006–2007 school year, there was a formal media literacy class whose focus was the analysis of media texts. The majority of students took this 10-week course, offered in the media/elective cycle throughout the school year. For many unfortunate reasons, there was a rotation of teachers in charge of the class, so there was no consistency between classes. Based on the principal's assumption that media literacy fundamentals were already infused across the curriculum, the class was not offered beyond the 2006–2007 school year. In the 2007–2008 school year, the only formal media class for all grades was video production. Though the teacher tried to include elements of media analysis, as a filmmaker himself he focused mostly on production. The students interviewed for this research have a range of understanding, articulation, and defining media education. Arguably, students' definitions should grow in complexity and sophistication as they move through high school. The ninth -raders entering in 2007 have had no formal media literacy training. The tenth to twelfth-graders have conceivably been exposed to formal media literacy, multiple courses in production, and attempts at media education integration across the curriculum.

Monica, Tom, José, and Marlo are all ninth-graders, presumably the least versed in media education, and they define it thus:

MONICA: Um, learning about communication and the outside world, like anything new that you want to learn.

TOM: Media education is you're learning about being on TV, all the media stuff, what you could learn possibly from this school.

JOSÉ: To have a study of our society.

MARLO: Um ... media education ... media, like, the word media.

The tenth- and eleventh-grade students have conceivably been exposed to media literacy and may be expected to have a more solid grasp of a definition. Tenth- and eleventh-graders have greater experience with media classes, and it should be expected that they are more thoroughly versed in definitions of media education. However, in hearing their definitions, it is clear they are not. Tenth-graders J-trout and Joan each explain media education:

J-TROUT: TV. I mean, learning how to work a camera, but it doesn't take rocket science for a person to learn how to use a camera or a computer or something.

JOAN: Media, when I think of media, I think of everything that I feel has to deal with the media. Um, computers, television, singing, dancing, art, um, so when I think of media, that's what I be lookin' forward to seeing.

Eleventh-grade Lucy does not have a thorough definition of media education but struggles with the following, "Media education. I don't know, I don't really have a definition for that." In contrast, Genevieve and Alex, both eleventh graders, discuss their understandings of media education in conversation with each other:

GENEVIEVE: Just educating us on the different types of mediums. Like we talked in our English class. Our English teacher said that, you know, editorials come in different mediums like newspapers, um video, magazines, cartoons. So, just educating ourselves on that.

ALEX: I think it's to educate ourselves on different stereotypes, things that are stereotypical in this world.

The most advanced definitions of media education presumably come from the twelfth-graders, who have ostensibly been through four years of media studies training. This, however, is not the reality:

NINE: Um, media education I think it's like, um, everything that can communicate what's going on in the world, like what's happening with anything, like, um, anything that informs us basically, I don't know.

NINO: I think we need it. We need to pay attention to the media. Even though they not very truthful most of the time, and sometimes they are, but we need to pay attention, we need to know how it works. It's like the media's the future, we need-a learn about technology. I think they need to put it in every school. So everyone knows like an idea of it. So they pay attention to it, you know.

In conversation with one another, twelfth-graders Bruce, Peter, and Popcorn discuss their definitions:

BRUCE: That's a really broad topic.
POPCORN: Yeah, it's a really broad topic.
PETER: It could be commercials.
POPCORN: It could go into anything.
BRUCE: Yeah, 'cause when you say 'media,' that could be from a magazine to like your favorite commercial.
PETER: Newspaper.
BRUCE: So when you do media studies, film drops in there, magazines drop in there, it's like a whole bunch of stuff is under the category of media, so that's very broad.
POPCORN: And how to like communicate—

BRUCE: —Yeah, communication—

POPCORN: —With people. I think that area should be in like every school. Like, they should just have a class for that, 'cause like, if you know how to communicate with people, I mean, 'cause a lot of people don't.

BRUCE: Yeah, 'cause ah, there is an art to communication, there's an art to everything. Like, yeah, like I said, media's very broad and, and everything falls under media, media's just how something is presented. So like that's why like media is so broad 'cause everything is presented.

There is no doubt that media education encompasses a host of topics, techniques, and areas of conversation. However, the repeated use of the word *broad* in this conversation is a method by which the boys distance themselves from appearing unaware of the topic.

These definitions do not grow in sophistication and do not reflect a formal knowledge of media education. No interviewed student was able to formally state the principles of analysis, production, critical inquiry, or multiple literacies. The absence of a coherent, developed definition is, presumably, the fault of LSHS for not providing a media literacy class with clear learning objectives and activities. However, LSHS operates within a larger environment whose interests increasingly focus on the test and simultaneously does not provide space or resources to equip or provide teachers to teach this material. "Blame" for failure is easily shifted across multiple locations. The absence of definitions explores the balance between test-centered and student-centered education. Media education is not a "test-ready" subject but rather draws liberally from student participation, provided they are versed in the guiding principles; this demands a teacher trained in media studies who is comfortable drawing from student knowledge and cultivating a space for critical autonomy. Unfortunately, LSHS teachers have not had this training explicitly. The teachers draw from their own colloquial knowledge and bring this knowledge into the classroom. The absence of coherent, sophisticated definitions of media education is representative of pedagogical difficulties within LSHS specifically and NYC schools broadly and is felt most directly and immediately by the students.

Video Production

For three-quarters of the 2007–2008 school year, video production was the one formal media class at LSHS. Context is vital to learning, and the space and time wherein video production occurred included a series of obstacles. The video production teacher was highly skilled in production but, by his own admission, not in pedagogy. In May, he abruptly resigned, and the principal took over the class, an imperfect, stopgap measure at best. The class cycle lasted only 10 weeks, each meeting time less than an hour, and many cycles were interrupted by holidays. Include the students' own attendance problems and there was very little consistency throughout the school year. All students were expected to complete a video within 10 weeks and were, in theory, required to document their process with storyboards, production notes, or scripts. Overall, if a student completed a video, these preparatory aspects were overlooked. This illustrates a disregard of video production as a viable, complex subject worthy of more time and materials. At no time would we expect students to master traditional literacy without significant draft work over time; indeed, the revision process is built into curricula, across grades and subject matters. Yet in video production, it is acceptable to create one video, in one "draft," without application of formal production work, and be considered "proficient." Most students who were interviewed express little beyond basic technical knowledge in talking about their video production class. Ninth-grade José explains, "In video production, I learned how to film. And like, break time codes and like how to cut up the movie." Pyro, a tenth-grader, explains video production as a class where "we get to make videos by using camcorders and cameras and using computers." In the interviews, I encouraged the participants to talk about their work in video production, but this was not a substantive part of any conversation. For example, when I asked Nino her favorite class, she replied, "I could say media?" I said yes; however, she followed up by saying, "Well, since I was little, I always liked math. But I really like photography. I wish I could take that all year." Many participants expressed a desire to have "more" or "real" media classes. Popcorn, for example, chose after-school programs in photography and art because he felt the video production class did not challenge him. The absence of challenge is manifested through a minimal quantity of equipment to be shared by all students; a lot of time was spent waiting for cameras or computers. During time scheduled for production, there was not enough preparatory or process work for students to complete while awaiting equipment. Because the class was only 10 weeks long, there was little room for development or reflection within the cycle.

Integration Across the Curriculum

Media studies is not integrated across the curriculum. Instead, well-intentioned teachers use technology and videos to bolster their curricula whereas less adept or less flexible teachers make no attempt to include media in their curricula. Without a common foundation or collective agreement, media integration is predicated on teacher discretion and skill. For the most part, students believe they receive media training in their classes and are generally supportive of their teachers' work. If students get along with their teachers, they are willing to take instructional risks; without a personal connection, however, they retreat. On media inclusion, Nine defends the teachers' use of technology. She explains, "Yeah, we're a media-based school, so it's like in every class, we try to integrate the media, like we try to watch movies that will relate to the class, like in math class, we watched *A Beautiful Mind*. That has to do with numbers, I guess." Watching movies is important and can be used to teach critical thinking and textual analysis skills, but it is not what makes a media-themed school unique. Eleventh-grade Ivette sums up the inclusion of technology-as-media-education. In her estimation, media education is integrated in all her classes and she explains,

> The way that we use media in our school is by typing, researching, using a Smart Board or the teacher uses a projector in order to tell us what he wants us to do, telling us what's right, what's wrong, you know, he uses the board, he writes on the board.

Genevieve, too, argues the media are worked into all the classes, especially in English. She explains:

> [In English] we break down the media, what we see everyday in newspapers, in magazines, and even on-line. We break that down and say what's your point of view on this? What's your interpretation of this piece? And how do you feel on it? What's the tone? And we start to see behind the layers of the media that things aren't what meet the eye. And we began to develop our own ideas.

Nine is more critical of the media inclusion but believes her teachers do their best to include media studies. She explains:

> I think the teachers, when they plan their curriculum, they try to bring the media into it, and at times they do, but I don't think that the students can sometimes tell the difference between when we're making connections with our media studies and when we're not. Like, they just know it's a math class or it's an English class, they don't really notice the times that they integrate the media into it.

These answers reflect the students' respect for and trust in their teachers' expertise. No participant says their teacher does *not* integrate the media into classes; however, their answers show their understanding of media studies inclusion is varied, with shifting notions of responsibility. Ivette discusses the use of technology, especially computers, Smart Boards and projectors, as tools for learning and equates the *use* of technology with the *infusion* of media studies. Genevieve's list of questions provided by her English teacher reveals work done to uncover how students know what they know. Nine's commentary about teacher planning and student awareness belies the overall trust in teacher awareness and authority. It is the student's responsibility to 'make connections' between the subject and the media infusion. Because students generally believe in the authority of their teachers and trust in the knowledge of their subject matter, it rests on the students to be responsible learners: to learn from technology, to articulate epistemological positions, and to recognize the presence or absence of media studies connection. In this iteration, students inadvertently draw from the neo-liberal orthodoxy that it is their own responsibility to learn about the media within the planned curricula.

Without a formal grounding in media education, the resulting curriculum gravitates toward an approach wherein the inclusion of "media" is largely about the inclusion of technology. Students rarely have opportunities to discuss audiences, analysis, and production topics within a critical media studies framework. They are invited to share their opinions though, in Nine's estimation, this might not happen with the knowledge that it is occurring in a media studies framework. The following shows how the participants articulate media studies integration in their core classes:

Social Studies

PYRO, 10TH GRADE: We use the computers to do Social Studies projects, you can make a slide show for any event in history.

GENEVIEVE, 11TH GRADE: And history, we looked at different articles like in the past. I know we looked at this article from um, from around the 1800s, um early 1900s about the women's movement.

POPCORN, 12TH GRADE: I mean, we look at news for political science, we look at newspapers about being on the debates.

Math

PYRO, 10TH GRADE: In math, yesterday we were watching Sweet 16 because we're on a budget project. So the assignment was to plan out a project for your Sweet 16, plan the ultimate birthday party. And you have to work on a certain budget.

Science

JOSÉ, 9TH GRADE: We were studying optical toys and that has to do with movement and that relates to media production.

PYRO, 10TH GRADE: Science, we've looked at videos like the Discovery show, Planet Earth. We watched basic educational programming.

GENEVIEVE, 11TH GRADE: In health class we're talking about viruses and vaccines, so we read an article about this town affected by this virus and how certain mothers didn't want their child vaccinated because they heard from the media that it harmed more than helped. So we learn a lot about health in America through articles and movies and television, like House, you know there was an episode where there was this virus that spread through a maternity ward. So, we studied the skills that House and his staff applied to find the sources of that virus.

POPCORN, 12TH GRADE: In science we read science articles, *New York Times*.

English

PYRO, 10TH GRADE: In English we watched a couple of movies for certain assignments. Like the movie *Speak* and we spoke about a current event that's somewhat like an epidemic, we talked about rape. We read a screenplay called *Fences*, which spoke on stereotypical stuff, like a black woman being the head of the family and everything.

GENEVIEVE, 11TH GRADE: In English we did editorials. Pick a social issue that affected us. The one that I picked, human trafficking, that's global. And the way I found out about it was from a movie on Lifetime, *Human Trafficking*. And also looked up on the website, which is also a form of media.

POPCORN, 12TH GRADE: In English, we watch movies and read movie reviews, you know just as another form of writing.

Media education at LSHS does not have a common definition or plan to integrate the theme across the curriculum. The use of computers, news articles, television shows, public health issues, and films can enhance subject learning. However, these cannot be "inserted" into a curriculum without corresponding work on their political implications. Moore (1991) details ways to include media across the curriculum and writes that one promise of media education is to "provide teachers of existing subjects with strategies for dealing anew with aspects of the media in their own teaching ... ideas for treating study texts as dynamic *producers of meaning* about history, geography, science or whatever" (p.173). Without analysis of the texts— and meta-analysis on the inclusion of such texts in the classroom space—the development of critical autonomy is lacking. The inclusion of technologies and texts can be used to open doors and make approachable discussions of political economy, construction and power of institutions, systematic racism/sexism/classism, and the history and purpose of schooling, among other subjects. That is, they can be used to draw directly from student experience and situate that experience in time and space. Use of technologies and texts can help make unfamiliar material familiar. To encourage students' critical autonomy and to help guide them beyond oppression and away from replicating their subjugated social positions, the study and use of the media is a necessary component. Approaching unfamiliar material and possibly controversial topics through familiar material may provide students with a strong multidisciplinary foundation and provide them space to be active participants in their classrooms. At LSHS, there is not a common community of learners with a coherent pedagogical approach to the study and inclusion of media. Media education *could* be successfully integrated into LSHS and, as it is, is reflective of the larger environment: A massive overhaul of each class, the curricula of the school, and the role of the school in the community is necessary.

Conclusion

For the most part, even the least motivated students know the "right" answers: they know what work needs to be done, and they know generally what to do to please their teachers. Many might choose not to do this, but overall, by high school, most students are familiar with the workings of the school system; there are very few curricular surprises. However, they are not always familiar with their immediate schools; the work done to adopt alternative pedagogies is not always transparent, and students bear the weight of experiments in curricular change. When students are presented with alternative curricula freedom of choice and are encouraged to develop and execute work in their own interests, many find this challenging and even overwhelming. From the outside, especially with the factory-like system of school and the emphasis on high-stakes testing, it seems like freedom of choice is a wholly good thing. However, it can be intimidating, and what students believe they are learning might not be the case. A curricular expectation with strict boundaries and clear scaffolding of goals and objectives is required. The goals need not be lofty and the technology need not be fancy, but the expectations and cohesion should be clear. Technology and text inclusion across the curriculum, like watching movies or TV shows, writing reviews of media, and using computers, is an exciting and fun part of class, but without complicating the work, with multiple levels of analysis and reflection, learning will not move beyond the superficial. The execution of the lessons in a media-infused class can involve students in a greater capacity than in a traditional or test-prep class. Moore's (1991) discussion of media studies inclusion introduces a variety of ways core courses can draw from media analysis; it does not need to be an "other" activity. When students begin to see texts as producers of meaning, they begin to unveil and make ideology material.

Popcorn illustrates that the use of media in his classes does not appear to be unique or extraordinary. Discussing the inclusion of watching movies or writing editorials or movie reviews, he retorts, "I mean, in what high school *don't* they use media? You know, like as a way of learning. I mean, every high school watches movies. Every high school uses the computer, so I don't really see a special thing about this high school." Popcorn taps into a key political problem in the attempt at media inclusion: what makes watching movies or using computers special? Popcorn is mostly disappointed by the undeserved reputation that the school is somehow unique because of its stated emphasis on self-expression. He argues, "I expect the school to like have a solid art class, but the only class we have that's like art-based, I would say, is film production. As far as intensity, it's not really intense, only if you're passionate about it." Popcorn struggles to explicate his frustration at the minimal access he feels he has to "real" arts- and media-based curricula. Through his and his fellow participants' iterations, media education is not clearly defined with explicit goals and objectives. The definitions provided by students are superficial and do not grow in complexity throughout their high school tenure. The work done in the name of media studies, according to the participants, belies technology inclusion, especially in the use of videos, computers, and the Internet. Popcorn reiterates the question of responsibility: is it the system or the student? Is it the motivated student who wants to do the work or the school system to make the work challenging? Popcorn observes that "we only have like one period a day that's media-based and most of the classes are not media based." He does believe it is possible to make the course work more complex and stronger but is not sure himself how to go about it. "Most definitely it is possible to, you know, make media a stronger base [and] force in this school," he says. As a graduating senior, he believes his role in the school is finished and does not think decision makers at the school would be interested in his critique.

His sense of defeat is reflective of the waning energy dedicated to media education inclusion. As the school year wound down, all bodies—adult and student—were restless. Class attendance and schoolwork were de-prioritized as the agony of state tests loomed and the excitement of prom and graduation grew.

The media are a major part of our culture, and they are worthy of study. Though this is an overly obvious statement, it has not worked its way into secondary schools in a significant manner. Media education—or work done in its name—will have no lasting impact without significant changes within individual schools and across the school system. Specifically, to fulfill its media theme, LSHS needs a series of media courses with clear goals and objectives that increase in analytic and production complexity from grades 9 to 12. Students should have courses in media literacy and media production that provide them with solid definitions and foundations of study, especially in analysis, roles of audience, construction of institutions, and dissemination of information. Without formal and systematic media literacy training, students will not move beyond their own colloquial analyses. They will not be able to explicate *why* studying the media is important, how the media inform our daily choices, or how the media are intricately a part of and mutually influenced by the material studied in their core courses. These media classes should not operate in isolation; teachers of media should make intellectual and curricular connections with teachers of core subjects, and all teachers should receive professional development courses in media education that are relevant and applicable to their subject matter.

Broadly, schools should not operate in isolation from one another or the larger communities. Further research should include conversations and work on professional development in media education for core subject teachers, licensure in media education, and theme-based and performance standards—regularly reviewed and improved upon—across the curriculum. The support that students and teachers need cannot be found only within the walls of individual schools. The language of new school reform needs to move beyond rhetoric. If they employ the language of radical change, schools and their communities need to be open to actual radical change. School systems themselves need solid foundations, not just rhetoric and political catchphrases. Without these, media education will continue to be incorrectly tagged as technology inclusion.

Given the rigid strictures of the school system, how should these statements of change be made manifest? The students who participated in this study, especially those who are highlighted in this chapter, show that there are serious gaps in media-specific classes and in the implementation of media studies across the curriculum. Upon graduation, students are not equipped with complex media-analysis skills and have encountered an education in technology inclusion, not media studies inclusion. At this stage, it is known what students do not know, are not learning and are not involved in. Despite the grim picture painted, I argue this is the clarion call to work toward a meaningful pedagogical intervention. This research begins inside the classroom with the emphasis that the walls are permeable and include the larger school, the community, and theories on education that deserve deeper examination. Media education will not alter the social or cultural capital of students, but it can provide the disruption that responds to the problematic test-as-education model and rattles the status quo.

Acknowledgments

I thank Kathleen Tyner for this opportunity and for her careful and immensely constructive editing; Wendy Chen for her curiosity, support, energy, and multiple readings; Robert for continued conversation and attention to detail; the students who participated, especially Popcorn: you have left an indelible mark on my heart.

Notes

1 All institutional and proper names and some identifying information have been changed to protect participants' confidentiality. Youth participants chose their own cover names.
2 In 2006–2007, four teachers left within the year; in 2007–2008, two teachers left within the school year.

References

Altman, L. K. (2008, March). Sex infections found in quarter of teenage girls. *New York Times*. Retrieved March 12, 2008, from nytimes.com

Anderson, P., & Summerfield, J. (2004). Why is urban education different from suburban and rural education? In S. R. Steinberg & J. L. Kincheloe (Eds.), *19 urban questions: Teaching in the city* (pp. 29–39). New York: Peter Lang.

Anonymous. (2002, March). Mayor Bloomberg's public schools. *New York Times*. Retrieved April 15, 2008, from nytimes.com

Anyon, J. (1997). *Ghetto schooling: A political economy of urban education reform*. New York: Teachers College Press.

Aronowitz, S. (2004, February). Against schooling: Education and social class. *Workplace: A Journal for Academic Labor*. Retrieved April 1, 2008, from cust. educ.ubc.ca/workplace.

Aufderheide, P. (1993). *Forum report: Media literacy—a report of the National Leadership Conference on Media Literacy*. Washington, DC: The Aspen Institute.

Bazalgette, C. (1992). Key aspects of media education. In M. Alvarado & O. Boyd-Barrett (Eds.), *Media education: An introduction* (pp. 199–219). London: The Open University Press.

Buckingham, D. (1990). *Watching media learning: Making sense of media education*. London: The Falmer Press.

Buckingham, D. (1991). Teaching about the media. In D. Lusted (Ed.), *The media studies book: A guide for teachers* (pp. 12–35). London: Routledge.

Buckingham, D. (1993). *Reading audiences: Young people and the media*. London: Manchester University Press.

Buckingham, D. (1998). *Teaching popular culture: Beyond radical pedagogy.* London: Routledge.

Buckingham, D. (2003). *Media education: Literacy, learning and contemporary culture.* London: Polity Press.

Buckingham, D., & Sefton-Greene, J. (1994). *Cultural studies goes to school: Reading and teaching popular media.* London: Taylor & Francis.

Buckingham, D., Grahame, J., & Sefton-Greene, J. (1995). *Making media: Practical production in media education.* London: English & Media Centre.

Carlson, D. (2004, February). Leaving children behind: Urban education, class politics, and the machines of transnational capitalism. *Workplace: A Journal for Academic Labor.* Retrieved April 1, 2008, from cust.educ.ubc.ca/workplace.

Coffey, A., & Atkinson, P. (1996). *Making sense of qualitative data: Complementary research strategies.* Thousand Oaks, CA: Sage.

Fine, M. (1998). Working the hyphens: Reinventing self and other in qualitative research. In N. K. Denzin & Y. S. Lincoln (Eds.), *The landscape of qualitative research* (pp. 130–155). Thousand Oaks, CA: Sage.

Fine, G. A., & Sandstrom, K. L. (1988). *Knowing children: Participant observation with minors.* Newbury Park, CA: Sage.

fisherkeller, J. (2002). *Growing up with television: Everyday learning among young adolescents.* Philadelphia: Temple University Press.

Giroux, H. A. (2004, February). Class casualties: Disappearing youth in the age of George W. Bush. *Workplace: A Journal of Academic Labor.* Retrieved April 1, 2008, from cust.educ.ubc.ca/workplace.

Goldstein, R. (2004). Who are our urban students and what makes them so different? In S. R. Steinberg & J. L. Kincheloe (Eds.), *19 urban questions: Teaching in the city* (pp. 41–51). New York: Peter Lang.

Goodman, S. (2003). *Teaching youth media: A critical guide to literacy, video production, and social change.* New York: Teachers College Press.

Goodnough, A. (2003, February). In picking top schools, Klein trips on urban politics. *New York Times.* Retrieved April 15, 2008, from nytimes.com.

Gorelick, S. (1996). Contradictions of feminist methodology. In H. Gottfried (Ed.), *Feminism and social change* (pp. 23–45). Urbana, IL: University of Illinois Press.

Grahame, J. (1991). The production process. In D. Lusted (Ed.), *The media studies book: A guide for teachers* (pp. 146–170). London: Routledge.

Greene, M. (1988). *The dialectic of freedom.* New York: Teachers College Press.

Guba, E. G., & Lincoln, Y. S. (1998). Competing paradigms in qualitative research. In N. K. Denzin & Y. S. Lincoln (Eds.), *The landscape of qualitative research* (pp.195–220). Thousand Oaks, CA: Sage.

Harris, G. (2007, December). Teenage birth rate rises for first time since '91. *New York Times.* Retrieved December 12, 2007, from nytimes.com.

Hartcollis, A. (2002, June). Consensus on city schools: History, growing outrage leads back to centralized leadership. *New York Times.* Retrieved April 15, 2008, from nytimes.com.

Heldke, L. (1998). On being a responsible traitor: A primer. In B. Bar-On & A. Ferguson (Eds.), *Daring to be good: Essays in feminist ethico-politics* (pp. 87–99). London: Routledge.

Leistyna, P. (2004, February). Introduction: Youth as a category through which class is lived. *Workplace: A Journal for Academic Labor*, 6. Retrieved April 1, 2008, from cust.educ.ubc.ca/workplace.

Lindlof, T. R. (1995). *Qualitative communication research methods*. Thousand Oaks, CA: Sage.

Liptak, A. (2008, February). 1 in 100 U.S. adults behind bars, new study says. *New York Times*. Retrieved February 28, 2008, from nytimes.com.

Miller, J. (2008, September). Tyranny of the test: One year as a Kaplan coach in the public schools. *Harper's* 35–46.

Moore, B. (1991). Media education. In D. Lusted (Ed.), *The media studies book: A guide for teachers* (pp. 171–190). London: Routledge.

New York City Department of Education. (2008). About us. Retrieved December 3, 2008, from http://schools.nyc.gov/AboutUs/default.htm

New York City Department of Education. (2008). Our schools. Retrieved November 1, 2008, from http://schools.nyc.gov/TeachNYC/teachinnyc/OurSchoolsOurStudents/ourschools.htm

Schwandt, T. A. (1998). Constructivist, interpretivist approaches to human inquiry. In N. K. Denzin & Y. S. Lincoln (Eds.), *The landscape of qualitative research* (pp. 221–259). Thousand Oaks, CA: Sage.

Tyner, K. (1998). *Literacy in a digital world: Teaching and learning in the age of information*. Mahwah, NJ: Lawrence Erlbaum Associates.

Way, N. (1998). *Everyday courage: The lives and stories of urban teenagers*. New York: New York University Press.

Western, B. (2006). *Punishment and inequality in America*. New York: Russell Sage.

Part III

The Next Generation

Media Literacy in Higher Education

Chapter 5

Composing and Reflecting

Integrating Digital Video in Teacher Education

David L. Bruce

Introduction

I have been using video as a mode of student composition in my former high school and current college classrooms for 18 years. During that time, I have seen powerful classroom learning experiences in reaching a wide range of students and accomplishing a number of English language arts (ELA) applications in meaningful group settings. Throughout my career, I have encountered non-print skeptics who asked, "So what"? *So what if they are making a video poem? They still need to pass a high-stakes test based around print literacy skills. So what if your teacher educators know how to use video in the classroom? They still need to follow standards-based instruction.*

Over the years, I have kept that "so what" question in the back of my mind as I have taught and researched video in the classroom. Rather than perceive those skeptical questions as mockery, I have thought of them as a good questions to ask: So what is really going on here? So what are students really learning?

The research presented in this chapter is a response to that "so what" question. The context of the study took place within an English education program during a two-course sequence taken in the senior year, prior to student teaching. These courses explored the teaching of reading, writing, and language within the socio-context of 7 to 12 adolescent classrooms. This assignment, composing a video in response to a written poem, was also designed to meet standards for teaching traditional ELA content but with a multimodal perspective.

The questions that guided this study were as follows:

1 What happens when students compose in a new medium?
2 How do they reflect on both the process and product of their compositions? What do their commentaries reveal?

Video in the Classroom

A growing body of teachers and researchers has documented the use of video in ELA classes. The numerous activities and applications of video include narratives, poems, advertisements, diaries, interpretations, documentaries, news features, interviews, music videos, public service announcements, reenactments, propaganda activities, and more (Bengtson, 2007; Brass, 2008; Brown, 2007; Bruce, 2008a, 2008b; Goodman, 2003; Hobbs, 2007; Kajder, 2006; Lund, 1998; Ranker, 2008; Tyner, 1998; Williams, 2007). Many of the activities are variations on traditional print ELA assignments that have been adapted to video.

The difference in the adaptation from print to video, however, is often profound. Not only does the modality of the response change, so does the number of options of representation. Albers (2006) calls this process *transmediation*, "a literacy strategy in which learners retranslate their understanding of an idea, concept, or text through another medium" (p. 90). Hull (2003) states that composing through new informational technologies "offer[s] distinctive contrasts to the primarily alphabetic texts and the forms of textual reasoning that predominated in schools and universities" (p. 230). Through the use of images and audio and words, the students are able to offer an interpretation with video that is different than with print alone (Bruce, 2008a; Miller & Borowicz, 2005).

Teacher education has also embraced the idea that students could represent their thoughts through the medium of video (Albers, 2006; Miller, 2007, 2008; Miller & Borowicz, 2005). This is an important step, as teacher training with new media is needed for this to filter into classroom practice (Fox, 2005; Goetze, Brown, & Schwarz, 2005; Hobbs, 2007). But to what end? What is beyond the novelty of using an emerging technology for student learning?

Cuban (2001) studied the policy and social embrace of providing computer-based technologies to classrooms and concluded, "the investment of billions of dollars over the last decade has yet to produce worthy outcomes" (p. 197). He stated that one of the reasons for this was unquestioned acceptance that computers themselves would fundamentally change pedagogy, student learning, and the manner in which classrooms would function. As digital video is computer-based, research of classroom uses of video cannot repeat those same faulty assumptions.

One such area for needed study is of the students' reflection on their learning processes with video. For example, in teacher education, encouraging candidates to reflect and comment upon their activities and experiences is crucial for critical awareness of both the process and product of communication in a variety of forms (Albers, 2006). One such reflective practice is the use of heuristics. Van Der Geest & Spyridakis (2000) state:

> The word heuristic comes from the Greek word for "discovering." Heuristics are procedures or principles that help their users work systematically toward a discovery, a decision, or a solution. Heuristics are typically used in situations where there is more than one good answer, more than one solution. They increase the chance that the solution chosen is the best possible solution among the many solutions possible. The Greek rhetoricians, for example, used heuristics to "discover" what to say in their speeches (p. 301).

Hillocks (1986) defined heuristics as a "systematic guide for investigating a phenomenon and may be as simple as the newswriting heuristic of who, what, when, where, why" (p. 178). In examining a number of studies that examined students' use of heuristics in their writing, he found that student writing improved in depth and breadth.

In my classes, I have used a heuristic as a means of getting students to describe what they videotaped and edited, to articulate their compositional choices, and to evaluate the final work. This uncovering became a way for students to explicate the intentionality and concepts behind their processes. Using a similar process with this study, when the teacher candidates had finished their videos, they reflected upon their compositional choices using a three-question heuristic:

1 Describe the shot.
2 Why did you choose to film the scene in this manner? What were you trying to show?
3 Evaluate the shot. How pleased were you with the final result? Please explain.

By using this heuristic, students were able to state their explicit knowledge of what they had done while also articulating the otherwise implicit aspects of reading and composition intentionality.

My own uses of and interest with video have primarily been to explore ways to get others to use the modality in meaningful ways for self-expression. This study explores how novices used these powerful compositional tools to provide alternative assessments to traditional English assignments (i.e. analyze a poem, respond to literary passage, and compose a narrative).

These students had relatively little experience prior to this assignment with any sort of formal (and informal) uses of reading and writing with video tools. Few had any media studies courses, and those who did took the classes in high school. None of them had professional video aspirations. The students' main experiences were dealing with print. Their print-centric experience became problematic when using terminology and talking about digital video.

To that end, I used words and phrases with which I knew they would be tacitly familiar regarding moving image media (cinema, film, footage, etc.) to make connections to the newer digital formats with which they would be working. Consequently, their inter-textual discussions fused terminology of print, film, and video, ironically mirroring the hybrid compositions with which they were working.

As part of their training to read and write with video, the class engaged in video analysis and deconstruction as they studied the language of a film clip. Students were taught a basic video grammar that consists of various combinations of establishing, reaction, and perspective shots (Begleiter, 2001). In addition, they considered the uses of other production elements such as audio, editing, graphics, special effects, and others. Students engaged in several whole-class deconstructions to model the assignment. They then individually completed a scene deconstruction for a film clip they might use in their own classroom.

Throughout the process, students engaged in storyboard activities to become more familiar with framing and sequencing. Students also viewed examples of classroom produced (both 7–12 and pre-service teacher) videos. Afterward, they received a brief tutorial on digital camera use and iMovie video editing software prior to beginning their assignments.

The Class

With 26 students in the class, students indicated limited experiences with digital video tools. Table 5.1 indicates the practice students had with any video equipment prior to the assignment.

The students who indicated experience with video cameras and editing had all recently taken a supplemental workshop college class as an elective offered in the English education program. Only two of them had prior experience in high school programs.

Assignment

Students were given the assignment of creating a response to a poem in digital video format. Table 5.2 displays the handout they were given for the assignment.

Table 5.1 Student experience with equipment (n=26)

Training	Yes	No
Storyboarding	5	21
Videocamera	9	18
Editing	9	18

Table 5.2 Create a video CinePoem assignment

You will create a CinePoem for which you will supply the video and audio to an existing poem text. The poem may be your own or may be one that you choose from a collection.

You will work in teams/groups of your choice of 3–4 people. In extenuating circumstances I may allow someone to work individually. However, due to the logistics of making a video, you are better off working collaboratively.

In addition to the time introducing this in class, you will be working together in several class sessions in your groups to select the poem and begin brainstorming images and planning your video. We will be completing these video poems this semester.

Requirements:
Treatment: Select a poem and write a brief (2–3 paragraphs) perspective of what you envision this video looking like. You will want to select a video that evokes images. Based on your concept, you must be able to capture an original moving image (i.e. most likely NO helicopter footage ...). All the digital video must be original. You may use still images that you have taken on a still camera.

Storyboard: Use the storyboard to create a representation that blends the text of the poem with the visuals you wish to create.

Raw Footage: Use a digital camera. If you do not have access to one, they are available in the Instructional Resource Center for sign out. PLEASE DO NOT USE THE VIDEO FUNCTIONS ON A STILL-FRAME CAMERA. THE FILE WILL NOT TRANSFER

Finished Version: Your finished version will include the text of the poem (written or spoken), all original video footage, and music (if appropriate). When you are finished with editing the video, download the finished version back to the DV tape (put it after your raw footage).

Reflection: When you turn in your final video, you are also going to turn in a two-part reflection. The fim is the attached sheet, answering questions regarding the shots/selections that you used. This part will be completed as a group. The second is to go back to your treatments and compare how you originally envisioned the video and how it actually turned out. What were surprises (serendipitous videography, etc.) and disappointments. How closely did your original idea relate to your final project?

Table 5.3 Poems selected by groups for CinePoem projects (*n*=26)

Number in group	Poem
4	*Anchor* by K. Noga
2	*Yesterday* by J. Castaldi
2	*The Pasture* by R. Frost
4	*Mirror* by S. Plath
2	*Dulce et Decorum Est* by W. Owen
4	*The Prepositions* by S. Odds

Data Sources

The data from this study were based on attributes of student work (initial concepts, storyboards, videos, heuristics, and reflections), surveys, interviews with two students, and a teacher journal.

Groups

Students were to work in groups of two to four people. Students could choose to respond to an existing poem or one of their own. The class self-selected their group members and divided into six groups. Table 5.3 details the number of groups and the poems they selected.

Of the six groups, five chose poems written by other authors. One group, *Anchor*, selected a poem written by one of the students in the group.

Anchor Group

The following section presents the work of one of the groups composed of three students. The poem the group selected, *Anchor*, was written by one of the members who kept a poetry notebook. They were interested in process of composing two original versions—print and video—of the poem.

ORIGINAL POEM

> *Anchor*
> I envy the butterfly.
> —so careless
> —so elegant
> Fluttering from one flower to the next,
> without a salt of care for the petal she last made her bed.

I envy the feather,
That gently drifts through the air.
—so fine
—so free
No responsibilities to mark of.
Able to visit the whole world,
without leaving a dent in the land she touches.

TREATMENT

TREATMENT

The following is the written treatment of how the group envisioned their poem translated to the modality of video.

> Our purpose in this CinePoem is to bring a poem to life, so to speak. This is ever more prominent of a goal since the poem has many allusions to nature and living a "full" life. Through the footage we hope to juxtapose several items—the clear, sheer beauty of nature with the fettered existence that many people live; the live action of video interspersed with shots of the actual writing of the poem.
>
> All of these goals really boil down to one single objective: we wish to interpret the poem through our choice of images. Seeing as we have the author of the poem in our group and that we have some very specific images drawn directly from the poem, we hope to give the poem a very literal interpretation.

In examining their initial treatment, the group was concerned with adapting an existing poem with corresponding visuals, yet they did not specifically articulate what those visuals would be. Rather, they focused more on the theme they wanted their video to convey, namely, the simplicity of nature compared to the harried manner in which people live. The group stated the images they envisioned represented a literal interpretation of the poem. However, I perceive they moved beyond a one-to-one correspondence of text to image. Through their use of juxtaposed visuals, the group used the conventions of digital video to convey their ideas in a manner not possible with a print interpretation of their poem.

HEURISTIC

The following section contains their heuristic of the project. I include the storyboards and video stills from their project to correspond with the images about which they were writing. Some of the scenes do not have a storyboard indicating changes they made to their initial concept for their project. In addition, they do not mention their music selection

Figure 5.1 Storyboard of sequence 2   *Figure 5.2* Video still of sequence 2

accompanying the video. They choose a Japanese instrumental, a slow song containing a meditative feel.

Sequence 1. Intro and credits to poem

Sequence 2. Writing "Anchor" in the notebook. This shot sets up the poem and the video. We were pleased with the shot because of how well it sets up the poem (Figures 5.1 and 5.2).

Sequence 3. Kathleen writing in her notebook with a feather in the background on the windowsill. There is a cross-fade to the next shot where Kathleen looks out the window and notices the feather and also sees Scott in the distan[ce]. We wanted to emphasize the connection between nature, individuals and the writing process. It opens the plot up to inside and outside characters. (Figure 5.3)

Sequence 4. Cross-fade to Scott gazing down with a look of wonder and happiness. We wanted to show Scott reacting, but the audience doesn't know to what so it creates intrigue. It works as a transition to the next shot. (Figure 5.4 and 5.5)

Sequence 5. Flower and butterfly sequence. Established the butterfly on the flower. Cross-fade to Scott's hands going towards the flower

Figure 5.3 Video still of sequence 3

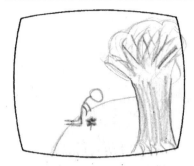

Figure 5.4 Storyboard of sequence 4

Figure 5.5 Video still of sequence 4

and him picking it up gently. He admires the butterfly and flower. Establishes Scott's connection and fascination with nature. We liked how the shots show the connection between man and nature. Also very effective camera angle and zoom. (Figures 5.6 and 5.7)

Sequence 6. More writing of the poem showing the first few lines. The writing ties the writer to Scott and the events happening outside. This is a broken sequence [sic]. We liked how it shows the thought process of the writer and the man on nature. (Figure 5.8)

Figure 5.6 Storyboard of sequence 5

Figure 5.7 Video still of sequence 5

Figure 5.8 Video still of sequence 6

Figure 5.9 Video still of sequence 7

Sequence 7. Scott admiring the butterfly on the flower. Also a broken sequence [sic]. The expressions on Scott's face confirm that his thoughts are the same as the writer's. We liked how we split this sequence with the writing sequence to show the connection between the two people (Figure 5.9)

Sequence 8. Looking through the window from outside at Kathleen writing and the feather is still on the window. There is a reflection of trees in the window showing another connection between man and nature. Kathleen begins to notice the feather. Kathleen writing more of the poem, writing about the feather, but from inside. We like how it shows the inspiration for the poem (Figures 5.10 and 5.11).

Sequence 9. The feather flies away and Kathleen notices. Kathleen continues to write about the feather. We originally were going to have a sequence of the feather floating/flying around, but the shots didn't turn out as we had hoped, so that was the original motivation for this shot (Figures 5.12 and 5.13).

Sequence 10. Looking out the window zooming in towards Scott. This was the establishing shot to show Scott as the subject for the

Figure 5.10 Storyboard of sequence 8

Figure 5.11 Video still of sequence 8

Figure 5.12 Storyboard of sequence 9   *Figure 5.13* Video still of sequence 9

rest of the video. We like the zoom and slow motion so the change wouldn't be so abrupt (Figures 5.14 and 5.15).

Sequence 11. Cross-fade into Scott putting the flower back into the ground as a show of his separateness from nature. We wanted to focus on the butterfly and nature, so we had to show Scott putting it away. (Figure 5.16)

Figure 5.14 Storyboard of sequence 10   *Figure 5.15* Video still of sequence 10

Figure 5.16 Video still of sequence 11

Figure 5.17 Storyboard of sequence 12

Figure 5.18 Video still of sequence 12

Sequence 12. Scott sequence. The snap back to reality with Scott realizing time as an issue. He looks at his watch and stands slowly up and begins to walk away and fades out. There are three shots showing the text of the rest of the poem. We wanted to show the weight of time and responsibilities on man in contrast to the butterfly and the feather Figures 5.17 and 5.18).

Sequence 13. A fade in to the butterfly flying freely and the scene whites out at the end. We wanted to show how the butterfly has a free life and he is not tied down like the man is. This was our favorite shot because of how real the butterfly looked and how it tied the video all together (Figures 5.19 and 5.20).

GROUP AND COMPOSITION ASPECTS

The *Anchor* group worked collaboratively and shared equitable workload between the members. They got all of their footage on one afternoon

Figure 5.19 Storyboard of sequence 13

Figure 5.20 Video still of sequence 13

outside of class. This was not typical of all the groups, as some of them took several sessions of videotaping to get all of their needed visuals. The *Anchor* group completed their editing over three class meetings and several sessions outside of scheduled class times. One member stated that she "loved seeing how all of our ideas and images came together to create something we are proud of."

It is worth noting that though there was a linear aspect to their video production (brainstorming, videotaping, editing), they also worked in an iterative fashion whereby those stages overlapped or occurred in a non-sequential manner. Though they all shared the same stages of creating the video, no one group worked in the same manner as the others to compose their video. For example, some groups began editing prior to all of their footage being completed, whereas others conceptualized new ideas and gathered additional video once they worked with the editing program.

Findings

The goal of the project was to have students in an English education program compose a response to a poem using digital video. The assignment took longer than I had originally planned, requiring an extension of the project deadline to accommodate technical and logistical issues that arose through the work. Despite the timeline issues, the project proved to be a rich assignment for the students. The questions guiding my research were as follows:

1 What happens when students compose in a new medium?
2 How do they reflect on both the process and product of their compositions? What do their commentaries reveal?

In this section, I address aspects of their composing processes, successes and frustrations, and reflections on their process and product.

Composing in Two Media

In analyzing their work, one finding deals with the ability to envision the poem through images. A striking element about placing the storyboards next to the final image is the verisimilitude between their initial thoughts and their final product. This is an explicit connection that the modality of video affords. Though the storyboards are rudimentary, they capture the essence of the shot the group envisioned. This is not to say that the final project looks exactly like the storyboards or that all ideas made it to the final version. There were several storyboard frames that this group was unable to film owing to logistics and/or not being able to represent the video footage as they had imagined. For example, they conceptualized a sequence of a floating feather (they got the idea from the closing sequence of *Forrest Gump*) but, as they stated in their heuristic "the shots didn't turn out as we had hoped," so they made changes.

The other five groups had similar experiences. Many of their envisioned storyboard shots were strikingly similar in shape and/or frame to their final takes. Time and time again, the frames of their storyboards served as a visual template for their final video. Each group discarded some of their original ideas for video-either because the moving images they envisioned were not satisfactorily captured or, more likely, they shot better video along the way.

Successes and Frustration

This assignment generated more positive feedback and enthusiasm than any other activity students completed during the two semesters they were in class. When asked in their post-project reflections what was their best moment in the project, the answers were distributed through a number of aspects of the composing process. Table 5.4 indicates the range of their responses.

Table 5.4 Student responses to best moments of the CinePoem project (*n*=26)

Favorite aspect of project	Number of students responding	Sample student comment
Viewing final project	7	We were able to see to share our "imagined" video and come together to create a linear, cohesive product.
Camerawork	6	When we filmed driving through steam coming up from the sewer. The poem is dingy and a little depressing and the shot captured the essence of the poem.
Editing	6	Editing was my favorite part of creating the video poem. I enjoyed adding text and music to the images as well as all the special effects you can add.
Conceptualizing the project	5	I had the most enjoyment from creating the storyboard and finding shots that really grasped the meaning of the poem.
Group work	2	We experienced a positive group dynamic during our first day of filming and we learned how group interaction promotes a sense of team ownership.

Table 5.5 Most frustrating aspect of the CinePoem project (n=26)

Most frustrating aspect of the video project	Numbers of student responses
Technology problems	12
Group dynamics	8
Videotaping issues	5
Conceptual problem	1

Despite their enthusiasm for the project, the video technology was problematic for many of the students. Of the 26 students in the class, 23 mentioned that they felt inadequately prepared for using the video program and/or video camera. Students felt they needed additional tutorials to become more familiar with using the technology. Even those who had some facility with the equipment mentioned they wanted more training and experience. One student said

> I still need training with the camera and the computer. If I had more experience with the technology, I could have further executed my ideas. I wish I would have the opportunity to do another video composition because I feel more prepared and decisive. I speculate my group would have more confidence and be more experimental. My skills concerning technology held me back.

Ironically, as no other assignment generated such enthusiasm from the students, no other generated as much frustration either. When asked in their post-project reflections what were their most frustrating moments in composing their videos, technology problems were cited as the number one frustration (Table 5.5).

Technology problems dealt primarily with the DV editing software, particularly glitches in the program such as ghost images of text they could not delete. More often, the main problem was the program shutting down and losing progress since they had last saved the project. Videotaping issues sometimes involved the camera equipment, such as videotaping a scene with poor lighting, but also logistical issues, such as finding common time to meet to videotape or encountering inclement weather when they had planned to shoot video. One student said, "There were times when we thought the footage would come out really great but in the end it was useless."

When responses about technology and videotaping frustrations were combined, nearly two-thirds of the class's roadblocks dealt with the technology issues. Some of the problems dealt with inexperience with the equipment, others dealt with technology not functioning properly and, owing to their inexperience, to their inability to efficiently perform the inevitable troubleshooting needed in the production process.

Not surprisingly, given the problematic nature of group work, one-third of the class related some aspect of group dynamics as their main source of frustration. Some of this revolved around leadership struggles ("as a group, we began editing. It wasn't that we couldn't agree on choices, it was just that some people take the reigns and refuse to relinquish them"); fair share of group work ("not all members of the group were willing to put in equal time and effort"); and/or personality conflicts ("I would have preferred working alone"). Though I have not systematically documented this phenomenon, I can anecdotally state that the group problems are not isolated to this study. I have seen some aspect of group dysfunction over the years in nearly every context I have used video in the classroom. Though many groups tend to work well, there are always groups that have difficulty sharing a common vision or sharing the work equitably. However, despite problems reported in the groups, there appeared to be a healthy tension in working collaboratively. One member of a group stated

> I had to keep in mind that other people are working with you. As much as I wanted this to be mine, I was working with others. At the time it frustrated me, but I realized all my ideas can't go with a group—they needed their time, and wanted it as much as I did ... Each person in the group came together and produced a piece I am very proud of.

Despite the setbacks of equipment or group issues, students overwhelmingly responded positively to the project. Many of them indicated they wanted to do another such project, not only to become more familiar with the equipment but to try variations of other ELA-based assignments with video.

Reflecting on Their Work

Students articulated their tacit and explicit ELA knowledge through the video composition and through their reflections. One of the goals the *Anchor* group stated in their treatment was to contrast "the clear, sheer beauty of nature with the fettered existence that many people live." In examining *Anchor's* heuristic, the students were clear to mention this juxtaposition several times. They were not only able to say they wanted to do it as articulated in their reflection; they were able to use the conventions of the video to express their vision.

For example, construction of the montage contributed to the expression of their CinePoem concept. In sequence 10, the group used a slow zoom toward Scott. They stated, "We like the zoom and slow motion so the change wouldn't be so abrupt." Other groups were also able to be explicit in their ability to state their intended result and use the equipment to articulate that vision. One of the many such examples was the *Yesterday* group. Their selected poem follows.

> *yesterday* (Jesse B. Castaldi)
> a long laundromat hour, an old fade,
> a familiar slide of time;
> soap in boxes, machines of it;
> a sign begs, "keep this place clean."
> outside, the bars are so wetly lit in their
> silent huddled storefronts;
> electric buses pass by in the rain
> with their peculiar leviathan sound
> noising in the night.
> electricity hums along wires
> strung above the street, fine web of wire.
> i wait to be inhabited, smoothing laundry,
> feeding the tumbling with coins, buses swim
> along the street, sighing those metal sighs.
> there isn't a thing i do today
> that does not have your name written, sounding into it;
> sounds like something maybe looking for air,
> breaching above the wetness,
> maybe calling a name
> out into that dark, folding sky.

The group envisioned a grainy, dingy look to their video. In their reflection they stated,

> We got footage as the description of the poem reads directly. We collected shots as they are described in the poem to get a true insight on how the poem reads. Once we put all of our shots together as they read in the poem, we put our own interpretations on how they should look by adding the special effects [turning the footage into black and white, adding aged effects to the footage].

Another finding is that students were able to integrate their existing knowledge of literary devices in the video production process. These students were all English education majors and would have been familiar with these in their coursework. The *Anchor* group explicitly mentioned plot, characters, and allusions. They made specific references to aspects of composition such as writing process, sequence, contrast, and transitions.

They also implicitly used concepts of coherence and point of view. In analyzing the class sets of treatments and heuristics, students made explicit reference (or demonstrated the implicit use of) the following ELA content knowledge:

- literary devices (mood, metaphor, tone, parallelism, contrast, foreshadowing, etc.);
- audience awareness;
- perspective/point of view;
- composition processes (brainstorming, drafting, revision, publishing);
- using composition tools for intended effect.

The heuristics and reflections also revealed that students were able to articulate and demonstrate their knowledge of video grammar. This was an important part of learning the visual language. The *Anchor* group specifically mentioned *establishing* ("to show Scott as the subject for the rest of the video"), *reaction* ("the expression on Scott's face confirm that his thoughts are the same as the writer's"), and *perspective* ("Kathleen looks out the window and notices the feather and also sees Scott in the distance") shots. Each of the other groups demonstrated the same sort of process knowledge. In fact, learning to use this rudimentary terminology seemed to allow all the groups a functioning understanding of how the three kinds of shots worked together in a purposeful manner.

Discussion

Although the use of personal video equipment dates back to at least the mid–twentieth century, the technology was "new media" to my students in a formal classroom setting. Few of them had any practice using video cameras, even for recreational purposes. Fewer still had any experience using DV editing programs. Thus, students faced the dual tasks of not only learning how to use the equipment but learning how to apply such technology in traditionally print-based classrooms. Nevertheless, with explicit training in reading and composing video, the students quickly picked up the skills needed to create their video responses to the poems.

Using an established research protocol, heuristics, for a new media assignment proved to be helpful. As the explosion of new media continues, so will the potential applications for out of school literacies to make their way into in school applications. Though teachers and researchers should continue to document the use and application of these new media, the field should not lose sight of the question "so what?" in studying these new applications. So what is happening in the classroom? So what are the students learning? Using the heuristic allowed the students time to reflect and evaluate their interpretive and compositional choices. In addition, the heuristic proved to be a valuable research tool by having a written articulation of their thoughts on the process and product. In many ways, it served much in the same function as a director's commentary feature on a DVD.

The social and audience components of the project were also important learning devices both in informal and formal ways. There was frequent and informal feedback as the students worked together in the lab. Often one group would ask another for some "how-to" advice regarding the DV editing program. It was not uncommon to have portions of the working video seen and commented by other students. This allowed for immediate feedback for the production group to perceive whether they were getting the kind of audience feedback they had imagined. At the completion of the project, all videos were premiered on a large screen for the entire class to view. Students were prompted to react with comments about what they enjoyed about the video: interpretation, visuals, audio/textual cues, and the like. This was a tremendous source of satisfaction with the class and one that resonated far after the assignment was over. I received verbal and course feedback regarding how important that part of the process was.

Though it takes class time—often an entire class session—I have found the public viewing of the project to be integral to the process. The audience feedback is immediate and powerful for the group presenting their work. They are able to entertain comments and questions about their projects. It also seems appropriate that for such a visually based assignment, part of the evaluation would be public. This is something difficult to do with print assignments, as the students in English classrooms are most often writing for the singular audience of teacher.

I have used this digital video assignment in various teacher education courses with hundreds of students. One of the biggest teaching considerations is time. Time is needed in class for video training both in learning to read and compose videos. Time is also needed to complete the heuristic. There is merit in students' articulation of interpretive and compositional choices. I have found that the most valuable manner of doing the heuristic is in groups. As nearly all the research on video in the classroom has focused on group production (Bruce, 2008b; Goodman, 2003; Hobbs, 2007; Kajder, 2006; Miller, 2007; Miller & Borowicz, 2005; Ranker, 2008), it follows that the reflections of their work should have a collaborative element as well. Typically, the students huddled around the screen while viewing their video. They discussed anecdotes that occurred throughout the process, what they wished they could have done differently, what they were pleased with, and so on. The reflection process tended to be dialogic between their video text and their experience in creating it. The group dynamic allowed for multiple viewpoints and, often, one member prompted an idea, event, or compositional choice the others had forgotten.

Another consideration that was present in this study mirrors what I have consistently seen throughout the years of working with video, namely the constant technology issues. There will be problems. It is endemic to the process. I have learned that stating this fact up front alleviates some of the anxiety and tension, particularly those technology novices who exclaim that the computer hates them. Articulating potential equipment issues sets an atmosphere of problem solving rather than panic when glitches inevitably arise. I have also learned that potential problems can be alleviated through anticipating some of the issues.

For example, computer and/or program crashes are the most common technological problem I have observed, particularly when a group loses unsaved changes when a crash occurs. To that end, our class began the practice of yelling "save!" whenever someone thought to do so, prompting the other groups to do the same. I have continued that practice with other populations. A program may not be able to be prevented from malfunctioning, but the simple act of frequent saving mitigates the losses.

A final point of discussion is the value students perceived in using video in their own ELA classrooms. Many students saw the assignment's potential in the connection between reading and writing. One student wrote:

> This project has great relevance because in it you are both reading and writing in the same stroke. You are reading a poem and then writing your interpretation of that poem using video images instead of words.

Other students commented on the visual and tactile elements that would engage students who struggle with print literacy. One such response said,

> This experience taught me how to interact with literature. Creating the video produced a technological reader response. We were allowed to read, examine, and interpret the poem without feeling restricted by pencil and paper. After this production experience, I learned another way to engage students and show the power of language arts. Producing a video poem appeals to popular culture because it imitates music videos, requires a computer, and allows students to integrate songs and pictures, which cannot be done when answering a two-part response question. This should be part of the English language arts classroom because students need hands-on opportunities to analyze literature and express perspectives. This assignment appeals to different intelligences, and students experience accountability.

Every student in the class responded positively to using some aspect of video in their own classrooms. Though some expressed concern about their ability to deal with the technological logistics or whether their school would have access to such technology, students perceived reading and writing with video to be an important part of ELA classrooms.

Conclusion

This chapter explored how students in an ELA teacher education course read and composed a multimodal text while also reflecting on their own learning. While adding to the growing body of research of video composition in the classroom—and in this case, teacher education—this study also explored the pedagogical and process issues related to learning design and the uses of electronic media production.

Prompted by the question *so what?* I wanted to explore what the students learned while they composed with video. Through the use of heuristics to prompt student reflection and meta-cognition and through exploring their processes and products, I found that students used video to meaningfully respond to a traditional ELA assignment, namely to analyze a piece of literature. The class project did not use the technology as an event but rather encouraged students to apply content-specific strategies to integrate new ways to read, write, and reflect on their learning.

Certainly video will be around for the foreseeable future. Though new advances will make video more accessible and user-friendly, manipulating visuals, text, audio, and special effects will remain fundamental aspects of composing with video. In a similar manner, new media and technologies will continue to find their way into the classroom. However, educators should never lose sight of the fundamental aspects of student learning— *so what is really happening here?*— that occur in the dazzle of emerging technology.

References

Albers, P. (2006). Imagining the possibilities in multimodal curriculum design. *English Education, 38*(2), 75–101.

Begleiter, M. (2001). *From word to image: Storyboarding and the filmmaking process.* Studio City, CA: Michael Wiese Productions.

Bengtson, D. (2007). Creating video poetry. In M. Christel & S. Sullivan (Eds.), *Lesson plans for creating media-rich classrooms* (pp. 97–104). Urbana, IL: National Council of Teachers of English.

Brass, J. (2008). Local knowledge and digital movie composing in an after-school literacy program. *Journal of Adult and Adolescent Literacy, 51*(6), 464–473.

Brown, L. (2007). Creating a public service announcement: Powerful persuasion in 60 seconds. In M. Christel & S. Sullivan (Eds.), *Lesson plans for creating media-rich classrooms* (pp. 225–231). Urbana, IL: National Council of Teachers of English.

Bruce, D. (2008a). Multimedia production as composition. In J. Flood, S. Heath, & D. Lapp (Eds.), *Handbook of research in teaching literacy through the communicative and visual arts*, vol. II (pp. 13–18). New York: Routledge.

Bruce, D. (2008b) Visualizing literacy: Building bridges with media. *Reading & Writing Quarterly, 24*(3), 264–282.

Cuban, L. (2001). *Oversold and underused: Computers in the classroom.* Cambridge, MA: Harvard University Press.

Fox, R. (2005). Researching media literacy: Pitfalls and possibilities. In G. Schwarz & P. Brown (Eds.), *Media literacy: Transforming curriculum and teaching. The one-hundred and fourth yearbook of the National Society for the Study of Education, Part I* (pp. 251–259). Malden, MA: Blackwell.

Goetze, S., Brown, D., & Schwarz, G. (2005). Teachers need media literacy, too! In G. Schwarz & P. Brown (Eds.), *Media literacy: Transforming curriculum and teaching. The one-hundred and fourth yearbook of the National Society for the Study of Education, Part I* (pp. 161–179). Malden, MA: Blackwell.

Goodman, S. (2003). *Teaching youth media: A critical guide to literacy, video production and social change.* New York: Teachers College Press.

Hillocks, G. (1986). *Research on written composition: New directions for teaching.* Urbana, IL: National Council of Teachers of English.

Hobbs, R. (2007). Reading the media: Media literacy in high school English. New York: Teachers College Press.

Hull, G. (2003). At last: Youth culture and digital media: New literacies for new times. *Research in the Teaching of English, 38*(2), 229–233.

Kajder, S. (2006). *Bringing the outside in: Visual ways to engage reluctant readers.* Portland, ME: Stenhouse Publishers.

Lund, D. (1998). Video production in the English language arts classroom. *English Journal, 87*(1), 78–82.

Miller, S. (2007). English teacher learning for new times: Digital video composing as multimodal literacy practice. *English Education, 40*, 61–83.

Miller, S. (2008). Teacher learning for new times: Repurposing new multimodal literacies and digital-video composing for schools. In J. Flood, S. Heath, & D. Lapp (Eds.), *Handbook of research in teaching literacy through the communicative and visual arts*, vol. II (pp. 441–453). New York: Routledge.

Miller, S., & Borowicz, S. (2005). City voices, city visions: Digital video as literacy/learning supertool in urban classrooms. In M. Finn, L. Johnson, & R. Lewis (Eds.), *Urban education with an attitude* (pp. 87–105). New York: State University of New York Press.

Ranker, J. (2008). Making meaning on the screen: Digital video production about the Dominican Republic. *Journal of Adult and Adolescent Literacy, 51*(5), 410–422.

Tyner, K. (1998). *Literacy in a digital world: Teaching and learning in the age of information.* Mahwah, NJ: Lawrence Erlbaum.

Van Der Geest, T., & Spyridakis, J. (2000). Developing heuristics for web communication: An introduction to this special issue. *Technical Communication*, *47*(3), 301–310.

Williams, S. (2007). Turning text into movie trailers: The Romeo and Juliet iMovie experience. In M. Christel & S. Sullivan (Eds.) *Lesson plans for creating media-rich classrooms* (pp. 105–110). Urbana, IL: National Council of Teachers of English.

Chapter 6

"Truthiness" and Trust

News Media Literacy Strategies in the Digital Age

Jennifer Fleming

Introduction

Digitalization not only diffuses media audiences at unprecedented rates, it fundamentally changes news media businesses and, in the process, the nature of news itself. The "trusted" news anchor is being replaced by an army of bipolar bloggers masquerading as experts; the *New York Times's* agenda-setting function in society is being eroded by so-called consensus journalists pointing, clicking, and capturing stories with their cell phones. The result is a new media mess of half-truths and lowest common denominator story selection.

Traditional media literacy strategies are helpful but not sufficient in this brave new world of online news. News media have, and will always be, produced and consumed differently than most other media. Journalists are often viewed as seekers of truth and protectors of democracy. Additionally, many people use news knowledge as "social currency"— as a way to bond with friends and family, to advance their careers and connect with others they don't know (Associated Press, 2008, p. 50). The purpose of this chapter is to contribute to the growing dialog about how best to approach critical analysis of news media as real and virtual worlds collide in newsrooms and classrooms. Building on various cultural theories and media literacy frameworks, the chapter will conclude with examples of what news media literacy practices might look like in higher education spaces. Although largely based on my own experiences, I look at traditional and emerging definitions of media literacy and approaches to its instruction.

Conceptual Orientations

News Values and the Cultural Value of News

For much of the 1960s and 1970s, legendary journalist Walter Cronkite ended the *CBS Evening News* broadcast with his trademark phrase, "... And that's the way it is." And, the way Cronkite framed the news each night was just that for millions of Americans during the golden age of journalism. Starting with CBS radio broadcaster Edward R. Murrow's reports during World War II to Bob Woodward and Carl Bernstein's Watergate investigations, the period is "celebrated not only for its seemingly permanent parade of important news stories but also because the journalists who provided them were thought to be different: coming out of the working class, less elitist and not treated, or paid, like celebrities" (Gans, 2004, p. xv). For example, Cronkite's 1968 public prediction that the bloody experience in Vietnam would end in a "stalemate" is credited with changing political and popular perspectives about the war (Hallin, 1989, p. 170). Cronkite not only solidified his place as the most "trusted" figure in public life; he played a role in the modern cultural expectation that news media should be trusted, they should be protectors of democracy, and they should tell the truth.

Bennett (1997) defined news as a "daily negotiation among various actors occupying different niches in the information ecosystem" (p. 108). During Cronkite's era, the national news information ecosystem was limited to three television networks and a few magazines. Gans (2004) examined the processes, considerations, values, and assumptions that underlie news judgment at several of these news-gathering operations in his seminal work *Deciding What's News: A Study of CBS Evening News, NBC Nightly News, Newsweek, and Time*. In his study of the values, professional standards, and external pressures that shaped journalists' judgments, Gans found that lack of time and space forced journalists to focus primarily on "known" sources for stories. Known sources include political, economic, or cultural leaders and officials (p. 8).

In the 1980s and 1990s, cable TV news dramatically changed the information ecosystem Gans examined, and Cronkite ruled. CNN (1980), the Fox News Channel (1996) and MSNBC (1996) turned the daily negotiation of news values and professional standards into an hourly, if not minute-by-minute, rush to fill their news holes. The *news hole* refers to amount of content a news provider—broadcast, print, and now online—needs to create in a news cycle. In traditional newspaper media production cycles, the news hole is often tied to the amount of advertising sold. When space is tight, it means that a large amount of advertising was sold on that day. As a result, less newsworthy stories might be dropped, inferring that the stories might have made it to print if there had been less advertising (Itule & Anderson, 2003). The same could be said for nightly national news programs; their news hole is often 22 minutes for a 30-minute broadcast. Twenty-four-hour cable news channels have to create hours of content each day to fill their holes. Despite the significant increase in the amount of time devoted to news, Gans (2004) argues that there has been a steady decrease in "hard" or important news covered.

> When war and politics are not making headlines, cable's hard news is apt to be about murder trials, celebrity scandals and the like ... Cable news [also] laces its news with opinion, largely from commentators and talk show hosts, only some of them expert on their topic (p. xiv).

Cable news thus spawned a technology-driven paradox of modern journalism; programmers had more time to fill, yet they seemed to fill it with less important, less newsworthy stories of the likes of OJ Simpson, the arrest of Paris Hilton, or the death of Anna Nicole Smith.

Digitalization has ripped the bottom off of the already deep news holes in the United States and globally. There are virtually no time or space constraints online, turning the once-limited news hole of a half-hour broadcast, or one-third of newspaper space, into a black hole. The online temporal and spatial free-for-all means that almost anyone with an Internet connection and an opinion can present his or her versions of news as journalism. As a result, Greenblatt & Kleba (2008) describe journalism in the twenty-first century as a "wide-open market" that makes it harder for traditional news agencies and sources to set themselves apart (p. 158).

John Hartley (1996) refers to news as the most important textual system in the world because it exemplifies the "sense-making practice of modernity" (p. 32). With the digitalization of media, the number of people *practicing* journalism—the number of people making sense of the world and publishing their findings—is growing exponentially. However, this is not because news organizations are hiring. In fact, most so-called mainstream news organizations are downsizing. In July 2008, the *Los Angeles Times* announced its plans to slash 250 jobs, 150 of those from its award-winning newsroom. Executives said the cuts were part of ongoing efforts to keep operating costs in line with declining revenues. Some current and former *Los Angeles Times* reporters disagree. They blame Tribune Company Chairman Samuel Zell's "recklessness" in the takeover of the newspaper in 2007 and launched a class action lawsuit. The lawsuit claims that the buyout tripled the newspaper's debt at a time of declining revenues—a deal described as an "imprudent transaction" (Perez-Pena, 2008, p. C4). Others, including *Los Angeles Times* editor Russ Stanton, blame his organization's cutbacks on the fragmentation of audiences and advertisers online. Stanton said his organization needed to adjust to an Internet-induced paradox: "Thanks to the Internet, we have more readers for our great journalism than at any time in our history. But also thanks to the Internet, our advertisers have more choices, and we have less money" (Hiltzik, 2008).

Nearly three decades after Gans's study, all four news organizations he examined—*NBC Nightly News*, *CBS Evening News*, *Time*, and

Newsweek—remain dominant brands in journalism, as does the *Los Angeles Times*, yet the journalists employed by these organizations are now competing for advertisers and audiences with often anonymous bloggers and ideologues online. For example, blogger Marcy Wheeler contributed to the discussion of the Valerie Plame–CIA leak case by taking aim at what she perceived to be the failures of modern journalism. Wheeler (2007), writing from her home in Michigan under the online moniker "emptywheel," called herself an "ordinary citizen" who gave up "billable hours and sleep to follow every twist and turn in the case" (p. 7). She turned her blog into a book, *Anatomy of Deceit: How the Bush Administration Used the Media to Sell the Iraq War and Out a Spy*. She argues the Plame case is an excellent example of how news media can be manipulated by dominant White House narratives and that bloggers like herself bring "perspective" and "persistence" to do what "the press should have done: call our leaders on their deceptions" (p. 9). It is clear Wheeler spent an enormous amount of time researching and writing about the case; interestingly, while she lambasted *New York Times* reporter Judith Miller for using anonymous sources, Wheeler's own "investigation" started with an argument she had with another blogger known as "Meteor Blades." According to Wheeler (2007), Meteor Blades is one of the "wise men" of the blogosphere with "life experience and perspective far exceeding my own" (p. 8). Conceptually, the point isn't to determine the identity (and motivations) of "Meteor Blades" or to argue that the news media have badly failed the public or democracy in high-profile stories such as the Plame case, or the run-up to the Iraq invasion. The perception that news media have a responsibility to the public and democracy is central to the understanding of news media literacy.

Kellner (2005) argues that news media are primarily to blame for a "crisis of democracy" in the United States. Through cultural studies analyses, Kellner opines that thoughtful, analytical news stories and arguments are overshadowed by oversimplified media "spectacles" marked by simple messages, dramatic images, and "binary categories of good and evil" (p. xiii). Kellner blames corporate news media specifically because, he argues, they favor narrative models aimed at attracting audiences instead of supporting independent thought and critical reflection. The answer, for Kellner, isn't restriction of speech but more speech from alternative media and the Internet. He argues that the Internet promises the possibility of a lively public sphere with a wider range of news and opinion that could serve as "an important check against our increasingly arrogant, incompetent, and cowardly mainstream corporate media" (p. xvii).

Similarly, McChesney (2008) argues that the "crisis" in modern journalism is largely due to commercialization and the tradition of relying on official, often government, sources for information and materials (p. 117). The cost to democracy, McChesney suggests, is that journalism based on official sources does not lead to rigorous examination of major issues. In McChesney's view, journalism today is better at "generating ignorance and apathy than informed and passionately engaged citizenry" (p. 34).

Political scientists, sociologists, and mass communication researchers such as McChesney pay particularly close attention to the agenda-setting function of news media in society. *Agenda-setting* refers to the ability of news media to define the significant issues of the day. The core hypothesis of agenda-setting studies relates to degree of emphasis in the belief that issues emphasized in news media influence public priorities (McCombs & Estrada, 1997). However, emphasis may become a moot point in the age of unlimited news media choice and unfiltered expression.

Salon.com blogger Farhad Manjoo (2008) argues that emphasis in news is being replaced by a "culture of niches." Niches are emerging because there is so much news content choice via so many devices. Manjoo goes as far as to declare that the modern era represents the "twilight of objectivity" in journalism (p. 143). According to Manjoo, flagrantly opinionated newscasters such as the *Fox News Channel's* Bill O'Reilly and Sean Hannity and *CNN's* Lou Dobbs are here to stay and audiences will see more of them because "attitude" journalism is a "natural response" to information fragmentation (p. 147).

Fragmenting Cultures and Constructivist Pedagogy

There is no denying that American citizens in every demographic sector are surrounded by media. Evidence that there are nearly as many TV sets and cell phones as there are people in United States is almost cliché (Central Intelligence Agency, 2008). The media literacy movement aims to address ubiquitous and influential media environments through pedagogies and assessment practices that enhance understanding of media. Media literacy educators to various degrees strive to teach students how to critically interpret, analyze, critique and, in some cases, create media in a variety of forms (Aufderheide, 1993). However, one need look no further than the staggering statistic that approximately 1.9 trillion text messages were sent worldwide in 2007 to understand that the modern media ecosystem at all levels—production, distribution and consumption—has changed dramatically since the widely cited definition of media literacy in the United States emerged in the early 1990s (Ingelbrecht *et al.*, 2007).

Contemporary students are not only media consumers, many are producers, distributors, and exhibitors of media content. Buckingham (2003) suggests "If media education is to help bridge the gap between the school and the world of children's out of school experience, it must surely begin with the knowledge that children already possess" (p. 34). In an age when two-thirds of American teenagers have cell phones, more than 90% use the Internet, more than half own an iPod or MP3 mobile music device, and virtually all of them play or have played video games, it would be useful to not only start with established knowledge but to understand youth media habits (Macgill, 2007). Thus, a constructivist approach to media literacy is arguably the most appropriate because the media experiences of twenty-first-century students are so diverse and anything but static.

Constructivist pedagogy is based on the belief that knowledge is best constructed from the learner's existing knowledge. The constructivist goal is to prompt students to discuss, question, debate, hypothesize, and investigate new areas of learning from existing foundations (Phillips & Soltis, 2004). Along these lines, constructivist approaches to media literacy would utilize student media knowledge and media habits to help them better understand the full spectrum of media tools, texts and practices. As Tyner (1998) notes, "Classroom teachers cannot fail to notice the mismatch between ... electronic literacy practices at home and in the community and those they use at school" (p. 69). Theories of media impact on individuals and communities are shifting from technological determinism to more process-based approaches examining the impact of new media tools and texts.

Kellner (1995) refers to modern mediated worlds of entertainment and information as "media culture" (p. 17). According to Kellner, television programs, popular songs, newspapers, magazines, films, and radio shows have replaced traditional socializing agents such as the family, church, and schools and are "reordering perceptions of space and time, erasing distinctions between reality and media image, while producing new modes of experience and subjectivity" (p. 17). In mediated cultures, social trends and cues are cultivated at a distance and communicated through various media culture artifacts. Kellner's analyses of 1980s and 1990s media culture artifacts such as the film *Poltergeist* and Madonna music videos reveals how social ideologies, values, and representations of race, gender, and class interact with and relate to one another in society. For Kellner, media culture texts represent "contested terrains" because they are often the sites of social, cultural, political and racial struggles (p. 56).

Zingrone (2001) focuses on the individual struggle and "stress" of "electric culture" (p. ix). Building on the works and writings of Marshall McLuhan, Zingrone argues information excess and the mediated nature of modern existence have destabilized society. According to Zingrone, the only way for people to exist in a state of constant information overload is to simplify human experience and suppress the true complexity of reality,

Under electric conditions, simple and complex are operating simultaneously; they drive the engine of critical meaning and, since much of what we take in is of the nature of entertainment, this makes it very difficult to find solid ground on which to base action or insightful perception (p. 25).

Jenkins (2006) introduces another digital age framework known as *convergence culture*. Convergence culture, according to Jenkins, is "where old and new media collide, where grassroots and corporate media intersect, where the power of the media producer and the power of the media consumer interact in unpredictable ways" (p. 2). Jenkins suggests it is more accurate to view convergence not as a technological tool but rather as a process that is both a top-down corporate-driven *and* bottom-up consumer-driven. "Convergence alters the relationships between existing technologies, industries, markets, genres and audiences. Convergence alters the logic by which media industries operate and by which media consumers process news and entertainment" (pp. 16–17).

Jenkins *et al.* (2007) conceptualize and define "participatory culture" as one with "relatively low barriers to artistic expression and civil engagement, strong support for creating and sharing one's creations, and some type of information mentorship whereby what is known by the most experiences is passed along to novices" (p. 3). The authors identify four general forms of participatory culture: affiliations (such as Facebook, MySpace, and game clans); expressions (digital sampling, zines, and mash-ups); collaborative problem solving (Wikipedia and reality gaming); and circulations (podcasting and blogging). Some theorists, however, view the fourth form of participatory culture— the ability to produce, publish, and distribute media—not as an act of empowerment but instead as evidence of information anarchy brewing online (Keen, 2007; Manjoo, 2008).

In contrast to Jenkins's (2006) optimistic hopes for convergence and participatory cultures, Keen takes a more pessimistic view. In *cult of the amateur,* Keen (2007) argues that the user-generated content available for free online can be dangerous because the distinction between trained expert and uninformed amateur is blurred. Keen rejects the idea that the blogosphere represents a vibrant democratic marketplace of ideas culture that thrives on debate. The problem for Keen lies not with the medium and its infinite number of information sources but with users: "The fact is that too many of us aren't innately honest creatures, either on- or offline … when we're left to our own amateur devices, we don't always behave well" (p. 80). Truth online, argues Keen, has become a commodity to bought, sold, packaged, and reinvented.

The End of Truth As We Know It?

Historian Nelson Goodman (1978) suggests that truth is constructed, contested, and fluid. He notes that societies are made and remade through a process of composition and decomposition, weighting, ordering, deletion and supplementation, and deformation. Goodman views truth as more of a process; a process built on judgments of individuals and the worlds they come from, the worlds they create, and the worlds they perpetuate, "Truth cannot be defined or tested by agreement with the world; for not only do truths differ for different world but the nature of agreement between a version and a world apart from it is notoriously nebulous" (p. 17).

Contemporary historian Marshall Poe (2006) argues that thanks to sites such as *Wikipedia*, truth in the digital age is determined not by historians, nor by journalists, but by online consensus. For Poe, the openness of *Wikipedia* to contribution and revision of content leads to interpretation and debate until the community negotiates and decides what "fact" is. "*Wikipedia* suggests a different theory of truth ... the community decides that two plus two equals four the same way it decides what an apple is: by consensus" (Poe, 2006).

The most prominent theory of truth in the digital age emerged not online but on cable TV. In 2005, comedian Stephen Colbert introduced the concept of "truthiness" on his "fake" news program, *The Colbert Report*. The word spread throughout media culture and was quickly referenced in the *New York Times*, the *Washington Post*, *Newsweek*, CNN, ABC, *Salon*, and *The Associated Press*, to name a few more traditional news organizations. Education theorists Welner & Molnar (2007) applied the concept to the field of education with their article "Truthiness in Education," which examined how ideology-driven think tanks influence policy reports. Leading dictionary publisher Merriam-Webster named the noun, defined as "truth that comes from the gut, not books," as its 2006 word of the year. Truthiness beat out Google for the honor by a five-to-one margin. In an interesting aside, the 2006 competition was the first time the dictionary publisher invited the public to vote with the help of an online survey (Khodarahmi, 2007).

Conceptually, Manjoo (2008) takes truthiness to a whole new level in his book, *True Enough: Learning to Live in a Post-Fact Society*. He argues that the "the limitless choice we now enjoy over the information we get about our world has loosened our grip on what is—and isn't—true" (p. 4). America is splitting into niches, he argues, and perceptions of reality are splitting right along with it. For Manjoo, the heart of the modern media system is not commercial or ideological. Instead, it is the audience, "In a world of unprecedented media choice we begin to select our reality according to our biases, and we interpret evidence and solicit expertise in a way that pleases us" (p. 147).

Media Literacy in a Post-Fact Society

Media literacy in the United States is a fractured field; one based on good intentions but marred by lack of consensus about how best to teach it, and lack of knowledge about different approaches. Tyner (1991) argues that media literacy educators and advocates apply "one small aspect of media education and conclude that they have the whole picture."

Tyner (1998) synthesizes the media literacy picture in *Literacy in a Digital World: Teaching and Learning in the Age of Information* by defining and describing various "multiliteracies" (p. 94). Tool literacies such as computer literacy, network literacy, and technology literacy focus on developing an understanding and awareness of computer and network technologies. Literacies of representation, including information literacy and media literacy, challenge students to critically evaluate media messages. Visual literacy is similar to literacies of representation, only the units of critical interpretation and analyses are images. Tyner (1998) also calls for a "fresh combination of multiliteracies as a response to new media" instead of an "unfortunate tendency to promote one multiliteracy over another" (p. 97).

Kellner (1995) argues that "multiperspectival" frameworks—approaches that draw from a variety of theoretical constructs—are ideal for scholars and educators because "all interpretation is necessarily mediated by one's perspectives and is thus inevitably laden with presuppositions, values, biases, and limitations" (p. 98). Kellner's own approach to media literacy draws predominantly from a cultural-critical theory base.

Kellner and Share (2007) welcome multiple literacy models but argue that most approaches to media literacy are inadequate because they ignore ideology and representations of gender, race, class, and sexuality in media. Kellner and Share theorize that "critical media literacy" could be used as a framework to enhance established media literacy models through deeper analysis of information and its link to power in society. The authors suggest that once power relationships are revealed, media and information technologies could be used as "tools for empowerment" by those traditional ignored by or misrepresented in mainstream media (p. 3).

In contrast to Kellner and Share's political media literacy lens, Potter's (2008) approach to media literacy empowerment starts and ends with the individual. He describes media literacy as a set of perspectives people use to guide media selection and interpretation. According to Potter, media literacy should focus on reflection of media perceptions and choices in addition to analysis of media content and the social construction of media industries. Potter identifies three personal "building blocks" of media literacy (p. 12). The first, *personal locus*, refers to choice. Potter argues that the more a person is aware of the reasons behind content choices, the more he or she can control the meaning-making process. The second media literacy building block for Potter is *knowledge structures*. Knowledge structures—sets of information in a person's memory—are important, argues Potter, because every student, no matter his or her age, already knows something about media. According to Potter, students can add to their established media knowledge and become more media-literate with a better understanding of media effects, media content, media industries, the real world, and self. Potter's third and final building block consists of analytical *skills* such as analysis, evaluation, and synthesis of media content.

Hanson (2008) also favors an analytical approach to media literacy framed around individual perceptions and knowledge structures. His *Seven Truths "They" Don't Want You to Know about the Media* resemble arguments often heard when ideology-driven pundits accuse the "liberal elite media" or "mainstream media" of bias and unfair treatment. Hanson's seven truths are the following:

1   The media are essential components of our lives.
2   There are no mainstream media.
3   Everything from the margin moves to the center.
4   Nothing's new: everything that happened in the past will happen again.
5   New media are always scary.
6   Activism and analysis are not the same thing.
7   There is no "they". (p. xxiii)

However, Hanson's (2008) and Potter's (2008) frameworks do not address digital media creation or participation: two things a growing number of media literacy advocates appear to emphasize. For example, the New Media Consortium (2005) defines twenty-first-century literacy as a "set" of analytical *and* technical abilities: "These include the ability to understand the power of images and sounds, to recognize and use that power, to manipulate and transform digital media, to distribute them persuasively, and to easily adapt them to new forms" (p. 19). Jenkins *et al.* (2007) argue the consortium's definition is incomplete and that contemporary concepts of media literacy should also emphasize the ability to interact in digital environments, "New media literacies should be seen as social skills, as ways of interacting with a larger community, and not simply an individual skill used for personal expression" (p. 20).

Merging Media Literacy Theory With Journalism Education Practice

Whether a media literacy educator's emphasis is on analysis, creation, interaction, or a combination of all three, journalism instructors are in a unique position because they have engaged students in the creation of media messages in a variety of forms for more than a century. Journalism education at the college-level can be traced to former Confederate General Robert E. Lee who, as president of Washington College in Virginia (now Washington and Lee University), conceptualized journalism education and offered student scholarships to support the study of "typography, stenography, and bookkeeping" (Crenshaw, 1969, p. 164). Obviously, the field has evolved since then in terms of approach and technology. However, Mihaliadis & Hiebert (2005) argue that journalism educators offer media literacy "added value" by means of a conceptual bridge between theory and practice, "Where the added value comes into play is in seeing media literacy as the connection between the practical role of the journalist and the theoretical construct within which the journalist exists" (p. 165).

According to the Accrediting Council on Education in Journalism and Mass Communications (2003), the mission of journalism and mass communication professions in a democratic society is to "inform, to enlighten and to champion freedom of speech and press" (p.1). Therefore, one of the goals of news media literacy is to champion freedom of speech and press, outcomes similar to those proposed by a number of curriculum efforts such as the *Media and American Democracy* curriculum, a collection of lessons for high school students that include examination of the historical foundations and limitations of the First Amendment: how media images influence understanding of current events and the role of bloggers in mainstream media (Burchard, 2005). Additional news media literacy outcomes in the digital age may include recognition and critical examination of hidden meanings in news media; news media source identification, including sources cited within news media texts; and understanding of news media consumption habits.

Drawing from the Canadian media literacy experience, an initiative that dates back to the 1960s, Pungente, Duncan, and Andersen (2005) identify four approaches to media literacy in the classroom: medium-based, theme-based, stand-alone units, and integration of media studies into other activities. Medium-based media literacy pedagogies focus on the characteristics, strengths, and weaknesses of each medium. The theme-based approach involves several media because it focuses on an issue such as stereotyping in media. The third approach identified by Pungente *et al.* (2005) is media literacy stand-alone units, meaning a genre or theme is selected and studied for a limited time, typically up to two weeks. The authors argue that the final approach, integrating media studies into other classroom activities, is the most effective because it provides opportunities to connect new media with older media such as books and [printed] newspapers. Regardless of the approach or combination of approaches taken, Pungente *et al.* (2005) suggest "authenticity is the key to relevant learning," that is, texts used in media literacy programs should have interest and relevance in students' lives (p. 153).

Along these lines, authentic news media consumption in the twenty-first century is marked by multitasking, according to an *Associated Press* (2008) ethnographic study of news consumers (18- to 24-year age group) from three countries—the United States, the United Kingdom, and India. The authors conclude that media multitasking limits the ability of young consumers to give news their full attention because they feel "so overwhelmed and inundated by news that they just did not know what to do" (p. 43). The authors refer to this as "news fatigue." According to the researchers, the irony in news fatigue is that consumers "felt helpless to change their news consumption at a time when they have more control and more choice than ever before" (p. 44).

Interestingly, the sources young news consumers appear to pay closer attention to are stories forwarded to them by peers they trust or stories they determine are worth sharing with their peers (Associated Press, 2008). *New York Times* journalist Brian Stetler (2008) wrote about an emerging online trend that suggests young people are replacing professional news filters with social filters. "Younger voters tend to be not just consumers of news and current events but conduits as well—sending out e-mailed links and videos to friends and their social networks" (p. A1). According to data from the market research firm The Intelligence Group, "recommendations from friends or text messages from a campaign—information that is shared not sought—is perceived as natural" (Selter, p. A1). "Natural" or "authentic" news media literacy experiences in the classroom should then reflect the multitasking nature of news of consumption while providing students the opportunity to share their findings with peers and fostering a spirit of critical inquiry concerning personal practices, preferences, and perceptions of news. There must also be an emphasis on the questioning of all news media sources, whether it's a story e-mailed by a friend, a blog, or an article from a "traditional" news source such as the *New York Times*.

Digital media allow for unprecedented access to multiple media platforms and sources; they allow for unprecedented opportunities to create, publish, distribute, and share media texts in a variety of formats. Participatory culture practices of expression and participation are acts of empowerment, as noted by Jenkins *et al.* (2007), who would like to see more opportunities for students "to participate and to develop the cultural competencies and social skills needed for full involvement" (p. 4). The emphasis on "full involvement" is noteworthy. However, from a journalism instructor's perspective, students can be taught to create news content in a variety of forms. They can be taught to publish or broadcast their work, and they can be taught to participate in news cultures both on- and off-line. The challenge remains to teach students the consistent critical thinking processes that they can use as they produce and consume news. McKinsey & Co. interviewed dozens of news media leaders and found that young journalists entering the field consistently lacked a strong sense of ethics and analytical thinking skills (Carnegie Corporation of New York, 2005).

Methods and Results

Based on the conceptual orientations and media consumption trends discussed, it could be argued that news in the digital age is as much a habit as it is a product, and it is as much about process at is it about profits. To that end, I conducted two exploratory case studies in my own classes at a large urban university approximately 25 miles south of Los Angeles. As the instructor, I was both a participant and observer. My objective was to gain a holistic understanding of how to merge student news media habits with journalism pedagogy and media literacy principles in college classroom environments and to assess the results. Case study methodology is useful in exploratory educational research of this kind because it is multiperspectival by design and strives to better understand how activities engaged in by the participants interrelate (Tellis, 1997). It was my hope that a combination of theories and strategies from multiple disciplines would illuminate the importance of critical reflection of news media in media literacy pedagogy. Two questions guided the pilot projects:

Q1: From the perspective of students, is a constructivist approach to media literacy effective in the development of habits that question news media sources and experiences?

Q2: From the perspective of instructors, how can we merge student media habits and digital cultures with educational spaces to achieve media literacy objectives?

The two exploratory case studies involved 71 students. The students ranged in age from 18 to 29; 66% were women, 34% were men, and all were undergraduates. I employed an embedded/integrated strategy to news media literacy during the first case study, which took place during a senior journalism class in spring 2007. I used a stand-alone unit strategy during the second case study, which was conducted during a freshman journalism course in spring 2008.

A number of qualitative descriptive instruments, including student assignments, notebooks, reflection essays, and instructor observations and comments, were used to analyze the effectiveness of the two strategies. I interpreted these materials for patterns that demonstrated the development of independent thinking. I was especially interested in evidence that suggested participants' fundamental beliefs about news media practices and personal habits were challenged. The results were illuminating. However, it is important to note that the case studies were based on my own experiences as a means to better inform practice and future research directions, thus their results are not generalizable.

Strategy 1: 'Embedding' News Media Literacy into the Curriculum

For the first project, 29 students in a senior journalism class examined war-themed news texts they found online. The primary pedagogical strategy was to regularly incorporate news media literacy principles of questioning sources and habits into student activities. The project lasted two months and focused primarily on weekly journal entries and in-class discussions. Students found two war-related news texts online, summarized and evaluated the texts based on prompts provided by the instructor, and then shared their findings with their peers. Prompts included straightforward media literacy concepts (e.g., "Discuss the text's key messages, or how the text's author, producer or director used words, images, metaphors to communicate meaning"); others combined critical media literacy with basic journalistic principles (e.g., "Analyze the credibility of a text's source, and the sources cited within the text"). Several referred to personal knowledge, experiences and consumption practices that connect with student prior knowledge and encourage dialogue (e.g., "Relate personal opinions and experiences whenever possible"). The purpose of the questions was to provide a more qualitative than quantitative view of how students responded to news media they encountered so that independent thinking patterns could be identified.

The results of the senior project were promising. From the student perspective, the senior project provided a high level of satisfaction and numerous opportunities for analysis. The senior project engaged students with course materials and discussions because they were often the sources of the topics and subjects addressed in class. Students also appeared to welcome the challenge and responsibility of leading the direction of the course and their learning.

From the instructor's perspective, evidence of independent thinking and changes in student perspectives about news media sources could be identified. By the end of the project, students reported a change in how they interpreted and questioned news stories. The stories they read and watched online before the project were increasingly cited as incomplete: "News media often cover wars based on single events, but they did not explain the further importance of those events, their causes, the context, and the relevance."

The most significant pattern to emerge from the project was how students developed habits of mind that included critical questioning of news media sources, the sources cited within news media texts, and their own reactions to texts. For example, through independent discovery and discussion, students identified a frequent source cited in news stories about the Iraq invasion: the American Enterprise Institute. This led to a collective investigation of the organization whose published purpose is to "defend the principles and improve the institutions of American freedom and democratic capitalism—limited government, private enterprise, individual liberty and responsibility" (American Enterprise Institute, 2005). The student-led investigation opened the door to deeper, more critical media literacy discussions about ideology-driven sources quoted often in news media texts, yet frequently positioned and interpreted as authoritative sources. Many students admitted they assumed the American Enterprise Institute was a politically-balanced source because it was framed as such. One student commented, "I didn't notice what sources were used in these articles until we discussed them in class. Every article I read is a chance for me to dissect media techniques. I ask myself why certain sources were used instead of others."

Another student discovery online was a disturbing Volkswagen advertisement posted on YouTube by "xooxs," who described the video as ""VW Polo commercial. Terrorists detonate a bomb inside the Volkswagen." At first glance, this may not seem like a news story but, within a constructivist paradigm, we agreed to address students' media contributions that were deemed worthy of discussion. It turned out that this particular segment generated some of the project's most thought-provoking discussions. The 22-second segment showed an Arab-looking man parking a Volkswagen Polo beside an outdoor café in what appeared to be a European city. The next scene showed the man detonating a bomb. The car contained the powerful explosion, saving sidewalk café patrons; they didn't notice the explosion because the car was "Small but tough." None of the students identified the piece as a parody nor questioned its authenticity. In fact, several thought it was funny, and an example of "European humor." Collectively, the class could not decide whether the YouTube text was "real" or not, which led to a valuable lesson according to one student, "Audiences should learn to pay more attention to the sources of media messages, and question them, even when they appear credible." For the students, the professional-looking nature of the mock ad made it appear credible; their prior knowledge (or lack thereof perhaps) of Middle Eastern politics added to their collective assessment of whether the ad was real or fake.

Three themes emerged from data from the first project. First, students initially resisted constructivist pedagogy. Next, a pattern of ownership of learning and collective knowledge emerged from class discussions based on student-generated content and analysis. And finally, student-generated dialog appears to be an effective way to merge media literacy principles, news media habits, and classroom spaces.

Students in the first project initially resisted the collaborative, investigative nature of constructivist pedagogy. It seemed that they wanted to know exactly what to read, exactly what to write and, most important, the exact questions to answer. Additionally, war was not a topic most students wanted to address on a regular basis, let alone try to understand. One student wrote, "Prior to this assignment, I used to be someone who avoided thinking too much about war. It was hard, unpleasant, and always made me sad." These comments hint at the alienation many young people face when they select [or avoid] news and could help explain the popularity of satirical news programs such as *The Colbert Report* (Associated Press, 2008).

What was most exciting to experience from the perspective of an instructor was the collaborative nature of the discussions and spirit of sharing content online and in the classroom. Once students understood their opinion and contributions mattered to the culture and quality of the class, they began to look deeper; they began to question more and push their content selections beyond their regular media habits, "My first news stories were boring ... I was not personally invested in the assignment yet. I didn't ask myself important questions about the articles."

The spirit of inquiry and personal discovery was palpable as students began to look inward for meaning as much as they looked to news content for information. "I began to choose stories that stood out to me; I chose stories that had meaning in my life, or that made me feel something." Their responses support Potter's (2008) arguments that personal understanding of media habits is just as important as understanding media content. They also appear to be consistent with Manjoo's (2008) argument that bias in modern media systems has more to do with the selection of content as opposed to the production of it. Overall, students who participated in the first project were satisfied with the constructivist strategy of integration:

I'd like to say thank you for conducting this class in a different way than other courses are designed. I feel that instead of lecturing about certain theories, you allowed us to teach ourselves and formulate our own perceptions. You gave us certain tools ... but didn't represent the interpretation of them, you left that to us ... I learned the key to understanding is to ask questions.

There were, of course, challenges inherent in this seemingly free-flowing approach to the analysis of news media and classroom organization. One of the most obvious challenges was how to reconcile courses standards without prior knowledge of the student-generated news content to be examined, discussed, questioned, and debated in class. Additionally, I believe there is a fine line between criticism and critical inquiry. All of the students who participated in the first project were senior journalism majors, and I did not want the project to seem like it was unfairly attacking the profession many hoped to enter after graduation. The goal was to help students question news media in a discriminating way to encourage critical, independent judgment. Students reported that they were appreciative of the opportunity to look at news industries from more critical perspectives and to share their findings with their peers.

Strategy 2: News Media Literacy Stand-Alone Unit

The second project consisted of 42 students who participated in a stand-alone media literacy unit. The second project lasted two weeks. I attempted to use students' prior cultural experiences by offering them an opportunity to analyze, deconstruct, and discuss a news media text found on YouTube, a Web site frequently used by college students for political information and news (Associated Press, 2008). The original source of the YouTube video was *Dateline NBC*, a popular investigative news magazine show in the United States. The seven-minute segment was pulled from an episode of *Dateline NBC's* "To Catch a Predator" series. The series merges vigilante justice with "gotcha" journalism techniques in a quest to catch so-called online sexual predators. A user identified as "wnwz" posted the YouTube video that generated more than one-and-a-half million views and 8,000 comments. The segment was useful in this exercise because students' responses revealed that issues related to the source of news texts, it seemed, was a matter of wide interpretation.

After viewing the segment, students were asked three open-ended questions that focused on critical evaluation of digital news sources: (1) Who/what is the source? (2) What is their purpose? The third question prompted students to assess truth: (3) Discuss the "truthiness" of the segment. The *Merriam-Webster* definition of *truthiness*, "truth that comes from the gut, not books," was included in the prompt posted online. As part of the online learning environment, students published their opinions in the "Truthiness Forum." In-class discussions and reflection essays followed the online responses and exchanges.

Student perceptions of source were the most useful from a pedagogical perspective because I could also use the student-generated data as discussion topics in class. The top three sources, as determined by the students, were: *Dateline NBC* (29%), "wnwz" (27%) and Olmbermannation.com (15%). I shared these findings with the students to demonstrate the indeterminate nature of sources in news media, in particular, as demonstrated in online news media. The layers of sources, the borrowing and perhaps stealing of copyrighted material, the thousands of comments about the segment, and the Keith Olbermann promotions embedded within the text demonstrate Jenkins's (2006) observation that convergence culture enables people to "archive, annotate, appropriate, and recirculate media content in powerful news ways" (p. 18). At the same time, it could be argued, the power to archive, annotate, appropriate, and recirculate media content reduces the power of consumers to evaluate the credibility of a source, and a source's motivation. One student wrote,

> The video is posted by a person under nick name "wnwz", which is really vague. But besides that, as we can see at the beginning of the video, the video was posted, or taken, from www.olbermannnation. com, a site that contains videos related to TV reporter and commentator Keith Olbermann. Keith Olbermann works for NBC as an anchorman, best known for hosting the show "Countdown with Keith Olbermann." On the website, www.olbermannnation.com, I could not find who posted it, so it probably was a just a home-made TiVo recorded excerpt or something like that.

The purpose of asking students the truthiness of the segment was to allow students to contextualize "truth" as a means of evaluating news media sources in a more critical light and understanding that truth is a matter of perspective, especially in digital media environments. We worked from the perspective that instead of assuming a news media text is truthful, it is best to start from assumption that news media texts are versions of the truth at best and outright misrepresentations of reality at worst. Not surprisingly, there was little consensus about the segment's truthiness, which provided more material for exchanges in-class and online. One student wrote,

> The "truthiness" of the segment is very difficult to come by. There is a lot of lying going on in the show. The men are fooled into coming

to the house by people that act as minors. At times they are begged to show up. Once they arrive they see the "minor" and are interviewed by the reporter. The "predator" then begins to lie to excuse his actions. Afterwards, they are arrested in a very dramatic fashion. The crime hasn't even been committed because it was a fake minor but they are already being arrested. Everything just seems too staged. I have to admit that the show is very interesting and leaves people wanting to see more.

Though online and in-class discussions about the YouTube segment were interesting, the stand-alone project provided little evidence that after the classroom tasks, students adopted new, more critical habits of mind related either to the questioning of news media or an increased understanding of news media consumption patterns. This is likely owing to a variety of reasons.

Outcomes for Each Strategy

The two approaches were difficult to compare because the embedded project lasted longer than the stand-alone strategy. In the embedded plan, students had more opportunities to share, discuss, and contextualize their discoveries through active questioning and collaborative learning. This active learning environment was not effectively replicated in the stand-alone project. Additionally, it seemed students who participated in the stand-alone project viewed their exercise as just another assignment. Upon reflection, their interpretation is understandable because the project could have been better integrated into course content. In comparison to the first, embedded strategy, the second cohort of students in the stand-alone project did not generate the content that was collectively examined, and therefore they did not seem to own their learning.

The experiences of two different strategies to news media literacy—a stand-alone and an embedded/integrated approach—support the suggestion by Pungente *et al.* (2005) that the most effective strategies are those that regularly integrate media literacy into course content and activities. Pungente *et al.* also argue that it is important to reflect student media environments so that media literacy lessons are authentic. Given my experiences with the two different approaches to the critical analysis of news media, I plan to better reflect student media habits in pedagogy and course activities. I recognize that I neglected to fully understand the news media choices of the students who participated in the stand-alone project. Instead, I selected news media texts on the basis of my perceptions of what the students would be interested in. In the future, I plan to collect data from students about where they get their news and what they consider news and then to build my pedagogy around their perceptions and consumptions habits. Otherwise, the tendency was for students to reflect my own.

Conclusions

An Associated Press (2008) study reported that the ubiquity of 24/7 news, available from a variety of technologies—television, Internet, mobile devices, radio, and newspapers—did not translate to a better news environment for consumers. Instead, many of the study's young subjects reported "news fatigue" (p. 52). Investigators also found that news consumers are accessing news by chance as much as by design. The evidence indicates that young people are turning their backs on television as a primary source for news. According to the Pew Research Center for the People and the Press (2008), the Internet was the leading source for young people seeking news about the 2008 U.S. presidential campaign. Internet news sources cited by survey respondents included MSNBC, CNN, Yahoo News, the Drudge Report, MySpace, and YouTube. To combat information fatigue in a fragmented, by-chance media environment, the cultural anthropologists hired by the Associated Press advised news organizations to redesign they way the frame, produce, and publish news online. "New value could be created if news producers and distributors can figure out ways to help consumers connect the dots more coherently" (p. 56).

In this context, the experiences of two exploratory news media literacy projects provide a way to connect the dots of media literacy with thought-provoking theories about digital cultures and traditional perceptions of news media. They provide a way to connect the dots of constructivist pedagogy with the multidimensional, personalized media environments of students. They also provide a way to connect the dots of journalist storytelling and truth-seeking with fragmented facts often masquerading as opinion online. Instructor observations and student feedback suggest that a constructivist approach to media literacy is effective in creating a habit of critical news media analysis. Media literacy lessons were more powerful when students were the sources of the content examined, questioned, deconstructed, and debated.

From the perspective of a journalism educator, the emphasis on building more critical habits of mind is important because news media have turned into easy targets for criticism while at a time their agenda-setting function is eroding with their market shares. Today's news media culture is complicated and convoluted. News media consumers are picking and choosing their own news media truths from an unprecedented number of sources. The Cronkite-era of the "trusted" news source is over. In its place is a free-speech free-for-all online. The goal of news media literacy then is to help students better understand, question, and challenge their own news media choices, perceptions, and habits. It's also to build a bedrock of independent thinking so students have the critical capacity and clarity of mind to continuously question the clutter of the Internet.

References

Accrediting Council on Education in Journalism and Mass Communications. (2003). Principles of Accreditation. Retrieved October 10, 2008, from http://www2.ku.edu/~acejmc/PROGRAM/PRINCIPLES.SHTML

Aufderheide, P. (Ed.) (1993). *Media literacy: A report of the National Leadership Conference on Media Literacy.* Aspen, CO: Aspen Institute.

American Enterprise Institute. (2005). AEI's organization and purposes. Retrieved August 16, 2008, from http://www.aei.org/about/

The Associated Press & Context-Based Research Group. (2008, June). *A new model for news: Studying the deep structure of young-adult news consumption.* Retrieved July 28, 2008, from http://www.ap.org/newmodel.pdf

Bennett, W. L. (1997). Cracking the news code: some rules that journalists live by. In S. Iyengar & R. Reeves (Eds.), *Do the media govern? Politicians, voters and reporters in America* (pp. 103–118). Thousand Oaks, CA: Sage.

Burchard, V. (Ed.). (2005). *Media and American democracy.* Arlington, VA: Bill of Rights Institute.

Buckingham, D. (2003). *Media education: Literacy, learning and contemporary culture.* Cambridge: Polity Press.

Carnegie Corporation of New York. (2005). *Improving the education of tomorrow's journalists.* New York: Carnegie Corporation. Retrieved July 26, 2007, from http://www.carnegie.org/sub/program/initiativedocs/Exec_Sum_Journalism.pdf

Central Intelligence Agency. (2008). The *World Factbook: United States.* Washington, DC: CIA. Retrieved December 9, 2008, from https://www.cia.gov/library/publications/the-world-factbook/

Crenshaw, O. (1969). *General Lee's college: The rise and growth of Washington and Lee University.* New York: Random House.

Gans, H. J. (2004). *Deciding what's news: A study of CBS Evening News, NBC Nightly News, Newsweek, and Time* (Rev. ed). Evanston, IL: Northwestern University Press.

Greenblatt A., & Kleba, H. (2008). Media bias. In *Issues in Media: Selections from CQ Researcher* (pp. 141–164). Washington DC: CG Press.

Goodman, N. (1978). *Ways of worldmaking.* Indianapolis, IN: Hackett Publishing.

Hallin, D. (1989). *The "uncensored war:" The media and Vietnam.* Berkeley, CA: University of California Press.

Hanson, R. (2008). *Mass communication: Living in a media world.* Washington, DC: CG Press.

Hartley, J. (1996). *Popular reality: Journalism, modernity, popular culture.* London: Arnold.

Hiltzik, M. A. (2008, July). Los Angeles Times to cut 250 jobs, including 150 from news staff. *Los Angeles Times*. Retrieved July 26, 2008, from http://www. latimes.com/business/la-fi-times3-2008jul03,0,657523.story

Ingelbrecht, N., Hart, T., Mitsuyama, N., Baghdassarian, S., Gupta, A., Gupta, M., *et al.* (2007). Market trends: Mobile messaging, worldwide, 2006–2011. *Gartner, Inc.* Retrieved December 9, 2008, from http://www.gartner.com/it/page.jsp?id=565124

Itule, B. & Anderson, D. (2003). *News writing and reporting for today's media* (6th ed.). New York: McGraw-Hill.

Jenkins, H. (2006). *Convergence culture: Where old and new media collide.* New York: New York University Press.

Jenkins, H., Clinton, K., Purushotma, R., Robison, A. J. & Weigel, M. (2007). *Confronting the challenges of participatory culture: Media education for the 21st century.* Retrieved August 10, 2008, from http://www. digitallearning.macfound.org/atf/cf/%7B7E45C7E0-A3E0-4B89-AC9C-E807E1B0AE4E%7D/JENKINS_WHITE_PAPER.PDF

Keen, A. (2007). *The cult of the amateur: How today's Internet is killing our culture.* New York: Doubleday.

Kellner, D. (1995). *Media culture: Cultural studies, identity and politics between the modern and the postmodern.* New York: Routledge.

Kellner, D. (2005). *Media spectacle and the crisis of democracy.* Boulder, CO: Paradigm Publishers.

Kellner, D., & Share, J. (2007). Critical media literacy is not an option. *Learning Inquiry 1*, 59–69.

Khodarahmi, S. (2007). Words of the year. *Communication World, 24*(2), 11–12.

Macgill, A. (2007). *Parent and teenager Internet use.* Pew Internet & American Life Project. Retrieved December 10, 2008, from http://www.pewinternet.org/pdfs/PIP_Teen_Parents_data_memo_Oct2007.pdf

McChesney, R. (2008). *The political economy of media: Enduring issues, emerging dilemmas.* New York: Monthly Review Press.

McCombs, M., & Estrada, G. (1997). The news media and the pictures in our heads. In S. Iyengar & R. Reeves (Eds.), *Do the media govern? Politicians, voters and reporters in America* (pp. 237–247). Thousand Oaks, CA: Sage.

Manjoo, F. (2008). *True enough: Learning to live in a post-fact society.* Hoboken, NJ: Wiley.

Mihailidis, P., & Hiebert, R. (2005). Media literacy in journalism education curriculum. *Academic Exchange Quarterly, 9(3)*, 162–166.

New Media Consortium. (2005). *A global imperative: The report of the 21st Century Literacy Summit.* Retrieved October 10, 2008, from http://archive. nmc.org/pdf/Global_Imperative.pdf

Perez-Pena, R. (2008, September). Reporters from paper suing chief of Tribune. *New York Times*, p. C4.

Pew Research Center for the People and the Press. (2008). *Social networking and online videos take off: Internet's broader role in campaign 2008.* Retrieved October 20, 2008, from http://people-press.org/reports/pdf/384.pdf

Phillips , D. C., & Soltis, J. F. (2004). *Perspectives on learning* (4th ed.). New York: Teachers College Press.

Poe, M. (2006, September). The hive. *The Atlantic*. Retrieved July 15, 2008, from http://www.theatlantic.com/doc/200609/wikipedia

Potter, W. J. (2008). *Media literacy* (4th ed.). Los Angeles: Sage Publications.

Pungente, J., Duncan, B., & Andersen, N. The Canadian experience: Leading the way. In G. Schwarz & P. U. Brown (Eds.), *Media literacy: Transforming curriculum and teaching* (pp. 140–160). Malden, MA: Blackwell Publishing.

Stetler, B. (2008, March). Finding political news online, young viewers pass it along. *New York Times*, p A1.

Tellis, W. (1997). Introduction to the case study. *The Qualitative Report, 3*(2). Retrieved December 12, 2008, from http://www.nova.edu/ssss/QR/QR3-2/tellis1.html

Tyner, K. (1991, Summer). The media education elephant. *Strategies Quarterly*. Retrieved October 10, 2008, from http://interact.uoregon.edu/Medialit/JCP/articles_mlr/tyner/elephant.html

Tyner, K. (1998). *Literacy in a digital world: Teaching and learning in the age of information*. Mahwah, NJ: Lawrence Erlbaum Associates.

Welner, K. G., & Molnar, A. (2007, February). Truthiness in education. *Education Week*. Retrieved August 15, 2008, from http://epsl.asu.edu/epru/articles/EPSL-0702-407-OWI.pdf

Wheeler, M. (2007). *Anatomy of deceit: How the Bush administration used the media to sell the Iraq War and out a spy*. Berkeley, CA: Vaster Books.

Zingrone, F. (2001). *The media symplex: At the edge of meaning in the age of chaos*. Toronto: Stoddart.

Chapter 7

A Safety Net?

Using New Technologies to Engage Education Students in Controversial Topics

J. Lynn McBrien

As new technological platforms for media increase, so do the calls to utilize them in the classroom. From online discussion boards to synchronous online learning, teachers hear claims of the relative advantages of new technology over the old. However, technologies seem to develop faster than they can be evaluated for effectiveness in the classroom, and more research is needed to inform practice (Fernández, 2007; Fisher, 2003; Garrison, Anderson, & Archer, 2000; Park & Bonk, 2007). As Snelbecker (1999) has suggested, teaching and learning theories ought to be driving the use of emerging technologies in the classroom, and not the reverse. However, practical considerations often take priority, such as nontraditional students' needs for flexible scheduling and even the rising cost of fuel to drive to a campus. Thus, in reality, it often falls to teachers to connect students' needs for emerging technology to effective pedagogy.

I currently teach undergraduate and graduate social foundations and media literacy courses in the College of Education at the University of South Florida, at both the main campus and a regional campus. Because our student population is spread out over the main Tampa campus and three regional campuses, online courses allow students who may live well more than 50 miles from professors' home campuses to take their course offerings. Three online technologies that I have been encouraged to use in my university course designs are BlackBoard (BB, an asynchronous online teaching and learning tool); podcasts (as an initiative by Apple, called iTunes University); and Elluminate Live! (E!), a synchronous distance learning platform that allows for oral communication via microphones, texting, projecting PowerPoints and videos, exploring Web sites, virtual small-group "rooms," and polling tools, all from the convenience of home. A glance at articles related to podcasts in the Education Full-Text database for the past five years revealed 156 articles, only 48 of which were peer-reviewed, and almost none that were evaluative. For E!, there were only seven articles (four peer-reviewed) and no analyses of its effectiveness. Using the keyword "BlackBoard" did not turn up any articles that were necessarily related to the online tool called BB.

The call to jump on the bandwagon of new media in education is reminiscent of Motion Picture Producers and Distributors Association leader Will Hays' appearance before the NEA in 1922 to gain support from educational leaders regarding the use of film for instructional purposes (Saettler, 1998). Indeed, film has since become an important educational tool, but media educators continue to explain the need for critical pedagogy when employing this now old technology in the classroom, as it continues to be used badly in many classrooms (Hobbs, 2006). Media educators and researchers such as Hobbs, Considine and Baker (2006), Buckingham (2003), and others argue that movies and films are excellent teaching tools but only when they are critically analyzed and used as springboards for thoughtful and serious discussions that include social and historical contexts, perspectives, and bias.

As an example, one exercise I use in my classes is to show several clips from the Iranian film *Color of Paradise* (Majidi, 1999). I ask my students where they think the film takes place and how the clips make them feel. The majority believe it was filmed in South America and that it makes them feel "warm" about family relationships. I follow their mistaken impressions with introductory scenes from several United States—made films for social studies classes about the Middle East, each of which includes iconic images of deserts, nomads, pyramids, camels, violence, and the Islamic call to prayer. This leads to a discussion of how media can humanize or can detach us from "the other." This is an example of how technology does not necessarily convey advanced skills in critical thinking without a facilitator who can help students reflect on media messages and editing. It is also an exercise in institutionalized prejudice and racism.

This example from the use of an established medium shapes my thoughts on the uses of emerging technologies in teaching and learning. My Social Foundations of Education course examines historical, political, legal, racial, social, and economic inequities affecting K–12 students. The regional campus at which I teach is located in a small city noted by Kiplinger research to have the seventh largest density of millionaires in the United States (Burt, 2006). Demographic information by the U.S. Census Bureau indicates a composition of 87% White and less than 10% of either Black or Latino residents in the two counties primarily served by this campus. Not surprisingly, many of my students have not previously been confronted with the concept of White privilege (Rothenberg, 2004), nor have many encountered ideas that would engage them to progress in their own racial identity. If these topics are not addressed with sensitivity in an environment of safety and trust, they are likely to produce defensive responses. My goal is to help students engage with subjects that may be painful for them and to progress beyond guilt to a healthy acknowledgement of institutionalized social problems and ways to combat inequities.

Along with my interest in media literacy, my specific research with refugees resettled in the United States requires me to address discrimination faced by these students (McBrien, 2005). For example, refugees are often from countries rife with war or political ideologies that U.S. citizens have come to fear—Iraq, Afghanistan, and Iran as examples. Many others come from African nations and, as such, encounter multiple forms of discrimination in the United States: they are from warring states, they may be Muslim, and they may experience racial discrimination. When discussing issues of diversity and global education with my students, I share narratives from my research detailing experiences of prejudice, discrimination, and racism. To respond, my students feel safe to speak their opinions and to consider diverse perspectives to advance their own thinking on controversial topics.

My teaching and my research focus have helped to shape specific questions surrounding the use of new technologies in teaching. Just as there are ineffective uses of film in classrooms, so too, using online teaching technologies purely for the sake of convenience is poor pedagogy. Thus, the question, "What constitutes effective use of online technologies in teaching?" is a question that all online instructors need to consider and is one of the research questions of this chapter. However, "effective" is a broad, vague concept, and its definition will be determined by course goals and contexts. As I reflect on the goals of my particular courses, "effectiveness" involves students' abilities to be at once safe, comfortable, and respectful in the online classroom context. These conditions are necessary to help students encounter diverse perspectives and be challenged in their own thought and belief processes. The social justice concepts we address involve the concept of how we approach the "other"—people who differ from those categories we use to define ourselves, by class, race, religion, gender, and so on. And so, in considering the use of online teaching technologies, key research questions for me are as follows: In what ways, if any, do online technologies further students' abilities to confront diverse perspectives? Does distance learning remove us further from one another, or can it be used to increase respect for and understanding of the "other"? Can distance learning create a "safe space" for students to actively engage with one another and with themselves to probe their personal prejudices and stereotypes?

Technology, Interaction, and Social Connection

In her discussion of emerging technological tools available for teaching and learning, Beldarrain (2006) stated that interactivity must be a primary concern in creating a successful online course (see also Jin, 2005). Moore (1993) broke interactivity down into four components: student-instructor, student-student, student-content, and student-interface interactions. Given geographical distance, Moore referred instead to "transactional distance" that can be reduced by careful consideration of dialogue, course structure, and learner autonomy. Dialogue is the cross-cutting component related to the four types of interactivity. It is also through dialogue, both written and spoken, that students can create a social presence in an online environment, which Beldarrain defines as "the degree to which individuals perceive intimacy, immediacy, and their particular role in a relationship" (p. 149). Garrison *et al.* (2000) explained this component as participants who can "project themselves socially and emotionally as 'real' people" (p. 94). As Picciano (2002) observed, students can interact in a class without gaining a sense of social presence or connection and belonging. In an analysis of both synchronous and asynchronous components of an online graduate education course, Fernández (2007) concluded that students created a social presence more through synchronous chat sessions than by asynchronous discussion boards. Picciano (2002), however, found a sense of social presence contributed to his asynchronous graduate student course on education in terms of students' perceptions of their learning.

Fernández (2007) noted that the exchange of ideas among students may be weakened when participants do not feel connected to one another. In her study of graduate students in a mathematics education course, she found that two-thirds of her students were disappointed if their discussion board postings did not receive a response from another student. Her analysis showed evidence of students' posts to one another resulting in "deeper thinking and growth in understanding of course content" (p. 144). Garrison *et al.* (2000) stated that social presence functioned as an affective element supporting the cognitive processes among learners. It can increase the depth of learning to effect a collaborative engagement and construction of knowledge rather than a simple interaction or delivery of information.

In a traditional classroom setting, physical presence and nonverbal cues contribute to the creation of social presence. In blended classrooms utilizing both face-to-face and online instruction, students have the ability to present themselves both physically and virtually. However, in courses that are fully online, the creation of a social presence occurs through language, types of responses (such as encouragement), use of symbols (such as emoticons) in discussion boards, voice inflection, frequency of response, and the use of symbols in synchronous sessions that allow for verbal communication.

Action Research

To provide a context for this research, I need to include some background about my own perspective on the role of the educator. I have tended to be a traditionalist in the sense that I enjoy a face-to-face classroom. I like to see the expressions on my students' faces and use their nonverbal cues to assess the classroom environment minute by minute. Thus, I was skeptical about moving portions of or entire courses onto a distance learning environment and somewhat grudgingly agreed to develop blended courses for which 4 to 6 of 15 sessions would be conducted via E! or BB beginning spring term, 2007. The courses were undergraduate and graduate Social Foundations of Education and a graduate seminar in media education entitled Communication, Education, and Change. In summer 2008, I conducted my first wholly online social foundations course with 18 graduate students of education.

Because the courses were experimental for me, I wanted to gauge the success of the distance features. Students completed surveys that assessed their competence in using new technologies and their impressions about using these technologies in their coursework. Questions included both quantitative and qualitative responses. I received 96 survey responses to using ipods, 97 regarding E! (62 with which I conducted an initial analysis with Cheng & Jones, 2009), and 64 student responses about the use of BB asynchronous interactive tools (such as discussion boards and small groups). Responses have been collected via online surveys and paper surveys. I also analyzed anonymous BB discussion posts to gain student viewpoints regarding their perceptions of these teaching techniques and student discussion board posts to understand ways in which students approached topics such as racism, immigration, and other controversial issues.

Of these new learning technologies, podcasts differ from BB and E! because they are not interactive. I include them because they were designed to offer students multiple perspectives on controversial topics. At my university, all students in the undergraduate sections of Social Foundations of Education must complete the same case study as their major writing assignment, and these cases are designed to address controversial topics and diversity. Recent topics have included undocumented immigrants, sex education, and the treatment of homosexual students. Professors teaching this course have been asked to record their perspectives on the case studies on the basis of their individual strands of research. In this way, we have hoped to offer students the benefit of the reflections of numerous academic perspectives to help generate their own thoughts about the case.

All of the data have come from undergraduate and graduate Social Foundations of Education courses at a research extension university in Florida. Students granted permission to use their survey and online discussion results through an IRB-accepted permission form. Data collection took place between fall 2007 and summer 2008.

Data analysis relied on Strauss and Corbin's (1990) open-ended coding approach, allowing themes to emerge rather than beginning with an a priori thesis. This resulted in a large variety of findings, not all of which related to my research questions. For example, one of the most common comments had to do with students' frustrations with numerous technical difficulties (45 instances), from inabilities to download podcasts and .pdf files from BB to problems with microphones and logging onto E!. A number of students commented, both positively and negatively, on the simultaneous methods of communicating on E!, such as texting, speaking, and polling. In spite of the popularity of ipods, only 15 of 29 students preferred listening to a podcast, 1 had no preference, 4 liked using both, and 9 students preferred reading the script.

Another frequent comment had to do with the convenience (31 instances) of using online technologies, in spite of the profusion of occasional technical difficulties. Students frequently noted that they appreciated not having to drive to campus. Many of the students work full-time, and they found it easier to make synchronous class schedules when they could stay home after work to attend class.

Findings

As mentioned, I initially began this research simply to assess whether students had or did not have a positive learning experience with various amounts and types of electronic learning platforms. Thus, I had not specifically planned to investigate what became for me the most critical theme of this project—that of a positive space to confront personal beliefs and unexplored prejudices. Such a positive environment involves feeling comfortable and safe. It also requires the presentation of a diversity of opinions through broad participation.

The theme that emerged with the greatest frequency was one I coded as "pleasure," at 59 instances. Words and phrases coded in this category included "fun," "enjoyed," and "I liked" or "I loved ..." Closely related to that theme was "comfort," at 17 instances. Most of these passages directly used the word "comfortable" to refer to their experience with E! or BB. General examples of these comments included the following:

> It was nice to have class in the comfort of my own home, especially because it takes me approximately an hour to get to school.

I loved the opportunity to work from home and be present for sessions.

Allows for a more comfortable learning environment.

Many of the student comments relating to comfort and pleasure indicated a cause-effect relationship between their positive affect and their learning experiences. These often addressed other themes important to confronting diverse perspectives, such as increased participation. The following student critiques indicate this theme:

I really enjoyed E!. I feel like we all got a chance to communicate and it felt almost like a debate, which was great.

I enjoyed using E!. I thought it was a great way for students who would not normally get involved in class discussions. I was encouraged to learn something new.

I feel that BB is helpful to get your thoughts out and it enables everyone to be able to speak and discuss, rather than just a few people in class.

I never thought I would like discussion boards. Then I began to read the input of other students. What a great technology tool! Not all students speak up in class; discussion boards allow me to understand other perspectives, and I grow in my knowledge and learning.

Comments such as these indicate that students noticed increased participation and valued the opportunity to learn from multiple perspectives.

Another important link to students' positive experiences with online technology related to their sense of safety. One student wrote,

I really enjoyed our E! sessions because everyone was able to converse in some way. People really took advantage of the chatting. I am sometimes embarrassed to speak about certain topics in class so it was nice that no one was looking at me or I felt that anyone knew who I was.

This comment also alludes to a sense of safety through anonymity. Numerous comments alluded to increased confidence resulting from a sense of invisibility:

I enjoyed the discussion among peers which I feel contributed to my learning experience. I could talk without feeling embarrassed to speak in front of a class staring back at me. In class I may feel uncomfortable to ask a question because everyone looks at you, but on E! I felt I could really think for myself without the influence of others and I really liked that.

Everyone seemed more comfortable talking and voicing their opinions, even the ones who are usually quiet in class. We held good conversations during the sessions, and I don't think we would have accomplished that in a regular classroom.

I felt the discussions were honest and open. I felt the ability to be more open, especially on controversial topics.

I personally dislike confrontation. I would not participate in a regular classroom discussion that would address subjects that make me uncomfortable. We are all equal online. No one knows that I'm one of the "older" students and won't dismiss what I say because they think my views are outdated. Everyone has an equal voice. I feel more comfortable to express my views online.

These comments indicate the students felt a sense of psychological comfort created by the physical distance. It helped many shy students overcome their tendency to remain silent in a traditional classroom setting, and it allowed them to speak out on topics they considered confrontational or controversial. One student said that the technology prevented her from feeling "intimidated." Two students who specifically described themselves as "older" stated that they felt more heard when other students could not physically perceive their age. This also allows for a diversity of opinion in terms of age and experiences.

Confronting Racism: A Textual Analysis

Overall, the student evaluations of the technologies as tools for learning were positive. However, does this assessment hold up when students are in the midst of confronting their own biases and encountering experiences radically different from their own?

To test the validity of my students' responses about learning online, I analyzed text messages and recordings from our Eluminate Live! (E!) classes and the content posted to the BB discussions. As an example of what is possible using new technologies for teaching, I will provide a textual analysis of typed messages in E! sessions and BB discussion boards by my summer 2008 graduate students in Social Foundations of Education. The class consisted of 18 students, 5 male and 13 female. One male self-identified as someone whose heritage was African American and Irish American (but who was considered by others only as African American) and who grew up during the Civil Rights era. One female identified as African American, another with American Indian heritage, and one as Hispanic. The students did not have a face-to-face meeting. I have given fictitious names to those quoted frequently in the following paragraphs.

Lawrence-Lightfoot and Hoffmann Davis (1997) describe tensions in qualitative data analysis "between organization and classification on one hand and maintaining the rich complexity of human experience on the other" (p. 192). In interpreting the rich interaction between the students' live and asynchronous conversations, I have tried to be mindful of this tension, coding for themes and patterns and including divergent opinions that provide "important contrasts with the norm" (p. 193). Such contrasts are important in addressing my questions on how distance learning can advance or hinder students' regard for diverse people and perspectives. Coding themes that emerged from BB and E! transcripts fell into two major categories:

1   Responses to course content (readings, videos)
    • Based on personal experiences
    • Backed by research or specific analysis of the content
    • Opinion not backed by experience or research (did not code for this in the E! transcripts, as most of it would be in this category)
    • Upset by materials: "stunned," "enraged" response to social injustice content
    • Asking questions of the texts
    • Denial of truth of content
    • Controversial (could be perceived as racist, stereotypical, prejudicial)
2   Personal interactions
    • Questions directed at other students
    • Agreement with one another/camaraderie (such as "I agree!" or "I'm sorry that happened to you!")
    • Disagreement with other students' comments (some were of the "I agree with __, but not ___") variety
    • Confrontational
    • Metacognition; self-reflective (such as "I am trying to understand...")

Table 7.1 displays the number of times these themes surfaced over four of the six weeks of the course. During the last two weeks, the course topics did not lend themselves to the same kind of personal exploration

Table 7.1 Coded themes from E! and BB transcripts

Response to course content	Wk 1	Wk 2	Wk 3	Wk 4*	Totals
Personal experience	43	18	25	30	116
Research backed	18	22	28	28	96
Opinion, not backed	20	9	8	14	51
Upset by content	12	9	10	4	35
Questioning content	15	5	9	5	34
Denial	2	3	2	8	15
Controversial	5	7	8	11	31
Totals	115	73	90	100	378
Student Interactions	*Wk 1*	*Wk 2*	*Wk 3*	*Wk 4**	*Totals*
Questioning	21	23	10	17	71
Agreement	50	46	40	39	175
Disagreement	18	13	6	20	57
Confrontational	2	6	3	18	29
Metacognition	1	15	9	15	40
Totals	92	103	68	109	372
Combined Totals	209	172	148	209	740
[Total Online Posts]	142	155	94	161	552

*In Week 4, only BB was utilized.

of controversial topics, so I did not include them in this analysis. During Week Four, we did not meet on E!, so there were only BB discussions to code. I did not analyze BB and E! comments separately, because remarks on E!, both typed and verbal, followed similar patterns to those on BB discussions. After the table, I provide a context for the patterns that are most related to the research questions and detailed examples of their emergence.

Week One

In the first week, the students considered opposite points of view about education in America. Along with primarily historical readings by John Dewey, Horace Mann, Thomas Jefferson, and others, they watched *20/20: Stupid in America*, in which John Stossel provides a carefully edited presentation showing expensive, fancy public schools that are failing children and poorly funded grassroots charter schools that are providing the academics and attention that children need. It is, more-or-less, an hour advertisement for school choice in the form of a news magazine. The students also watched *Children in America's Schools*, a documentary by Jonathan Kozol about deplorable conditions in poorly financed areas in the United States (the film highlights Ohio), contrasting them with rich public schools. The message of this film is that students in run-down schools come to believe they are worthless, and those in the well-financed schools have high self-esteem, motivation, and achievement. This film is carefully edited to indict the system of financing public schools in America.

Student responses, especially regarding the videos, clearly introduced diverse personalities and comments that would be uncommon to encounter in a traditional classroom because some of the comments could be regarded as stereotypical or racist (coded "controversial"). For instance, one student wrote, "Poor inner city students will always lag in achievement. Is this due to genetics or the environment?" In a response to the question, a student began by writing, "It is clearly the environment ..." but as she continued her argument, she convinced herself that "it is genetics. Or maybe both." Another student commented, "It seems that all the grants and corp money that I have browsed through is for low income schools." In a later discussion, this comment was reflected in several student posts commenting that most scholarships are for Blacks and other minorities.

Many initial responses to the videos came from students who were persuaded by their messages. However, other student responses recognized the potential for bias. About *20/20*, one student wrote,

> I felt like the report was biased and much like propaganda. While I assume that they did not make up things that were reported, it was not presented in a way that left the viewer with a choice to make. It was presented in a way (I feel) that the public would hate teachers and public schools. Why wouldn't they? The "report" did not say anything positive about public schools.

Another wrote, "I concur we can make anything sound positive or negative when we report and highlight the elements that we choose. Only one side of the story was told in each of these reports." Comments such as these indicate that some students were able to analyze the media and be active participants as they considered the messages.

Many students determined their responses to the videos based on personal experiences. Some had negative experiences with charter schools, for example, or they had worked in both poorly and well-funded schools. The student who backed most of his comments with evidence, theories, scholarly resources, and specific historical references was the student who self-identified as an African American male who was a child during the Civil Rights movement. A former teacher and current assistant principal himself, "Kevin" asserted that teachers were poorly trained and that the system that both films depicted as "broken" were, in fact, doing just what they were designed to do: oppress minorities. In a reference to Apple's (2001) work, Kevin wrote:

> The hegemonic alliance that is the right would like to return to a partly mythological past where the United States dominated the world economy unchallenged. People were mostly married and God was White like most of the people who were middle class or rich.

He also confronted "White thinking" when other students wrote generalizations that would not tend to hold true for minorities. For instance, when one student wrote, "Sadly some teachers are just in it for a paycheck, although I wonder why they would pick teaching as an easy and lucrative career," Kevin responded,

> There is a lot of truth to what you're saying for White men. Historically Blacks and women could not get into a lot of other professions. So the best and brightest of their ranks became teachers ... While I think that a lot of people get into teaching as a plan B (who do not get into their first choice of careers) I wouldn't necessarily say it is that way for a lot of Black people and women that have been in the profession for decades. I would agree that for many new teachers and White men this may be true. I think it may be a jump to say most people.

Kevin's remarks drew varied replies from classmates. A couple students disagreed with his assertion that teachers were poorly trained. One student replied to him that finances were not the only cause of problems in schools; many wrote that they believed problems were due to lack of parental support and involvement. One student, "John," who self-identified as a libertarian, confronted Kevin with the following comment:

> So Kevin, you don't believe the system will heal itself yet you seem to rail against the movements to change it. Am I misreading you? Or, are you just not satisfied with the "right's" positions on how to bring about change?

Kevin replied by suggesting that John read Michael Apple's (2001) *Educating the "Right" Way*. Personalities and personal viewpoints were apparent, creating a sense of social presence early in the course.

Week Two

In the second week, students read pieces by Booker T. Washington and W. E. B. DuBois and watched *The Children's March* and *A Time for Justice*, both distributed by Southern Poverty Law Center. Some students who had not seen photos of lynchings and news videos depicting violence against Blacks during the Civil Rights era responded that they were "horrified," "upset," or "outraged." Responses also indicated various common naïve beliefs, such as the belief that we are past racism (coded as "denial") and that it is best to view people from a color blind perspective. One female student's words, "Carol's," indicated her desire for growth in understanding (coded "personal search" and "personal experience"):

> I think we all are ignorant to some extent, regardless of our race, religion, or otherwise. I don't think most people are sensitive at all, rather they have been taught how to behave more "PC" in public. I have often seen people being very culturally sensitive and supporting in public, but behind closed doors behave quite the opposite. I often plead ignorance and ask lots of questions when I don't understand. Some people are very gracious and want to help me learn more, and others are offended. I was brought up in Colorado in an area they referred to as Vanilla Valley. I was never exposed to some of the things I have experienced living in the South. Recently, I had a co-worker who was very offended because I said I don't see her color when I look at her, I see "Jane" who can type faster than I and has a beautiful smile. She wanted me to see that she is a black woman, that is her identity.

Kevin reiterated the viewpoint of the Black woman by writing,

> People have culture and ethnicity. You can't divorce a person from their color or culture. They do not exist without it. If you do not see culture or ethnicity or some blend of the two you can not see a person.

By doing this, he is furthering Carol's education and enlarging her perspective to see through the eyes of a person of color.

Several posts later, Carol added,

> I don't understand why we need to label people. I don't refer to myself as any "color" because I don't want to be labeled and I very rarely share with anyone that I am Native American. I don't necessarily

think I don't really "see" color, rather I just don't think that color alone makes up a person. I try not to judge people on appearances whether it be their skin color, eye color, clothes, or weight. The point is, everyone has different views and opinions, mostly formed by their families and upbringing. As long as these opinions aren't hurtful towards someone, should we all be a little more tolerant and sensitive? Or maybe we should all just never say or think anything and never have the opportunity to hear the other side and how they perceive things. My comments are not to offend anyone. I was trying to explain my experiences and how I have tried to grow as a person and how I have tried to understand. I guess I should learn to keep my opinions to myself and just stick with the status quo.

In this post, Carol identifies as a member of a minority ethnicity and defends her position to perceive people in a "color-blind" way. She indicates both a desire not to be provocative and a sense of frustration ("I should learn to keep my opinions to myself …") Another female student, "Meg," responded with support and encouragement:

I think you are absolutely right in being able to share how we think and feel. We ought not ever feel that we own the truth but only wish to expand our understanding. How can we do that if we don't ask and don't share with one another? Please don't stop expressing your opinions—I very much want to hear them!

What followed was a series of posts from Carol and Meg that showed a desire to advance and understand a complicated and controversial topic: what is racist? What is not? How can I know? Carol wrote,

Thanks Meg, I appreciate that. I'm not even sure they are really opinions, really. I'm just looking for answers! There's text book answers to what racism is and what is and isn't P.C., but it's like getting a test back with an answer wrong. Sure, you can say what the correct answer is, but I want to know how do get to that correct answer? Why is it the correct answer? Does that make sense?

Later in the discussion thread, Carol admitted to feeling like a minority in Florida because she does not speak Spanish, and "Maria" added her voice to frustration about "politically correct" views:

I believe that people are so quick to yell "racism" that they don't take the time to look at the facts. The melting pot theory does not work. We are all unique individuals from diverse backgrounds, and we should all be proud of where we came from, regardless of where it was. This country is so scared of insulting someone and being sued that we bend over backwards to be "politically correct," and not just with regard to race. Case in point—no more Christmas parties at work—they're "holiday" parties. Every one of us needs to recognize and appreciate every culture, whether it's European, Asian, African, or American. Why do we differentiate certain groups of people by referring to them as African-American or Asian-American? Aren't we all just Americans? For those of you who are African-American or Asian-American, I'm not saying this to be insulting —I'm just pointing out yet another aspect of what could be considered racism.

Like Carol, Maria was concerned about offending others. At the same time, she felt safe to voice an emotionally charged opinion.

After viewing the films on the Civil Rights era, Kevin's responses became personal, and he related his childhood experiences of signs for "Coloreds Only" and being moved to the back of the bus or being told to stand so a White person could have his seat. Several female students responded to this personal narrative with appreciation:

> Wow, thanks for sharing your personal history. It puts a perspective on how bland my childhood was.
>
> Thanks for sharing your thoughts and experiences. I enjoyed your post.

Carol's response again shows her desire to understand and progress:

> How many movies have you watched where the actor's dialogue is about getting some "chocolate love" or similar? A lot of these are from Black writers and directors, too. It's like when you hear how horrible it is to say "nxxxxx" (or the n-word as some call it) yet Black people call each other that all the time. I personally think there is a history of that word being used to hurt people so I don't approve of its use regardless, but it's not my place to tell someone using it in a different context that it's wrong. It's wrong for me and I am the only one I can answer to. I really hope some of you respond to this because I am really curious if anyone else shares this view or has another opinion.

Carol's posts indicate a desire to learn from others and to arrive at a deeper understanding of race. In another thread, a female student disclosed that she was African American and wrote, "I'm still learning about my history and there is still a great deal I don't know."

A related controversial issue, that of affirmative action, came up in this week's postings. Several students' comments were similar to this representative post:

> I don't know a great deal about Affirmative Action except my own experience with it. I was denied a full time position while the woman hired was given it. She was not nearly as qualified as me. I was never given a straight answer as to why she received the job and I did not. The only explanation that was given to me in secret was that the school had to keep the ratio of minorities to whites up.

The implication is that a person of a minority group got the job simply because she was a minority candidate. In response, Kevin wrote of a time when he hired a person with lesser academic credentials for a job because it was not a job in which those with high credentials were likely to remain, as indicated by people who left this position previously. He was accused of reverse discrimination for his decision. This interplay allowed for controversial and diverse opinions to be voiced and acknowledged.

John engaged in another round of confrontation with Kevin when he wrote that Jews had "moved on" from oppression but Blacks had not:

> I remember distinctly in the videos images of the U.S. military attempting to protect the Blacks from the mobs of crazy Southern bigots. I am not saying they were always successful in providing protection, but an attempt was made. In my mind, getting beat, sprayed with hoses and treated badly doesn't compare to getting starved half to death and then being sent en mass to lethal chemical showers. This is no argument to justify what happened to either party, or to conclude that one party's suffering is more important than the other. One way I see how this has played out differently for each party is that I see Jews have moved on from the holocaust. Back in New York when I attended my synagogue regularly the holocaust was not something that was brought up too often. However it seems in the Black community people have not moved on as is evidenced by Obama's pastor and his remarks. I think people like to think of his views and actions as being obscure and not representative of the culture, but I get a different impression. I don't know if it's people like Obama's pastor and Al Sharpton who misrepresent their people or if Blacks really can't move on from what has happened like the Jews have.

Kevin responded with an equally pointed comment:

I have always wondered why the Jews would wear the Star of David that identified them as Jewish? I probably would have taken mine off and moved to an area where I wasn't known to be Jewish. Sounds simple; I'm sure that this was not as simple as it sounds. Blacks could not camouflage their skin color. The blanket statement that Blacks have not been able to move on the way Jews have is, I think inaccurate. Even though many of the men who committed the atrocities against Jews have not faced war crimes and are not dead, almost none of the criminals of the civil rights area have been punished. Yet Emmit Tills mother who just died last year said that she forgave the men who murdered her son and so did the wife of Medger Evers. I feel that the act of bringing war criminals to trial in Nuremburg helped the healing process. There probably would be less healing if the Nazi atrocities had been trivialized the way that the Civil Rights Movement has. Also racism against Blacks has not been confined only to the South. There have been and continue to be many instances of institutionalized racism in the North.

During this week, there were many more student interactions (103) than comments on course materials (69), and several students dared to express opinions about race, religion, privilege, and justice that occasionally indicated personal biases, stereotypes, or prejudice. The total of controversial and confrontational comments nearly doubled (13) from the first week's total (7).

Week Three

Midway through the course, Week Three, the students had readings on welfare and racial differences regarding cultural and economic capital. As I expected, there were students who took the attitude that "because I worked two jobs and avoided welfare, everyone can" and those who believed in welfare as a temporary aid to gaining financial independence. Kevin felt validated by the readings, writing, "I have always believed that people who feel that a person should be able to pass on their accumulated wealth to their offspring but were against Affirmative Action were hypocrites." Though not directly stated, this comment may have been in response to those who had written indicating that the policy unfairly discriminated against Whites the previous week. This was the only issue that students dealt with in terms of controversy and confrontation for the week, and overall, there was less intensity in the interactions.

Week Four

In Week Four, the students watched *A Place at the Table*, which included not only the stories of those typically represented as minorities in the United States but the story of an Irish American, a Japanese American, and a gay youth. This caused most of the students to reflect on their personal heritages. One student wrote that her mother was a member of the famous Hatfields, of the Hatfield and McCoy feud, to which several students responded that they appreciated a light reprieve in the conversation.

The levity however, did not last. A female student, "Mandy," wrote that she could understand that slaves were still resentful of their past treatment but that America had reached a turning point and "is past all this prejudice." Kevin responded that he felt sure the slaves were not resentful as they were all dead, that he taught his children not to expect fair treatment, and that "If you are Black and have a "C" average you will probably not get into a four year college unless you are very very rich. If you are White, on the other hand, with a "C" average you could become president." Mandy responded,

> Obama was raised in Hawaii with only 2% black. White is the minority there. So I doubt he witnessed any bias until he moved to the mainland ... My niece was turned down for UF. Extra credit is putting kids at 4.0 average now. Which I do not agree with. But don't you think you are being racist by believing a white can get in with a "C" average??

Kevin responded to Mandy's logical fallacy regarding Obama's time in Hawaii. As to the charge of being racist, he wrote,

> Am I racist if tell my child that you need to prepare yourself? If I were Asian I would tell them you're going to need to compete with the alumni's kids. I don't think you will be judged the same as the alumni kids. In fact the application even has a place to mark something called legacy! Because the school cares about what the alumni thinks (mostly because there is some monetary reward or penalty associated with that thought process) am I racist? Do you even know what it means to be racist? I am telling them that you are not competing against things that are meant to be fair. If believing the truth makes me a racist well ....

He went on to cite instances of President Bush's low GPA and concluded,

If you and your ancestors had always been denied admission even Affirmative Action would not offset the 300 years of exclusion! I went to segregated schools that used textbooks that had missing pages because we got them when the White schools were done with them or they were considered unusable! So as I do the math: prep schools that cater to the child and family, for George. Decrepit facilities with books that were substandard for me. I know that I couldn't get into Harvard or Yale. Yet between George W. and me, I got a higher SAT score. Who really got the benefit of Affirmative Action?

In a thread a day later, one of the female students accused me of being monocultural:

> I also believe that you, Professor McBrien are guilty of not being multicultural. The readings are only based on the Black view, it would be better to also include the White view and perhaps another culture's view towards the subject. How does someone not directly involved with America's racism see the situation? That way we could discuss the issue from different viewpoints. Bring both sides out in the open (then I would not be compelled to stick up for the Whites, and be indirectly accused of underlying racism :-))

The student's emoticon at the end of her post perhaps indicates concern about how I might respond. Thus, though she felt safe enough to voice what could be taken as a critical comment towards her instructor, she also was concerned about the potential of an offensive post. I responded by citing multiple ethnicities of the authors we had read, most of whom were not Black. Kevin, however, responded with high emotion:

> "… compelled to stick up for the Whites, and be indirectly accused of underlying racism." Interesting! I have a tendency toward sarcasm but sometimes I wonder what purpose would sarcasm serve? When I read the postings of Pam I think, hmm religious and I would like to say … XYZ and then I realize that it would really be hypocritical to criticize her because I disagree. In addition to the fact that when the support for an argument is faith I have to respect that I am in unfamiliar territory. When I read the postings of John, I say, intelligent mainstream perspective but myopic perspective … not in touch with the injustices. But when I read the last posting I thought these interactions are not going to allow me to finish my other assignments! Because I would like to respond and research and create an argument that I COULD DEFEND. NOW I REALIZE THAT THAT ARGUMENT COULD REALLY GO ON FOREVER.

Responses were immediate. One student suggested that the posting "hit a nerve." John wrote, "I don't believe that I am the one who is narrow-minded Kevin. It seems as though I have really gotten under your skin. This isn't even my post and yet I am brought up."

At that point, Kevin began to apologize for mentioning names. And he acknowledged emotion towards his mixed heritage:

> I am truly talking about my great grandfather the slave master who, because my grandmother was not also White, left everything to my half brother's line. And my brother who has inherited much of the wealth that my line worked to accumulate for the family does not feel that I am worthy of his help. I do not deserve to share in our grandfather's wealth or attend his schools. Even if I work hard for what I am given unless there is some new way that I could benefit him.

As the discussion escalated, I sent out a post about racial identity theory (Carter, 1995; Helms, 1990), reminding students that examinations of racism and personal bias are challenging and emotional and asking them to maintain a safe space by avoiding personal attacks. In response, Kevin wrote a highly self-reflective and confessional post:

> I shouldn't personalize my responses. I apologize to Pam and John for doing this. I now realize that I shouldn't respond when I feel a sense of frustration. I know that sometimes I can be perceived as a tad arrogant. I do try to continuously evaluate where I am both by reading and reflecting. I think that I probably exhibit elements of Bank's multiethnicity but I also remember when I didn't see myself as a racial being ... curious. I don't believe that I am objective (or that a person can be objective) even though I try to be in matters of race. Because many of our memories of love and hate have faces and those faces have races. I do not believe that racial hatred is instinctive as I have said many times. When I've interacted through the postings with members of this class I have tried to draw them into discussions that make them (and me) think about why they feel the way they do. Sometimes I feel that through discussion forums it is possible to examine the intractable irrationalities enough to at least get people questioning some of the premises that the irrationality rests on. In this pursuit I have personally attacked some people. In other words I have tried to get them to see something from my perspective. In that I perceive myself to be more scientific in my thought process than the people I am trying to convince. I also realize that while I have gained my indoctrination from scientifically trained people, they

were just people, as am I. Therefore I must assume that they, as I, have fallibility. This was never more apparent to me than when James Watson recently correlated race and intelligence. So I will try to be more topic centered in the future.

In response to his very personal and reflective post, Kevin received several encouraging messages, such as "I applaud you for your passion" and "I have enjoyed our honest discussions. This is what a university education is about right?" There was a thread of 14 posts in which students seemed to rally to support Kevin. One sent a link to a blog that discredited James Watson's assertion that Blacks are less intelligent than Whites. Pam wrote that she was not offended by Kevin's comments but that she "had to giggle though at your impression of me as religious. Being in my mid-forties I have just begun my deconstruction process and have learned in the past few years that everything they taught me in church is a lie." By this comment, Pam alerts Kevin to the problem of making assumptions about people's beliefs.

In the next discussion thread, John moved the conversation away from a matter of race and made a generalization about Hispanic immigrants:

No matter what the white majority does it will never be good enough to satisfy the minority … The readings brought up the issue of language and I strongly disagree with the multicultural idealist's view on that. In America we speak English and I think it is outrageous that places like California can mandate teaching in anything other than English. And that places like Miami have street signs in Spanish. Do you really think that schools in a foreign country teach in anything other than their language? Today it's not how can I assimilate and become an American, it's how can I be an (insert alternative nationality here) and still reap the benefits of this country without becoming an American. When I get asked what I am, I answer I am an American, but if you ask an American of Latin American or Mexican Decent they will tell you they are Puerto Rican, Guatemalan, Mexican, etc. Don't come to America if you don't want to become an American.

Students took issue with John. However, they did so by beginning with points of agreement. Kevin began his response with,

You echo my thoughts when you say that hate is passed on from generation to generation, and while I agree that things in this country are more equal than they have ever been that doesn't make them more equal than they need to be.

This introduction attempts to demonstrate points of unity before arguing a point of contention. Kevin went on,

> I was talking to U_ B_ today, an exemplary teacher in my school who came from Germany about a decade ago, I was actually commending her for her command of the English language to which she replied every one in Germany takes a foreign language from elementary school on; it's no big deal ... One last note—the original languages spoken when the Europeans came to America have been supplanted by English or Spanish or German or what ever European language you are referring to as not being American!!!

Glenda also began by mentioning respect before discussing her disagreement:

> Although I respect your viewpoints, I have to say that you may be misinformed regarding the deep issues that minorities face on a daily basis. Being a Black woman, I can speak from experience ... You state in your closing sentence—"Don't come to America if you don't want to become American." Well I was born here so I didn't have a choice—and overall I love it. My challenge though is for Americans to make others feel like they are American. Remember—we must confront the problem before we can conquer the problem.

More conciliatory language was found in a strand commenting on *A Place at the Table*. A male student was bothered by the fact that the movie placed blame on White men for selling slaves without also recognizing that Black Africans rounded up Blacks in their own countries to sell. Kevin responded, "Absolutely true. I thought about the same thing. The patent on greed has never been owned by one group."

Weeks Two and Four included the most intense student interactions, expressing personal prejudices and confronting one another's viewpoints. Students also employed the greatest use of exclamation marks, capitalizations, and emoticons during these weeks, especially Week Four. Additionally, both weeks included the greatest number of self-reflective posts that indicated a desire for understanding and a search for meaning.

During the remaining two weeks, the topics changed, and students were not confrontational with one another. However, as the summer session neared the end, I received seven unsolicited e-mails from students who thanked me for the course. Phrases they used included "thought-provoking," "interesting and enjoyable," and "visionary." A female student wrote, "Thanks for everything. This has been a truly enlightening course and invigorating, mind-boggling experience! (that's a good thing!)"

A male student wrote that it was "the most moving class" he had taken as a graduate student. A female student commented on the use of combined technologies:

> In case I didn't say it before, thank you for an enlightening class. I found it refreshing to share ideas that were so controversial. I found that the conversations and the topics were very intriguing and this was by far one of the best online classes because of the Elluminate sessions. At first, I was dreading it because of time constraints, but really found the communication opportunities better than just writing on BB. Anyway, thank you again.

Discussion

To review, I conducted this research as a professor who was somewhat wary of the value of emerging online technologies in teaching and learning. Because of the nature of my course content, I found myself asking the following questions:

- In what ways, if any, do current distance educational platforms or other online technologies further students' abilities to confront diverse perspectives?
- Does distance learning remove us further from one another or can it be used to increase respect for and understanding of the "other"?
- Can distance learning create a "safe space" for students to actively engage with one another and with themselves to probe their personal prejudices and stereotypes?

On the basis of responses to open-ended surveys and a textual analysis of student comments in an online graduate class, I found that new technologies provided a sense of comfort, relaxation, and enjoyment for most of my students, in spite of occasional technical problems. Several students noted the benefit of learning everyone's opinions and beliefs owing to online course requirements as opposed to traditional settings in which dominant students typically make most of the comments. Many also commented on increased feelings of safety owing to their physical absence from their peers. They stated that they were less embarrassed to voice their opinions.

Because all students were required to contribute to online conversations, students became privy to a broad range of diverse perspectives. They frequently asked questions of one another, creating a sense of social presence and willingness to learn from others' perspectives. In responding to course content, the highest response rate was that of comparing readings and videos to personal experiences, showing that the students were making meaning between their own lives and the more abstract world of research articles and documentaries. In 175 instances, agreement or supportive responsive comments were, by far, the highest amount of student interactions. However, dissenting comments totaled 57 instances (33%). Students' willingness to express their own biases and to confront one another with diverse beliefs indicates that using distance learning tools effectively can allow students to engage with difficult social topics to expand their own understanding. Finally, the 40 instances of self-reflection indicate that this form of teaching and learning can help students grow in their personal search for meaning and respect for divergent points of view.

This study is not generalizable. The unique combination of students in the graduate course clearly contributed to the findings and conclusions. However, this case provides grounds for further research and indicates that distance learning has the potential to contribute to reflection about the way that students perceive the "other" by creating a safe space to explore their biases and to encounter diversity and controversy.

References

Apple, M. W. (2001). *Educating the "right" way: Markets, standards, God, and inequality.* New York: Routledge/Falmer.

Beldarrain, Y. (2006). Distance education trends: Integrating new technologies to foster student interaction and collaboration. *Distance Education, 27*(2), 139–153.

Buckingham, D. (2003). *Media education: Literacy,learning and contemporary culture* Cambridge: Polity Press.

Burt, E. (2006, May). Where the millionaires are. Retrieved September 16, 2008, from http://www.kiplinger.com/features/archives/2006/03/millionaireintro.html

Carter, R. T. (1995). *The influence of race and racial identity on psychotherapy.* New York: John Wiley & Sons, Inc.

Considine, D. M., and Baker, F. (2006). Focus on film: They learn it thru the movies. *The Journal of Media Literacy, 53*(2), 24–32.

Fernández, M. L (2007). Communication and instruction in an online graduate education course. *Teaching Education, 18*(2), 137–150.

Fisher, M. (2003). Online collaborative learning: Relating theory to practice. *Journal of Educational Technology Systems, 31*(3), 227–249.

Garrison, D. R., Anderson, T., & Archer, W. (2000). Critical inquiry in a text-based environment: Computer conferencing in higher education. *The Internet and Higher Education, 2*(2-3), 87–105.

Helms, J. (1990). *Black and white racial identity: Theory, research, and practice.* New York: Greenwood Press.

Hobbs, R. (2006). Non-optimal uses of video in the classroom. *Learning, Media, and Technology, 31*, 35–50.

Jin, S. H. (2005). Analyzing student-student and student-instructor interaction through multiple communication tools in web-based learning. *International Journal of Instructional Media, 32*, 59–67.

Lawrence-Lightfoot, S., & Hoffmann Davis, J. (1997). *The art and science of portraiture*. San Francisco, CA: Jossey-Bass.

Majidi, M. (Director). (1999). *Color of paradise*. Sony Pictures.

McBrien, J. L. (2005). Educational needs and barriers for refugee students in the United States: A review of the literature. *Review of Educational Research, 75*, 329–364.

McBrien, J. L., Jones, P. & Cheng, R. (2009). Virtual spaces: Employing a synchronous online classroom to facilitate student engagement in online learning. *The International Review of Research in Open and Distance Learning, 10*(3), http://www.irrodl.org/index.php/irrodl/article/view/605/1298

Moore, M. G. (1993). Theory of transactional distance. In D. Keegan (Ed.), *Theoretical principles of distance education*. New York: Routledge.

Park, Y. J., & Bonk, C. J. (2007). Synchronous learning experiences: Distance and residential learners' perspectives in a blended graduate course. *Journal of Interactive Online Learning, 6*, 245–264.

Picciano, A. G. (2002). Beyond student perceptions: Issues of interaction, presence, and performance in an online course. *Journal for Asynchronous Learning Networks, 6*(1), 21–40.

Rothenberg, P. S. (2004). *White privilege: Essential readings on the other side of racism*. New York: Worth Publishers.

Saettler, P. (1998). Antecedents, origins, and theoretical evolution of AECT. *TechTrends, 43*, 51–57.

Snelbecker, G. E. (1999). Current progress, historical perspective, and some tasks for the future of instructional theory. In C. M. Reigeluth (Ed.), *Instructional-design theories and models, a new paradigm of instructional theory* (vol. 2, pp. 653– 674). Mahwah, NJ: Lawrence Erlbaum Associates.

Strauss, A., & Corbin, J. (1990). *Basics of qualitative research: Grounded theory procedures and techniques*. London: Sage.

Part IV

Beyond the Classroom

Media Literacy in Virtual Environments

Chapter 8

Media Literacy 2.0

Unique Characteristics of Video Games

Aaron Delwiche

In a landmark document published in the early 1990s, the Aspen Institute Report of the National Leadership Conference on Media Literacy (NLCML) stressed that the "fundamental objective of media literacy is critical autonomy in relationship to *all* media" (Aufderheide, 1993, p. x; emphasis added). Since that time, the communication landscape has changed dramatically, but the media literacy curriculum has not kept up with the changing media habits of contemporary youth. This is particularly true when it comes to video games.

By all measures, the video game industry is an increasingly powerful force on the media landscape. From the gaming parlors of China and South Korea to the living rooms of American suburbs, game hardware and software manufacturers generated more than $42 billion in global sales in 2007, and analysts predict that this figure will approach $70 billion by the year 2012 (Bond, 2008). Within the United States, two of three households are home to at least one gamer (Entertainment Software Association, 2008), and dedicated gaming consoles are found in four of ten American homes (Nielsen Media Research, 2007). This growth is fueled by an increasingly diverse audience. Contrary to the stereotypical notion that gaming is the exclusive province of adolescent boys, the average gamer is 35 years old, and approximately one of four gamers is older than the age of 50 (Entertainment Software Association, 2008). Women purchase half of all video games sold in the United States and account for 44% of the nation's total gaming population. Among online gamers between the ages of 25 and 34, two-thirds are women (Colvile, 2006).

Not surprisingly, the market for video game advertising alone exceeds $1 billion and is expected to reach $2.3 billion within the next four years (Bond, 2008). A portion of this money is spent on traditional billboards and product placement within franchises such as *Need for Speed* and *Guitar Hero*, but interactive media can also be used to deliver entertainment experiences that are essentially playable commercials. The most persuasive games are those that subtly integrate narrative and game-play mechanics with political and commercial messages (Delwiche, 2007).

A classic example of such integration is the game *America's Army*. Developed for the U.S. Army by the Modeling, Simulation and Virtual Environments Institute (MOVES) at the Naval Postgraduate School, *America's Army* is a free, downloadable game that leverages conventions of the first-person shooter genre to recruit young Americans into military service. Boasting more than 9 million registered players, America's Army has been described as "the most successful game launch in history" (O' Hagan 2004). According to one internal report, the game has been a wild success, engendering "positive awareness of Soldiering among twenty-nine percent of young Americans age 16 to 24" (Wardynski, 2004).

One might think that media literacy educators would be closely monitoring these developments, but existing analytical frameworks have limited applicability to the unique medium of video games. When it comes to television, film, and print, educators are equipped with a set of critical terms (e.g., editing, framing, lighting, sound) that can help students become more critically aware media consumers. So far, there is no comparable framework for teaching students to understand video games. Educators regularly critique titles such as *Grand Theft Auto* and *Fat Princess* for violent, racist, and sexist representations, but there has been little attention to the underlying characteristics of video games that make them uniquely powerful persuasive tools. As Steven Poole (2003) points out, "videogames are an increasingly pervasive part of the modern cultural landscape, but we have no way of speaking critically about them" (p. 12).

This chapter proposes a simple conceptual framework that can be used to promote critical consumption and production of video game content. After establishing the basic case for video game literacy, it sketches the broad outlines of an interpretive framework for understanding the medium. Focusing on key properties of video games, it suggests that the medium's persuasive power is directly related to four characteristics: immersion, engagement, identification, and interactivity. Because exposure to media production is a crucial component of media literacy, the chapter closes with a consideration of ways that cheat codes, level editors, and other modification tools can empower students to design their own game experiences without engaging in complex computer programming.

The Case for Video Game Literacy

The absence of a critical framework for analyzing video games is understandable when one considers the cultural history of this controversial medium. Throughout the 1980s and 1990s, the reaction to video games on the part of educators, researchers, and policymakers was lopsided at best and hysterical at worst. When video games first arrived on the scene, arcades and home gaming consoles generated a sustained wave of negative coverage (Williams, 2006). Early studies focused primarily on the effects of violent content, and the United States Surgeon General publicly worried in 1982 that youth were addicted "body and soul" to dangerous machines (Varadarajan, 1997). A decade later, relatives of students who died in the Columbine massacre filed a $5 billion lawsuit against game manufacturers, accusing them of turning young people into "monster killers" (Ward, 2001).

In recent years, video games have been deemed less of a threat. Though the possibility of censorship continues to lurk on the periphery of American politics, established institutions demonstrate growing open-mindedness about the civic potential of video games. In 2006, the John D. and Catherine T. MacArthur Foundation announced a $50 million initiative to fund research related to digital media and learning. Two years later, the Federal Consortium of Virtual Worlds organized a conference bringing together government employees, educators, and the nascent virtual world industry. The National Aeronautics and Space Administration (NASA), the National Oceanic and Atmospheric Administration (NOAA), the Center for Disease Control (CDC), and the National Institute of Health (NIH) are just a few of the government agencies that have announced substantial funding for innovative proposals related to virtual worlds and video games. Video games were further legitimized during the 2008 presidential campaign when Barak Obama purchased advertising space in 18 titles, including *Madden NFL 09* and *Guitar Hero 3* (Barrett, 2008).

In part, the changing cultural climate can be credited to groundbreaking works such as Sherry Turkle's *Life on the Screen* (1997); James Paul Gee's *What Video Games Have to Teach Us about Learning and Literacy* (2003); and Steven Johnson's *Everything Bad Is Good for You: How Today's Popular Culture Is Actually Making Us Smarter* (2005). Aimed at general audiences, these books delivered a clear-headed look at the far-reaching potential of video games. Meanwhile, the Digital Games Research Association (DiGRA) and the Association of Internet Researchers (AoIR)— along with conferences such as State of Play and Games, Learning and Society—have connected a far-flung global network of researchers and designers who share a mutual passion for understanding the possible influence of video games and virtual worlds.

Though the cultural climate is more receptive, games researchers have not engaged in a sustained effort to design interpretive frameworks that educators can use to critically analyze video games in the same way media literacy educators critique magazines, newspapers, and television. For many years, games scholars have been reluctant to criticize the medium, worrying that negative remarks might provide ammunition to would-be censors. There have been some attempts to explore the manipulative potential of video games—most notably in the work of Ian Bogost (2006, 2007) and Gonzalo Frasca (2001)—but the field as a whole is remarkably silent on the ways video games can serve as vehicles for commercial and political propaganda.

To be fair, media literacy researchers have not been clamoring for an interpretive framework that could be used to critique video games. Despite the fact that audiences of all ages spend more time than ever immersed in video games and virtual worlds, few in the media literacy movement seem to spend time actually *playing* video games. On those rare occasions when games are mentioned in the media literacy literature, theorists reach for the same set of analytical tools they use to critique film and television. For example, in the package of lesson plans developed by the Center for Media Literacy (Share, Jolls, & Thoman, 2007), video games are mentioned only twice in passing in the context of a lesson on product placement.

This is not to suggest that media educators ignore video games completely. David Hutchison's *Playing to Learn: Video Games in the Classroom* (2007) describes more than 100 ways games can be deployed in primary and secondary classrooms. Though infused with great creativity, Hutchison's work is primarily concerned with games as vehicles for teaching other subjects rather than as objects of critical scrutiny in their own right. As Duncan (2005) points out, there is a vital distinction between pedagogical approaches that "teach through" media and those that "teach about" the underlying characteristics that constitute media.

The absence of a conceptual framework for dissecting video games is particularly troubling when one considers their persuasive power. "Whatever the power of images," Penny (2004) writes, "interactive media is more. 'Not just a picture,' it is an interactive picture that responds to my actions" (p. 80). The pioneer game designer Chris Crawford argues that video games can be leveraged to shape attitudes in dangerous ways. "Goebbels was so frightening," he predicts, "because he had a pretty good grip on how to use modern media for propaganda purposes. Right now, we're all too dumb to figure it out. Someday, we'll have our interactive Goebbels" (Crawford, cited in Peabody, 1997).

We may have been "too dumb to figure it out" when Crawford was interviewed, but the past decade has witnessed the publication of dozens of important game-related studies across disciplines by researchers, leveraging both quantitative and qualitative methods (Wolf & Perron, 2003; Raessens & Goldstein, 2005; Williams, 2005; Vorderer & Bryant, 2006). As the first decade of the twenty-first century draws to a close, we understand much more about video games than we did in the mid-1990s. The problem is that these insights have not been folded back into the media literacy curriculum. Assuming that educators and game theorists are smart enough to "figure it out," what would be the key elements of an interpretive framework for critiquing video games?

At the core, such a framework would reflect the NLCML's fundamental definition of media literacy as the ability to "access, analyze, evaluate and communicate messages in a variety of forms." According to Aufderheide's (1997) interpretation of this definition, a media literate person is one who "can decode, evaluate, analyze, and produce both print and electronic media" (p. 79). In the specific context of video games, a literate player should understand the medium's defining characteristics while also reflecting on the implications of different production choices made by game designers. Drawing on the key concepts that provide the basis for media literacy education in Canada (Association for Media Literacy, 2008), a literate gamer should do the following:

1 understand that video game messages are constructed and that these messages construct their own immersive realities;
2 realize that different players negotiate the meaning of game content in different ways;
3 understand the commercial dimensions of video games;
4 identify ideological and political implications of video game content;
5 recognize the ways that unique characteristics of the medium shape video game content.

It is important to note that students are most likely to reach these objectives when they have the opportunity to behave as game creators. Across all forms of media, true literacy is about more than the mere consumption of messages; it also requires a basic understanding of how messages are produced. Discussing the constructivist objectives of traditional media literacy educators, Van Buren and Christ (2000) remind us that "it is through actively working with material, with peers or alone, that students solidify their understanding on a deep cognitive level" (p. 42). This is just as true of video games as it is of television and film.

Interpretive Framework: Immersion, Engagement, Interactivity, and Identification

Several factors complicate efforts to develop an interpretive framework for analyzing video games. For one thing, the video game medium is evolving in step with the accelerated growth of computing technology. Since 1958, computer processing has grown at an exponential rate, doubling approximately every two years (Moore, 1965). Sometimes referred to as Moore's Law, this trend has serious implications for all aspects of the video game interface. From the kinesthetic controls popularized by the Nintendo Wii to three-dimensional cameras that translate user movements into virtual spaces (Terdiman, 2008), user input devices continue to change dramatically. This is also true when it comes to game output. Affordable game displays already exceed the level of visual detail found in films like *Shrek* and *Wall-E*, and improved processing power enables increasingly complex simulations, more convincing computer-controlled game characters (rudimentary artificial intelligence), and the ability to tell stories in dramatically new ways. If these trends continue, gaming audiences of 2015 may view today's most acclaimed video games as the technological equivalent of *Pong*.

Matters are further complicated by the range of user experiences encouraged by different gaming genres. From the cerebral problem solving of classic adventure games to the twitch responses of action games and the psychological character investments found in role-playing games, the physical and cognitive demands of game-play can vary widely. Thus, media literacy educators need an interpretive framework that is specific enough to address the characteristics that differentiate video games from movies and television, yet flexible enough to accommodate a range of genres and gaming platforms.

In developing such a framework, we can learn much by mining game studies anthologies for recurring themes. From *The Videogame Theory Reader* (Wolf and Perron, 2003) to *First Person: New Media as Story, Performance and Game* (Wardrip-Fruin & Harrigan, 2004), researchers regularly highlight four essential characteristics. Video games are *immersive*, which means that they are capable of transporting users into compelling virtual environments (McMahan, 2003; Murray, 1997). They are *engaging* and have been known to provoke states of intense concentration that can last for hours (Oblinger, 2004). They foster intense *identification* between players and game characters (Filiciak, 2003), and they are *interactive* media that dynamically modify their messaging in response to user actions (Smith, 1999). All four of these characteristics are essential to the gaming experience, and each of these dimensions has been independently linked to attitude change. Their combined persuasive strength is multiplied as players compulsively revisit their favorite gaming titles.

As we consider each of these dimensions, it is important to remember that this framework is intended as a simple and evolving tool that can be used by students of all ages to think critically about their interactions with video games. Game scholars continue to deepen the field's understanding of these concepts, and a truly exhaustive treatment of any one of these topics would keep researchers busy for years. Yet, from the standpoint of media literacy, it is not necessary for students to become bogged down in debates between ludologists and narratologists or to drown in pedantic disputes about the meanings of individual terms. The objective is to spark critical reflection on the part of gaming audiences, and a rudimentary understanding of video game characteristics should provide a sufficient basis for such reflection.

Immersion

Television and radio can be easily consumed by distracted viewers, but video games demand and receive rapt audience attention. Murray (1997) refers to this domination of player senses as "immersion" and compares participation in virtual environments to the act of swimming. She explains that we experience "the sensation of being surrounded by a completely other reality, as different as water is from air, that takes over all of our attention, our whole perceptual apparatus" (p. 98). The sensory domination experienced from video games can be particularly profound. Whereas film and television content enter via two perceptual channels, video games make it possible for would-be persuaders to influence sight, sound, touch, and even proprioception (the perception of bodily movement). Indeed, gamers often perceive representations on the screen as haptic extensions of their bodies (Lahti, 2003).

Of course, immersive states have been observed in audience relationships to other media forms. Many of us can relate to the feeling of "being lost" in a good book. Cinema operators dim the lights, widen the screens, and encourage silence in an attempt to intensify immersion. More than 70 years ago, Herbert Blumer (1933) recognized that this immersive power of cinema contributes to a sort of "emotional possession." In this state,

> the individual suffers some loss of ordinary control over his feelings, his thoughts, and his actions. Such a condition results usually from an intense preoccupation with a theme, in this case that of a picture. The individual identifies himself so thoroughly with the plot or loses himself so much in the picture that he is carried away from the usual trend of conduct. His mind becomes fixed on certain imagery, and impulses usually latent or kept under restraint gain expression or seriously threaten to gain such expression.

The French theorist Jacques Ellul (1973) would later note that this is precisely how propaganda operates. It:

> tends to make the individual live in a separate world; he must not have outside points of reference. He must not be allowed a moment of meditation or reflection in which to see himself *vis-à-vis* the

propagandist, as happens when the propaganda is not continuous. At that moment, the individual emerges from the grip of propaganda.

(p. 17)

Recently, Green, Brock, and Kaufman (2004) have drawn our attention to an audience phenomenon called *transportation*: a "convergent mental process, a focusing of attention that may occur in response to either fiction or nonfiction. The components of transportation include emotional reactions, mental imagery, and a loss of access to real-world information" (p. 703). Noting that transported individuals are less likely to break the spell by challenging a story's embedded assumptions, Green and Brock (2000) argue that transportation potentially amplifies a narrative's persuasive effects. They observe that the feeling of "being there" approaches the feeling of real experience, which is also known to affect attitude formation. In four separate experiments. Green and Brock correlate the mechanism of transportation with changed beliefs, even when "belief change dimensions were not explicitly articulated in the story" (p. 718).

From a media literacy standpoint, the concept of immersion is a useful tool for getting students to think critically about their gaming experiences. For example, one might ask students to describe what happens to their own sensory apparatus when they are immersed in a favorite game. Students could be encouraged to reflect on elements that intensify immersion, whether related to audiovisual characteristics, narrative themes, underlying game-play mechanics, or the physical environment in which they are playing. More advanced students could be prodded to reflect on the highly artificial nature of video game spaces, and awareness that these immersive representations are constructed could then be folded back into a critique of the equally artificial representations of reality found in other forms of mediated experience.

Engagement

Video game immersion is sometimes confused with intense player engagement, but the two phenomena are not always connected. Whereas immersion describes the ability of a game to situate our senses within another world, engagement refers to our intense focus on the activities in the game. Mini-games such as *Jewel Quest* and *Solitaire* are not particularly immersive, but they are capable of fostering intense engagement. Focused gamers display many characteristics of what Csikzentmihalyi terms a "flow state" (Douglas and Hargadon, 2000). This state is characterized by focused concentration, time distortion, a sense of control over one's actions, and satisfaction derived from factors intrinsic to the activity being practiced (Nakamura and Csikszentmihalyi, 2002). As Funk, Chan, Brouwer, and Curtiss (2006) explain, this enjoyment is most likely "when a balance between skill and challenge is attained in an activity that is intrinsically rewarding." Sherry (2004) suggests that video games are uniquely well suited to induce the flow state because they offer clear objectives, precise feedback, immersive audiovisual material, and content that is dynamically adapted to reflect user choices.

This has important implications for persuasion, because the "motivation for an extended engagement" is crucial to mastering complex bodies of knowledge (Gee, 2004). Peng (2004) suggests that "students learn in a flow state where they are not just passive recipients of knowledge, but active learners who are in control of the learning activity and are challenged to reach a certain goal" (pp. 10–11). Garris, Ahlers, and Driskell (2002) agree, pointing out that "motivated learners more readily choose to engage in target activities, they pursue those activities more vigorously, and they persist longer at those activities than do less motivated learners" (p. 454). Such claims apply equally well to political persuasion: when audiences are motivated and engaged, they are presumably more likely to interact with a game's ideational content.

From a media literacy standpoint, the concept of intense engagement offers an opportunity for encouraging students to reflect on their own cognitive processes as both players and learners. For example, educators might assign students to small groups and ask them to identify elements of games they find compelling and those elements that do not grab their attention. Or, students could talk about how they deal with frustration when they fail to complete a game level, what compels them to pick up the controller and try again, and the feelings of mastery when they succeed. As a follow-up, insights from this exercise could be applied to their experiences as learners of other subjects. To what extent do feelings of personal efficacy and students' perceived ability to master a new body of knowledge relate to their engagement with traditional coursework? How do reward structures built into various video games relate to student engagement? What sorts of incidental lessons are students receiving from the games in which they are most engaged?

Such questions might seem too complicated for some learners, but this type of discussion can be enormously powerful for students of all ages. Thinking about *how* we think and learn is at the core of self-directed learning, and video game literacy discussions are a safe way to introduce this type of self-reflection.

Identification

In many of the most popular video games, players identify themselves *bodily* with their character in the game-world and *psychologically* with the broader narrative arc defined by that character's choices. We have come a long way from early video games such as *Pong* and *Asteroids*, which relied on distancing third-person perspectives. Today's game interfaces continually evolve to invite greater bodily identification with on-screen characters (Rehak, 2003). This type of corporeal identification is closely linked to the notion of presence. As Rob Fullup puts it, "in a game, Mario isn't a hero. I don't want to be him: he's me. Mario is a cursor" (cited in Frasca, 2001). Video game identification is potentially far more powerful than that fostered by cinema. "It is easier to identify ourselves with something that is partly created by us," argues Filiciak (2003) "than with pictures imposed on us by somebody else" (p. 91).

Filmmakers have long recognized the psychological power of such identification processes. In the opening sequence of Fritz Lang's *Man Hunt* (1941), the spectator views Adolph Hitler through a British hunter's rifle scope. Arguing that this "compulsively allies the spectator with the whole motivation of the picture and its main character," Furhammer and Isaakson (1971) explain that the "audience has been placed in a situation which forcibly produces exactly the moral perspective that the film itself will eventually arrive at" (p. 187). In this example, identification is corporeal in nature—extending the viewer's eyesight to the scope of the rifle and even the bullet itself. Other propaganda films, such as *Casablanca* (1941), encourage viewers to identify with the protagonists' psychological struggles and moral choices (Nachbar, 2000).

From the standpoint of those who seek to influence cognition and behavior, player identification with game characters is particularly intriguing. Gee (2003) observes that three types of identity are at work when gaming: virtual identity, real-world identity, and a projective identity that synthesizes both. Unlike the identification experienced with film and literature, video game identification is active (making choices that develop the character) and reactive (responding to conditions that stem from those choices). Players learn, "through their projective identities, new identities, new values, and new ways of being in the world, based on the powerful juxtaposition of their real-world identities ... and the virtual identity at stake in the learning" (p. 66). Ultimately, "the power of video games for good or ill, resides in the ways in which they meld learning and identity" (p. 199). This is as true of games that seek to impart political messages as of those that are explicitly educational.

Interactivity

Unlike movies and television programs, video games are interactive. In single-player games, the player makes choices, and the computer responds. In multiplayer environments such as *World of Warcraft* and *Call of Duty*, player decisions provoke responses from the computer and from other players. In the context of video games, Smith (1999) argues that interactivity most usefully refers to interaction with virtual objects (what players can do to those objects, the ways those objects can respond, and the ability of those objects to act upon avatars without prompting) and with the game's underlying narrative. In all of these situations, there is a cybernetic feedback loop between the user and the machine. According to Penny (2004), "it is the ongoing interaction between these representations and the embodied behavior of the user that makes such images more than images" (p. 83).

Similar feedback systems are used in video games. Garris *et al.* (2002), theorists with extensive experience in designing military simulations, argue that judgment-behavior-feedback loops are crucial to recognizing any instructional benefits from games. In their view, "the game cycle focuses attention to a critical chain of dependencies: (a) To elicit desirable behaviors from learners, (b) they first need to experience desirable emotional or cognitive reactions, (c) which result from interaction with and feedback generated from game play" (p. 452). This loop underpins all video games from *Pac Man* to *Counter-Strike*. Players are rewarded for engaging in certain behaviors (e.g., eating dots, shooting their opponents), and they experience positive feelings when such rewards are given. When players make choices discouraged by the game designers (e.g., walking off a cliff or shooting civilians), they are punished. For example, *America's Army* "rewards Soldierly behavior and penalizes rotten eggs" (Davis *et al.*, 2004, p. 11). Friedman (1998) argues that the cognitive outcomes of such interactive loops are particularly pronounced. After all, "the way computer games teach structures of thought—the way they reorganize perception—is by getting you to internalize the logic of the program." This means "thinking *along with* the computer, becoming an extension of the computer's processes" (p. 4).

Bogost (2006) notes that this dimension of interactivity describes the intersection of player objectives and those of the game developer. "Procedural environments are appealing to us not just because they exhibit rule-generated behavior," he explains, "but because we can induce the behavior ... the primary representational property of the computer is the codified rendering of responsive behaviors" (p. 42). He argues that the antidote to this is "procedural literacy," which he defines as "learning to read processes as a critic. This means playing a videogame or using procedural systems with an eye toward identifying and interpreting the rules that drive that system" (p. 64).

The Production Component

The four characteristics described heretofore constitute a powerful framework for critically analyzing the unique characteristics of video games. When fortified by traditional media literacy themes such as the significance of political economy and sensitization to the constructed nature of media representations, this approach paves the way for a broad range of lesson plans and classroom activities that are appropriate for students of all ages. However, this interpretive toolkit is only part of the solution. It is also important for students to think from the standpoint of message creators. As Renee Hobbs (2005) notes, "producing media messages has long been understood as one of the most valuable methods to gain insight on how messages are constructed" (p. 20). Weber and Dixon (2007) observe that "work by Buckingham and Sefton-Green (1994), among others, indicates that involving young people in forms of critical media production can be empowering for them, making them less vulnerable to manipulation by commercial interests" (p. 248).

Such a strategy does not require complex computer programming courses, intensive tutorials in 3-D modeling, or access to cutting-edge computer equipment. Design exercises, cheat codes, level editors, and game authoring toolkits are just a few ways in which students can modify existing games and create entirely new ones.

In many educational settings, hands-on computer access for each student in the classroom is not possible. However, these resource constraints can be overcome by immersing students in conceptual design. For years, media literacy educators have taught students to think about editing, framing, and layered audio by asking them to make design choices in visual storyboards. The same approach is possible when it comes to game design. For example, Hutchison (2007) describes an exercise called *Kid-Friendly Grand Theft Auto* in which students are encouraged to "take back the streets" by brainstorming "as many game play tasks they can think of that would suit a kid-friendly version of an open world game" (p. 111).

In a similar vein, students can be encouraged to use "cheat codes" to modify the underlying mechanics of their favorite games. During the early years of the video game industry, developers used undocumented codes to experiment with the effects of various parameters on game-play. As Consalvo (2007) documents in *Cheating: Gaining Advantage in Video Games*, "cheats existed, but as insider knowledge among game creators and a few committed players" (p. 10). For example, on the Nintendo Entertainment System, players could unlock hidden attributes of Konami games by pressing the joystick up twice, down twice, left, right, left, right, and then pressing the B button followed by the A button. Today, "cheat codes" are standard in most new games. Gamers can find books, magazines, and Web sites dedicated to the newest codes, and titles such as *Lego Indiana Jones* have explicitly folded cheat code sections into the narrative of their games. In many games, cheat codes can be used to make players invulnerable or invisible, to free up infinite resources, and to allow players to fly through the air or walk through walls. By tweaking underlying parameters of a given game, students could be encouraged to reflect on ways that environmental conditions constrain their range of potential choices.

Giving students hands-on experience with rudimentary aspects of video game production may also help us tackle the persistent gender imbalances within the industry. Pelletier (2007) analyzes game designs created by young men and women between the ages of 12 and 14. She argues that making game design courses more widely available to young women may not remove the many structural barriers that perpetuate the male dominated industry, but "making game design more popular and widespread perhaps begins to denaturalize the situation and thereby makes the stakes, as well as the possible options, clearer."

Conclusion

In closing, it should be noted that this article represents a *preliminary* attempt at sketching out the parameters of an interpretive framework media literacy educators can use to critically analyze video games. Each of the defining characteristics discussed in this article is currently the subject of intense scrutiny by games researchers, and there is a long way to travel before reaching critical consensus about any of these concepts.

Then again, the same could be said about the frameworks media literacy educators use to critically analyze traditional media. From print and radio to film and television, there is an enormous range of perspectives and tools that might theoretically be leveraged in the classroom. However, theoretical closure is not the goal of media literacy research. Sectarian debates are merely a distraction. Our most urgent need is the identification of useful interpretive tools, and this is the need to which this chapter is addressed. My hope is that other researchers will choose to improve this framework by modifying and extending it and by collaboratively building something better. These are still the early days. Simply starting the conversation is an important first step.

References

Association for Media Literacy. (2008). *What is media literacy?* Retrieved October 20, 2008, from http://www.aml.ca/whatis/

Aufderheide, P. (Ed.). (1993). *Media literacy: A report of the National Leadership Conference on Media Literacy*. Aspen, CO: Aspen Institute.

Aufderheide, P. (1997). Media literacy: From a report of the National Leadership Conference on Media Literacy. In R. Kubey (Ed.), *Media literacy in the information age*. New Brunswick, NJ: Transaction Publishers.

Barrett, D. (2008, October). Obama ads: It's in the game. *The London Free Press*. Retrieved October 20, 2008, from http://lfpress.ca/newsstand/Today/Thursday Ticket/2008/10/30/7249546-sun.html

Blumer, H. (1933). *Movies and conduct*. New York: Macmillan.

Bogost, I. (2006). *Unit operations: An approach to videogame criticism*. Cambridge, MA: MIT Press.

Bond, P. (2008, June). PwC: Video game market to soar. *Adweek.Com*. Retrieved October 20, 2008, from http://www.adweek.com/aw/content_display/news/agency/e3i19e4b7b8d9d4f265f4246d56ee69e9cd

Colvile, R. (2006, November). How women got in on the game video—games makers are waking up to a boom in female players—and offering more than pink consoles. *The Daily Telegraph* [London], p. 21.

Consalvo, M. (2007). *Cheating: Gaining advantage in videogames*. Cambridge, MA: MIT Press.

Davis, M., Schilling, R., Mayberry, A., Bossant, P., McCree, J., Dossett, S., et al. (2004). Making *America's Army*: The wizardry behind the US Army's hit PC game. In *America's Army PC game: Vision and realization*. Monterey, CA: The Wecker Group.

Delwiche, A. (2007). From *The Green Berets* to *America's Army*: Video games as a vehicle for political propaganda. In J. P. Williams & J. H. Smith (Eds.), *The players' realm: Studies on the culture of video games and gaming* (pp. 91–109). London: McFarland and Company.

Douglas, Y., & Hargadon, A. (2000). The pleasure principle: Immersion, engagement, flow. *Hypertext 2000*. San Antonio, TX: ACM.

Duncan, B. (2005). Media literacy: Essential survival skills for the new millennium. *Orbit Magazine*, 35(2). Retrieved October 20, 2008, from http://www.oise.utoronto.ca/orbit/mediaed_sample.html

Ellul, J. (1973). *Propaganda: The formation of men's attitudes*. New York: Alfred A. Knopf.

Entertainment Software Association (2008). Industry facts. Retrieved October 20, 2008, from http://www.theesa.com/facts/index.asp

Filiciak, M. (2003). Hyperidentities: Postmodern identity patterns in massively multiplayer online role-playing games. In M. Wolf and B. Perron (Eds.), *Video game theory reader* (pp. 87–102). London: Routledge.

Frasca, G. (2001). Rethinking agency and immersion: Video games as a means of consciousness-raising. *Digital Creativity*, 12(3), 167–174.

Friedman, T. (1998). Civilization and its discontents: Simulation, subjectivity, and space. In G. Smith (Ed.), *Discovering discs: Transforming space and place on CD-ROM*. New York: New York University Press.

Funk, J., Chan, M., Brouwer, J., & Curtiss, K. (2006). A biopsychosocial analysis of the video game-playing experience of children and adults in the United States. *Simile*, 6(3), 1–11.

Furhammer, L., & Isaksson, F. (1971). *Politics and film*. London: Studio Vista.

Garris, R., Ahlers, R., & Driskell, J. E. (2002). Games, motivation, and learning: A research and practice model. *Simulation & Gaming, 33*(4), 441–467.

Gee, J. P. (2003). *What video games have to teach us about learning and literacy*. New York: Palgrave.

Green, M., & Brock, T. (2000). The role of transportation in the persuasiveness of public narratives. *Journal of Personality and Social Psychology, 79*(5),701–721.

Green, M., Brock, T., & Kaufman, G. (2004). Understanding media enjoyment: The role of transportation into narrative worlds. *Communication Theory, 14*(4), 311–327.

Hobbs, R. (2005, March). Strengthening media education in the twenty-first century: Opportunities for the State of Pennsylvania. *Arts Education Policy Review, 106*(4), 13–23.

Hutchison, D. (2007). *Playing to learn: Video games in the classroom*. Westport, CT: Teacher Ideas Press.

Johnson, S. (2005). *Everything bad is good for you: How today's popular culture is actually making us smarter*. New York: Riverhead Books.

Lahti, M. (2003). As we become machines: Corporealized pleasures in video games. In M. Wolf & B. Perron (Eds.), *Video game theory reader* (pp. 157–170). London: Routledge.

McMahan, A. (2003). Immersion, engagement and presence: A method for analyzing 3-D video games. In M. Wolf & B. Perron (Eds.), *Video game theory reader* (pp. 67–86). London: Routledge.

Moore, G. (1965). Cramming more components onto integrated circuits. *Electronics Magazine, 38*(8): 114–117.

Murray, J. H. (1997). *Hamlet on the holodeck: The future of narrative in cyberspace*. New York: Free Press.

Nachbar, J. (2000). Doing all of our thinking for us: *Casablanca* and the home front. *Journal of Popular Film and Television, 27*(4), 5–15.

Nakamura, J., & Csikszentmihalyi, M. (2002). The concept of flow. In C. Snyder & S. Lopez (Eds.), *Handbook of positive psychology* (pp. 89–105). New York: Oxford University Press.

Nielsen Media Research. (2007, March 5). Nielsen says video game penetration in US TV households grew 18% during the past two years. Press release.

Oblinger, D. (2004). The next generation of educational engagement. *Journal of Interactive Media in Education*. Retrieved October 20, 2008, from http://www-jime.open.ac.uk/2004/8/oblinger-2004-8-disc-paper.html

O' Hagan, S. (2004). Recruitment hard drive: The U.S. Army is the world's biggest games developer, pumping billions into new software. *The Guardian* [London], June 19. Available: LEXIS-NEXIS Academic Universe.

Peabody, S. (1997, June). Interview with Chris Crawford: Fifteen years after *Excalibur* and *The Art of Computer Game Design*. Retrieved October 20, 2008, from http://www.vancouver.wsu.edu/fac/peabody/game-book/Chris-talk.html

Pelletier, C. (2007). Producing gender through digital interactions: The social purposes which young people set out to achieve through computer game design. In S. Dixon & S. Weber (Eds.), *Digital girls: Growing up online*. London: Palgrave Macmillan.

Peng, W. (2004). Is playing games all bad? Positive effects of computer and video games in learning. Paper presented at 54th annual meeting of the International Communication Association. New Orleans. May 27–31.

Penny, S. (2004). Representation, enaction and the ethics of simulation. In N. Wardrip-Fruin & P. Harrigan (Eds.), *First person: New media as story, performance and game*. Cambridge, MA: MIT Press.

Poole, S. (2003). *Trigger happy: videogames and the entertainment revolution*. New York: Arcade.

Raessens, J., & Goldstein, J. H. (2005). *Handbook of computer game studies*. Cambridge, MA: MIT Press.

Rehak, B. (2003). Playing at being: Psychoanalysis and the avatar. In M. Wolf & B. Perron (Eds.), *Video game theory reader* (pp. 103–128). London: Routledge.

Share, J., Jolls, T., & Thoman, E. (2007). *Five key questions that can change the world: Lesson plans for media literacy*. Malibu, CA: Center for Media Literacy.

Sherry, J. (2004). Flow and media enjoyment. *Communication Theory 14*(4), 328–347.

Smith, G. (1999). Introduction: A few words about interactivity. In G. Smith (Ed.), *On a silver platter: CD-ROMs and the promises of a new technology* (pp. 1–34). New York: New York University Press.

Terdiman, D. (2008, February). Mitch Kapor: 3D cameras will make virtual worlds easier to use. *CNET News*. Retrieved from http://news.cnet.com/8301-13772_3-9873205-52.html?tag=mncol;title

Tsikalas, K. (2001). When the SIMS get real: An analysis of how digital play spaces promote learning in low income, diverse communities. New York: Computers for Youth and CILT, PlaySpace Project. Retrieved October 20, 2008 from http://playspace.concord.org/Documents/Learning%20from%20The%20SIMS.pdf

Turkle, S. (1997). *Life on the screen: Identity in the age of the Internet*. New York: Simon & Schuster.

Van Buren, C., & Christ, W. G. (2000). Responsive essay: To why the production vs. theory dichotomy in curricular decision-making should be eliminated. *Feedback, 41*(3) 41–50.

Varadarajan, T. (1997, December 23). A misspent youth helps the joystick generation. *The Times* [London]. Retrieved Lexis Nexis on October 20, 2008.

Vorderer, P., & Bryant, J. (2006). *Playing video games: Motives, responses, and consequences*. LEA's communication series. Mahwah, NJ: Lawrence Erlbaum Associates.

Ward, M. (2001, May). Columbine family sues computer game makers. *BBC News*. Retrieved October 20, 2008, from http://news.bbc.co.uk/1/hi/sci/tech/1295920.stm

Wardrip-Fruin, N., & Harrigan, P. (2004). *First person: New media as story, performance, and game*. Cambridge, MA: MIT Press.

Wardynski, C. (2004). Informing popular culture: The *America's Army* game concept. In *America's Army PC Game: Vision and Realization* (pp. 6–7). Monterey, CA: The Wecker Group.

Weber, S., & Dixon, S. (2007). Young people's engagement with technology. In S. Dixon & S. Weber (Eds.), *Growing up online: Young people and digital technologies*. New York: Palgrave MacMillan.

Williams, D. (2005). Bridging the methodological divide in game research. *Simulation & Gaming, 36*(4), 447–463.

Williams, D. (2006). A (brief) social history of video games. In P. Vorderer & J. Bryant (Eds.), *Playing computer games: Motives, responses, and consequences.* Mahwah, NJ: Lawrence Erlbaum Associates.

Williams, J. P., & Smith, J. H. (2007). *The players' realm: Studies on the culture of video games and gaming.* Jefferson, NC: McFarland & Co.

Wolf, M., & Perron, B. (2003). *The video game theory reader.* New York: Routledge.

Chapter 9

New Media Literacies By Design

The Game School

Alice Robison

In late 2006, Henry Jenkins *et al.* produced a working paper that debuted alongside a new commitment from the John D. and Catherine T. MacArthur Foundation. In the paper, Jenkins and his co-authors characterized the emerging field of media literacy as focused on consumption of media and called for an extension of the traditional concepts of media literacy to connect with theories for new media and learning. To propel media literacy research forward, they argued, it is important to investigate media consumption and production but also participation. Participation within a culture "shifts the focus of literacy from one of individual expression to one of community involvement" (Jenkins, Purushotma, Clinton, Weigel, & Robison, 2006, p. 7). These Massachusetts Institute of Technology (MIT) researchers' perspective on media literacy education argues for an organic understanding of learning and knowing, one built on the scholarship of researchers in an emerging, trans-disciplinary area of scholarship referred to as the learning sciences (Sawyer, 2006).

"Confronting the Challenges of Participatory Culture," the Jenkins *et al.* white paper, describes a view of media literacy education that includes analysis and interpretation. At the same time, they posit that for media literacy education to keep pace with contemporary youth culture, we must also include the culture of media production, which combines newer tools and changing contexts of use. Jenkins and his co-authors envision a "new media literacies" approach to media education in which a richer understanding of media production and use can be better theorized and applied when considered alongside the emerging research studies in cognitive science, literacy studies, anthropology, and education (Ito *et al.*, 2008; James *et al.*, 2008; Peppler & Kafai, 2007; Steinkuehler & Duncan, 2008). These studies, though housed in various disciplines and departments, are generally characterized by a drive to amend traditional instructionist pedagogies based in cognitive-psychological studies of human learning that focused solely on the individual mind as a receiver of information (Piaget, 1977). Since the 1970s, researchers have gained a richer understanding of human learning as it happens in situated contexts of social participation and collaboration (Bereiter & Scardamalia, 1993; Kafai & Resnick, 1996; Lave & Wenger, 1991; Papert, 1991).

The shift in understanding how humans learn has inspired educators to try to understand how best to design learning environments that provide rich situations for experiencing, doing, and knowing (Barab & Squire, 2004; Brown, 1992). Often those environments include multimedia tools and computer networks that enable learners to cooperate in shared situations and solve problems collaboratively. However, it isn't always the case that newer technologies necessarily enable new ways of learning. It may be that some of the tools are new and that they might enable new forms of production, but what matters most in a new media literacies framework is how a community of producers makes those tools meaningful to themselves and their audiences.

As academic advisor to MIT's New Media Literacies Project from 2006 to 2008, I was often asked to help clarify what was meant by the term *new media literacies*. There was some question about whether the term referred to literacy practices with and around new media. That interpretation is accurate to the extent that the media themselves are actually new (e.g., software, digital hardware), but the truth is that most of what we refer to as "new" media aren't wholly new. Indeed, most of the media literacy practices discussed in the New Media Literacies paper (Jenkins *et al.*, 2006) describe new dispositions toward the "perceived affordances" (Norman, 2008) and (re)applications of media as they exist within their contexts of use. Put that way, it becomes easier to see that the new media literacies are about an appropriation of what the learning sciences have shown to be particularly salient ways of knowing and learning, making and doing.

Ultimately, the "new media literacies" assign cutting-edge research in the learning sciences to a media literacy context. The main point of the Jenkins *et al.* paper is that these literacy practices with and around media are wonderful instantiations of the most contemporary knowledge of about how students *learn and participate with media communities in their contexts of use*. The authors write, "Participatory culture shifts the focus of literacy from one of individual expression to community involvement" (Jenkins, *et al.*, 2006, p. 4), a sentiment that builds upon the collective opinions shared by learning sciences researchers (Design Based Research Collective, 2002). Educational technologists Sasha Barab and Kurt Squire (2004) summarize the view of cognition shared by current learning sciences researchers:

> A fundamental assumption of many learning scientists is that cognition is not a thing located within the individual thinker but is a process that is distributed across the knower, the environment in which knowing

occurs, and the activity in which the learner participates. In other words, learning, cognition, knowing, and context are irreducibly co-constituted and cannot be treated as isolated entities or processes.

(p. 1)

The new media literacies interpretation of the distributed, environmental, and activity-based concerns of the learning sciences is that of media use and production within the context of a community of participants. In other words, media literacy education should enable students to analyze and understand the usefulness and limitations of Wikipedia, for example. We can teach students to make edits to Wikipedia pages, and all of that is important to students making and using media. And yet, without knowing what it means to participate in the Wikipedia community, students might never see their efforts move beyond a beginner's understanding of what it means to be a Wikipedia user.

The principle of learning in a participatory context of media consumption and production is one that necessitates new designs for teaching and learning about media. Consequently, it becomes important to move the conversation temporarily away from media tools and texts and instead toward the spaces, places, and communities in and from which they are made and considered. Doing so allows us to consider the situated processes of making meaning with media at the same time that we examine the finished products, which allows for a more holistic conception of best practices for media literacy education.

Case Study: The Game School

A progressive example of the participatory, contextual, process-based approaches to media literacy education is Quest to Learn, a proposed new sixth- to twelfth-grade public school to be opened to sixth-graders beginning with the 2009 school year. The Quest to Learn school was conceived by the Institute of Play, a New York City-based nonprofit that supports game-based learning contexts in a variety of settings. Led by Associate Professor Katie Salen of the Parsons New School for Design, The Institute of Play collaborates with citizens seeking to partner with academics, scientists, policy makers, and artists on several projects. In the case of Quest to Learn, The Institute of Play consults with New Visions for Public Schools, a leader in helping redesign and administer many of New York City's public schools, which include its New Century High Schools. New Visions for Public Schools is guiding the important steps required to ensure that the school meets New York city and state curriculum requirements, as it has with many city schools like Quest to Learn that are part of the small schools movement in the United States (smallschools.org, 2008). However, the research and design choices that influence how those content standards are taught are made by the Institute of Play team and the educators at the school.

The mission of Quest to Learn is to build an innovative learning experience for kids that is based in both traditional content learning and what are now being called "gaming literacies" (Salen, 2007). Put simply, Quest to Learn is a school created to provide kids with an experience of learning that is based on the acts of designing, playing, and knowing. Building on the growing research and development in games-based learning, Quest to Learn formally extends the reach of current gaming literacy initiatives already in place in after-school programs, museums, and libraries throughout the United States. In particular, the school builds on initiatives wherein social interaction and critical reflection are expected learning outcomes (Fields & Kafai, in press; Hayes, 2008; Hull & Schultz, 2001; Joseph, 2008; Santo, 2007). Students are invited to experiment with potential solutions to problems and to design and test new ones. Perhaps most important, learning and gaming literacies are predicated on deep considerations of the contexts in which they exist and the terms under which they are encountered.

Quest to Learn is set to open to 60 sixth-graders for the 2009–2010 school year and will scale out to twelfth grade over several years. At the writing of this chapter, the Institute of Play and New Visions for Public Schools have just presented the school's proposal to the New York State Department of Education. As the curricular development process has just begun, the details of the school are still undergoing active revisions. Therefore this case study illustrates the foundations for the proposed Quest to Learn practices and activities in order to elucidate the overarching aims and concepts used to build a school based on the principles of games, gameplay, and game design.

The school's curriculum design team initially established core principles of learning for game design and play and then set out to integrate these principles into the development of supportive learning spaces. As such, the Quest to Learn approach to critical literacies is founded on a triad of interpretation, creative production, and situated contexts. The development team contends that by using gaming literacies as the school's core design principle, students are taught to see the world as a series of designed systems, each with its own rich, interrelated parts, puzzles, and problems. Furthermore, educators might work together to develop lessons that link various content areas to one another through an appreciation for and an understanding of that system and how its elements are treated in other subjects.

Quest to Learn's curricular and instructional model is designed to bring together methods for solving a variety of problems: technological,

Table 9.1 Game School ways of knowing

Ways of knowing	Description
Systems-based thinking	Students design and analyze dynamic systems, a characteristic activity in both the media and in science today.
Interdisciplinary thinking	Students solve problems that require them to seek out and synthesize knowledge from different domains. They become intelligent and resourceful as they learn how to find and use information in meaningful ways.
User-centered design	Students act as socio-technical engineers, thinking about how people interact with systems and how systems shape both competitive and collaborative social interaction.
Specialist language	Students learn to use complex technical linguistic and symbolic elements from a variety of domains, at a variety of different levels, and for a variety of different purposes.
Meta-level reflection	Students learn to explicate and define their ideas, describe issues and interactions at a meta-level, create and test hypotheses, and reflect on the impact of their solutions to others.
Network literacy	Students learn how to integrate knowledge from multiple sources, including music, video, online databases, other media, as well as from other students. In doing so they participate in the kinds of collaboration that new communication and information technologies enable.
Productive/tool literacy	Students gain an ability to use digital technologies to produce both meanings and tangible artifacts, including games.

From Salen, K., Torres, R. & Wolozin, L. (2008a). *The Game School Planning Document*: Draft 1.0. New York: Institute of Play.

social, communicational, scientific, and creative concerns, including those expressed in Table 9.1.

Students are immersed in the process of collaborating to solve shared problems through case- and model-based reasoning, project-based learning, and computer-supportive collaborative learning, all hallmarks of contemporary learning sciences research (Sawyer, 2006). And though students will surely play and design games, the principles of learning are informed by game design and play experiences. Furthermore, the participatory culture framework provided by the new media literacies (Jenkins *et al.*, 2006) offers the key distinction between what it means to add media literacy as a content area to an existing school curriculum and integrating it fully into the design of the curriculum itself. The new media literacies are about understanding and producing meaning, but they are also about participating in media communities, thereby offering context to what is produced and what it means.

As part of its mission, Quest to Learn also seeks to develop learning systems that recruit complex thinking about how things work and what students need to know to design, test, and reiterate those systems to make new ones. At present, the school has identified a series of principles, goals, and beliefs that underlie the curriculum and system of the school's design and operation. Although the school is still in its planning stages, it has been proposed according to 10 core practices that support every aspect of its design, as described in Table 9.2.

The overarching questions that drive curriculum development throughout the school are questions of systems, especially with regard to the "internal architecture of games—rules, components, core mechanics, goals, conflict, choice, and space" (Salen *et al.*, 2008b). In line with current research in the learning sciences that show the importance of situated cognition (Lave & Wenger, 1991), and project-based learning (Barron *et al.*, 1998), the school's contexts for learning are imagined as practice spaces wherein goal-based challenges motivate achievement. Expectations for success will be high, yet every piece of the curriculum will be designed to encourage students to meet those expectations. Taken together, each of these elements defines the overall praxis of Quest to Learn.

From the outset, Quest to Learn was conceived as a unique learning space meant to address the needs of students who are have been underserved by traditional school models. As a consultant to the project since 2007, I have participated in the conceptualization process and reviewed internal design documents written by members of the core Quest to Learn design team. These design documents (Salen *et al.*, 2008a, 2008b) cite multiple studies and reports (Kaiser Family Foundation, 2005; Pew Internet and American Life Project, 2005) that point to the need to re-think and re-design educational institutions to reflect both current research in the learning sciences and cultural shifts in dispositions toward digital technologies and "habits of mind" (Dewey, 1933).

The Quest to Learn development team envisions a curriculum based on an understanding of designed systems (Salen *et al.*, 2008a). Students will be encouraged to "quest to learn" as they move through a series of content areas packaged as media-rich, sequential coursework meant to help students succeed in four primary domains. Domains reflect an integrated system of learning meant to encourage students to see and understand dynamic relationships between parts of a whole. Quest to Learn's initial plans define each of the four central domains: "The Way Things Work," (science and math); "Codeworlds," (math and English

Table 9.2 Ten core practices defining the Game School

Core practice	Description
Taking on identities	My identity as a learner is complex and evolving as a member within my own community of practice. I am a writer, designer, reader, producer, teacher, student, and gamer.
Using game design and systems thinking	Everything I do in school connects to my life outside of school through a game design and systems perspective.
Practicing in context	School is a practice space where life systems I inhabit and share with others are modeled, designed, taken apart, re-engineered, and gamed as ways of knowing.
Playing and reflecting	I play games and reflect on my learning with them.
Theorizing and testing	I am learning as I propose, test, play with, and validate theories about the world.
Responding to a need to know	I am motivated to ask hard questions, to look for complex answers and take on the responsibility to imagine solutions with others.
Interacting with others	Games are not only a model for helping me think about how the world works, but also a dynamic medium through which to engage socially and develop a deeper understanding of myself in the world.
Experimenting and imagining possibilities	I take risks, make meaning, and act creatively and resourcefully within many different kinds of systems.
Giving and receiving feedback	My learning is visible to me, and I know how to anticipate what I will need to learn next.
Inventing solutions	I solve problems, using a game design and systems methodology: I identify the rules, invent a process, execute and evaluate.

From Salen, K., Torres, R. & Wolozin, L. (2008a). *The Game School Planning Document*: Draft 1.0. New York: Institute of Play.

language acquisition); "Being, Space and Place," (social studies/English language arts); and "Wellness" (health/physical education). Additionally, the team includes two supporting domains called "Sports for the Mind" and "Foreign Language Lab." Sports for the Mind includes instructed practice with making and using media; the Foreign Language Lab helps students with language learning, which at this school includes coding and the use of software tools. The Game Design and Systems graphic is a draft diagram used by the Quest to Learn planning team to communicate its vision for the Quest to Learn Domains of Learning concept. Domains reflect an integrated system of learning meant to encourage students to see and understand dynamic relationships between parts of a whole.

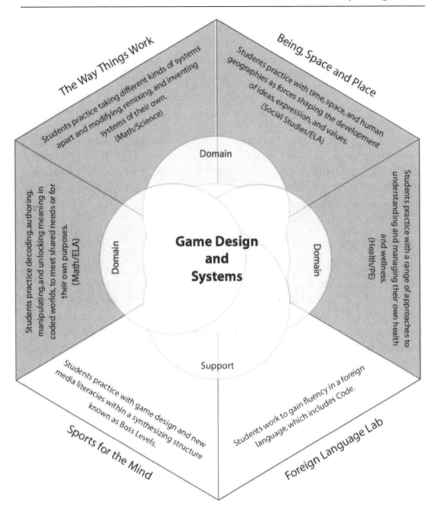

The Way Things Work

Students practice taking different kinds of systems apart and modifying, remixing, and inventing systems of their own. (Math/Science)

Being, Space and Place

Students practice with time, space, and human geographies as forces shaping the development of ideas, expression, and values. (Social Studies/ELA)

Students practice decoding, authoring, manipulating, and unlocking meaning in coded worlds, to meet shared needs or for their own purposes. (Math/ELA)

Students practice with a range of approaches to understanding and managing their own health and wellness. (Health/PE)

Domain

Domain

Domain

Domain

Game Design and Systems

Support

Students practice with game design and new media literacies within a synthesizing structure known as Boss Levels.

Sports for the Mind

Students work to gain fluency in a foreign language, which includes Code.

Foreign Language Lab

Figure 9.1 Games design and systems

Based on traditional content areas, the Quest to Learn Domains are defined in such a way as to provide a foundation for a curriculum that reflects systems-based thinking. Moreover, Quest to Learn Domains are meant to enable students to understand content areas as interrelated parts of a whole. The development team explains that its goal is to enable learners to move beyond the analytic process of deconstructing a problem "into component parts for discrete examination" (Salen *et al.*, 2008a, p. 46).

By examining the interrelationships of elements within whole systems via a game design pedagogy, learners are better equipped to recognize patterns that offer critical insights into the nature and complexity of systems (social, technological, natural, and imaginary) shaping their worlds.

(pp. 46–47)

Learning Domains are thus ways of organizing Quest to Learn's theme of game design and systems thinking by aligning the core learning practices described in Table 9.1 with the relationships between traditional content areas. The result is a curriculum that both reflects and is shaped by the ways in which these content areas interrelate.

Curriculum Structure

Whereas the Quest to Learn team conceives of game design and systems thinking as the "master context" for the four main and two supporting domains, the units and lesson plans take shape in the forms of "Missions" and "Quests." These terms are taken from two fundamental gaming activities whereby players are presented with expeditions and assignments designed to help them advance. Missions and Quests can also be thought of as macro-level challenges consisting of micro-level sets of problems collectively developed across domains of learning.

Over three trimesters, every grade level would base its curriculum on an "overarching question" that thematically guides curriculum and instructional design for each domain. Perhaps a sixth-grade overarching question might be, "What is the architecture of a dynamic system?" Each of the domains would use this quest to guide its pedagogy as evidenced in Table 9.3. For example, "The Way Things Work" teaches math and science concepts and skills. So perhaps its own overarching question would invite students to identify and analyze elements of simple machines in the first trimester, relationships between elements in a second trimester, and the functional significance of those relationships in a third trimester. Each of those questions is thus a more content-specific version of the grade's main overarching question: What is the architecture of a dynamic system? The trimesters are therefore organized by content areas (domains) but also the guiding question posited to the entire grade over the course of a year.

Consider the "Being, Space and Place" domain in which the traditional content areas of history, social studies, and geography might be integrated. Within this domain, the authors of the Quest to Learn planning document suggest a Mission titled "Spartan Private Investigators" that could be developed to build upon a year's worth of systems-understanding curricula. So let's say the first trimester in the Being, Space, and Place

Table 9.3 The new media literacies: participatory culture

A participatory culture is also one in which members believe their contributions matter, and feel some degree of social connection with one another (at the least they care what other people think about what they have created). Forms of participatory culture include:

Affiliations — memberships, formal and informal, in online communities centered around various forms of media, such as Friendster, Facebook, message boards, metagaming, game clans, or MySpace).

Expressions — producing new creative forms, such as digital sampling, skinning and modding, fan videomaking, fan fiction writing, zines, mash-ups).

Collaborative Problem-solving — working together in teams, formal and informal, to complete tasks and develop new knowledge (such as through Wikipedia, alternative reality gaming, spoiling).

Circulations — Shaping the flow of media (such as podcasting, blogging).

A growing body of scholarship suggests potential benefits of these forms of participatory culture, including opportunities for peer-to-peer learning, a changed attitude toward intellectual property, the diversification of cultural expression, the development of skills valued in the modern workplace, and a more empowered conception of citizenship. Access to this participatory culture functions as a new form of the hidden curriculum, shaping which youth will succeed and which will be left behind as they enter school and the workplace.

From Jenkins, H., Purushotma, R., Clinton, K., Weigel, M., & Robison, A. (2006). *Confronting the challenges of participatory culture: Media education for the 21st century.* Chicago, IL: The John D. and Catherine T. MacArthur Foundation, Digital Media and Learning Initiative (p. 5).

domain of sixth grade asks students to think about the qualities and elements of a system. The Spartan Private Investigators Mission might be introduced in the second trimester to intensify their understandings of how human civilizations develop through a consideration of how systems function as parts of a whole.

As it is described in the Quest to Learn planning document, students would be presented with an international conflict and then would be expected to build on previously learned understandings of the contexts in which conflicts occur between civilizations (Salen *et al.*, 2008b, p. 73). The Spartan Private Investigators mission directs students toward a specific context—in this case, the era when Sparta must consider the best strategies for reacting to Athens's hostilities toward them. In the process, historical events, physical geographies, and the implications of various resolution strategies (war, diplomacy, neutrality) are variables that must be understood and reckoned with to move toward a winning decision on Sparta's best methods for resolving the conflict. Students then present a final argument to the political leadership of Sparta, a "Council of Elders," whose makeup might include other students, teachers, support staff, or older peers.

Each proposed Mission for Quest to Learn Knowledge Domain is designed to address the learning goals aligned with New York State standards across the curriculum (in this case, English language arts and social studies). Additionally, educators specify what are called "Enduring Understandings," which are outcomes particular to this lesson. As Spartan Private Investigators is conceived, its Enduring Understandings are that "Students will understand that 1) societies interact with each other through a variety of hierarchical systems, and 2) complexity comes from the interaction of multiple elements" (Salen *et al.*, 2008b, p. 74). Furthermore, "Essential Questions" are meant to guide the shorter "quest" assignments: "How does conflict arise and how is it resolved for a system (Sparta) within a larger system (ancient Greece)? How do the actions of one society impact other societies?" (p. 74). Taken together, these guiding principles for lesson plan and activity development provide the grounding for a learning experience from which new media literacies emerge.

Quests—the segmented activities that together make up and speak to the larger Missions—are to be developed by teachers in collaboration with one another. Quests might be designed to take a week or more from a 10-week trimester to give students practice with the larger concepts of the Mission. Because the final piece of assessment for the mission is a formal oral presentation in which students develop policy briefs and engage in policy discussions from the perspectives of Greeks and Spartans, the Quests should prepare them for that exercise. Along the way are incremental, lower-stakes assessments such as journals, tests, notes, vocabulary, podcasts, maps, and simulations. However, each of these pieces is tied directly to its quest and serves as a scaffolding tool to incrementally move students toward the goal of the Mission itself. In other words, these assessment pieces provide the necessary means by which students contribute to the problem that they are working on together. The conditions for which a participatory culture exists are met: students are creating artifacts in a collaborative, social way and are "meant to believe that their contributions matter" (Jenkins *et al.*, 2006, p.5).

As a proposed unit and lesson plan, Spartan Private Investigators has integrated the new media literacies concept of participatory culture in such a way that opportunities to affiliate, express, collaborate, and circulate are fully integrated into its curriculum. Instead of adding a new media literacies–influenced lesson plan to an already packed curriculum, Spartan Private Investigators is *by its design* an example of participatory culture. Students participate in the culture of narratives, histories, objects, and archives of ancient Greece and Sparta, but how they do so is cultivated from the context of the problem they're trying to solve. If a Quest requires them to "gather, document and synthesize information on the culture, history, and politics of Sparta," they do so together as they read, write, discuss, and share what they are learning with the distinct purpose of understanding the cultural contexts that support those activities (Salen *et al.*, 2008b, p. 75). Writing is not directed to a generic, unknown reader; students know their audiences and speak directly to them in a voice attached to the identity they assume (a Spartan warrior, for example). The sharing of information and artifacts is purposeful; critiques and responses to what is shared are directed toward the reasons for doing so.

As systems-based thinking is a foundational learning goal at Quest to Learn, each Mission design and its series of Quests should encourage students' reflection on their learning in other domains. For example, during the 10-week Spartan Private Investigators Mission, a Quest invites students to participate in a role-playing exercise that recruits knowledge from a previous trimester. As outlined in the Quest to Learn planning document, students are presented with the mythical Pythia, Apollo's high priestess, who inspires students to "travel back in time to solve a pressing problem in Ancient Greece between Sparta and Athens" (Salen *et al.* 2008b, p. 75).

> Pythia communicates to the students through oracles (riddles) that are embedded with key vocabulary. Her messages are delivered to students via the pathways of light that students developed in the previous trimester in The Way Things Work [domain]. Pythia's oracles present challenges to students, which require them to gather, document, and synthesize information on the culture, history, and politics of Sparta. They use this information to develop believable identities as Spartans.
>
> (Salen, *et al.* 2008b, p. 75)

Even though students are participating in a different knowledge domain, the design of the Quest makes it necessary for them to understand how this learning context makes previously learned material more relevant. Therefore, when educators develop curriculum around systems-based thinking, they must work with one another to ensure a reciprocal relationship among the students' learning experiences.

Toward Participatory Media Contexts for Future Learning

It cannot be emphasized enough that the contexts in which media are produced are at the heart of participatory media: these contexts are what inspire and regenerate their emerging artifacts and activities. Any kind of focus on individual performance then must come from a context of meaningful participation. Likewise, it should be assessed on the basis of its perceived acceptance in the community with which it is affiliated. By this model, the purpose of instructional design involves creating interesting problem spaces, many of these linked to already established participatory communities.

The concept that new media literacies can and should be emphasized in learning spaces like the Quest to Learn school extends beyond the 11 "skills and competencies" from Jenkins and his co-authors: in short, these include social and collaborative skills like negotiation, networking, appropriation, and performance (Jenkins *et al.*, 2006, p. 4). Though it may be true that each is important to twenty-first-century learning and instruction, it is important to note that these skills and competencies are not necessarily new or even unique to digital tools and technologies and are already in wide use in the culture of participation. In fact, the New Media Literacies Project at MIT seeks to develop curriculum and professional development activities that highlight both digital and analog media experiences, because it is often at the intersection of both where the most interesting learning and production happens (Black, 2008). Quest to Learn's curriculum makes clear that a school built on game-based learning is about a particular orientation toward the underlying systems of the world and how they operate with, connect to, and influence one another. That concept is by no means limited to analog or digital hardware, software, or media. More important, it fosters knowledge creation with the context of their use.

For example, when a student makes a mash-up of his favorite three hip artists' videos, he needs to know how to use the software. However, he also needs to know which distribution channels are best for that creation. YouTube will get him the most hits for sure, but if it's a video that samples copyrighted work, it's likely that YouTube will remove it from their site, regardless of whether a formal complaint exists. As YouTube's popularity is so high, if the student's video is removed, it could be said that it's been "killed" on the Internet, lest it be captured by sites like YouTomb, which stores any metadata related to YouTube's complaint (MIT Free Culture Group, n.d.). There is the possibility that other video-sharing Web sites might not use the same violation-searching algorithm that YouTube does, but students would have to immerse themselves in the video mash-up communities to learn that it might be better to share a video on Vimeo or BlipTV instead. Making these decisions is why learning about and understanding various systems of media participation is just as meaningful and valuable as knowing how to use the tools to make these media.

Knowing how, why, when, and to what to degree we can express ourselves with media texts, tools, and cultures are the foundations for meaningful participation and affiliation with media communities. Indeed, as Jenkins and his co-authors explain, affiliations are at the heart of participatory media (Jenkins *et al.*, 2006, p. 9). However, perhaps the term *affiliation* isn't as accurate as it could be, because when taken out of the context of full-fledged participation, it seems to effect an idea of simple sponsorship rather than immersive connectedness to a media activity, community, brand, franchise, or set of practices.

For example, I might affiliate myself with people who like the Internet music sites and radio stations Last.fm or Pandora, but that affiliation becomes more than a "checked box" when I consider the fact that these music-listening communities are built on a shared social network of listeners and "genomic data" that classifies artists, genres, and songs, all of it culled from the listening habits of its users. Those listening experiences are made richer by our interactions with them. For me, Last.fm is made more interactive when I use its "scrobbling" feature, which tracks the music I listen to and stores the data so that my friends and I can keep track of one another's current favorites. Some users have begun using that data to generate sophisticated visualizations, which they then post on the Web for others to share. At that point, listening to music on the Web isn't the same as listening to it on the radio. However, it's not just about the tools, either. Understandably, the tools are important but only to the degree that they enable me to affiliate and participate in a more meaningful way with the shared media experience.

Another good example of the participatory culture concept can be seen in the uses of the popular Flickr photo-sharing Web site. When I first learned of Flickr, I saw it only as a place for online storage of my digital photos. I uploaded all my photos and organized them neatly into sets, where I could title them individually and describe each set. Soon I learned that I could also invite others to see the photos by sharing individual links that would direct them to each one. Then I learned that I could tag them with words used to describe them, so photos of my dog were tagged with her name, Annie. For fun I also tagged them with the words "dog" and "pug." As I have more than 1,000 photos altogether, assigning the tag "Annie" helped me find hers more easily when I searched through my personal photo archive.

I was surprised when one day I received a message from an owner of a group on Flickr called "Pugs." She had done a search of all the photos on Flickr and found mine. She asked me to join the group so that I could contribute my pug photos, too. I did, and now I enjoy seeing photos of other people's pugs. Of course, then I wondered what other Flickr groups were out there, and I soon started tagging my photos with broader terms in hopes that other users doing a wider range of searches would see my photos. After a while, I was asked to join several different groups whose subject is signs—road signs, historic signs, funny signs, and the like. Therefore, if I see the photo sharing Web site Flickr as just a place to upload my photos and keep them organized, I'm not a full participant in the affordances offered by it. However, my experiences with the site make it clear to me that Flickr is about much more than its technological offerings.

Literacy scholars Colin Lankshear and Michele Knobel (2005) also support the more ecological approach to media literacy education described by Jenkins and his co-authors. For example, Jenkins *et al.* state, "It matters what tools are available to a culture, but it matters more what that culture chooses to do with those tools" (2006, p. 8). To Lankshear and Knobel, the shift from focusing primarily on media tools toward a focus on culture is an ontological one. Lankshear and Knobel state plainly that they see new (media) literacies as indicative of a participatory, collaborative, and distributed ethos, one that can be contrasted with a technical, physical, and material mindset. Throughout their book, titled *New Literacies: Everyday Practice and Classroom Learning* (2006), they argue that too often we characterize the value of emerging creative tools and practices as just new ways of doing the same things we used to do, only with new objects that make our jobs speedier and more productive, an attitude that unfortunately fails to understand the cultural shift that goes along with a new literacies disposition.

Lankshear and Knobel (2006) emphasize that traditional literacies (and schooling) are still entrenched in a "physical-industrial" mindset that is "individualized, enclosed, product-centered, and hierarchical" (p. 38). What's changed is that the physical-industrial mindset coexists with a "cyberspatial, post-industrial" mindset in which our ways of knowing, being, and doing are more collective, distributed, change-based, and de-centered (Lankshear & Knobel, 2006, p. 38). In other words, what's "new" about new literacies is not just that we are working with new tools: It's not just about the products. What's new is the coexistence of new products and old tools and of habits and orientations toward both. That is, it is less important to note whether one's creative affiliations are centered on costume play or knitting; what matters is the depth of involvement, the peer-to-peer relationships, and the levels of expertise and ethos community members feel and exercise in that space. A focus on the commodity misses the point: It is what we do, think, and know within the context of its community that is significant.

The Quest to Learn school is designed on a model of media literacy that reflects a holistic experience of immersion within a context of problem-solving, co-designing, and systems-based thinking. Newly available tools and technologies are already part of the curricular package, which means that the focus of instruction is on the activities that are enabled by them. Education at Quest to Learn is based on new media literacies to the extent that, from the bottom to the top, lessons reflect the culture of our participation with media and our everyday use of it. With this school, we have a particular model of learning with new media tools that is inclusive of their cultures, which means that there can be no means for learning without deep immersion in the contexts of the problems we're trying to solve. By its design, the Quest to Learn school is an acute example of a formal learning environment built to reflect developing insights into the valuable expressions and experiences surrounding new media literacies.

References

Barab, S., and Squire, K. (2004). Design-based research: Putting a stake in the ground. *International Journal of the Learning Sciences, 13*(1), 1–14.

Barron, B., Schwartz, D., Vye, N., Moore, A., Petrosino, A., & Zech, L. (1998). Doing with understanding: Lessons from research on problem- and project-based learning. *International Journal of the Learning Sciences, 7*(3-4), 271–312.

Bereiter, C., & Scardamalia, M. (1993). *Surpassing ourselves: An inquiry into the nature and implications of expertise.* Chicago, IL: Open Court Press.

Black, R.W. (2008). *Adolescents and online fan fiction.* New York: Peter Lang.

Brown, A. L. (1992). Design experiments: Theoretical and methodological challenges in creating complex interventions in classroom settings. *Journal of the Learning Sciences, 2,* 141–178.

Design-Based Research Collective. (2003). Design-based research: An emerging paradigm for educational inquiry. *Educational Researcher, 32*(1), 5–8.

Dewey, J. (1933). The product and process of reflective activity: Psychological process and logical forms. In J. Boydston (Ed.), *The later works of John Dewey* (vol. 8, pp. 171–186). Carbondale, IL: Southern Illinois University Press.

Fields, D.A., & Kafai, Y.B. (in press). "du u wanna go 2 the moon??" A connective ethnography of peer knowledge sharing and diffusion across class, club, and home spaces in a tween virtual world. *International Journal of Computer Supported Collaborative Learning.*

Free Culture Group, YouTomb Project. (n.d.). Accessed December 30, 2008, from http://youtomb.mit.edu/

Hayes, E. R. (2008). Game content creation and IT proficiency: An exploratory study. *Computers and Education, 51*(1), 97–108.

Hull, G., & Schultz, K. (2001). Literacy and learning out of school: A review of theory and research. *Review of Educational Research, 71*(4), 575–611.

Ito, M., Horst, H., Bittanti, M., boyd, d., Herr-Stephenson, B., Lange, P.G., *et al.* (2008). *Living and learning with new media: Summary of findings from the Digital Youth Project.* Chicago: The John D. and Catherine T. MacArthur Foundation, Digital Media and Learning Initiative. Retrieved December 10, 2008, from http://digitalyouth.ischool.berkeley.edu

James, C. (with Davis, K., Flores, A., Francis, J.M., Pettingill, L., Rundle, M., & Gardner, H.) (2008). *Young people, ethics, and the new digital media: A synthesis from the Good Play Project.* (Good Work Project Report Series No. 54). Cambridge, MA: Harvard University Press.

Jenkins, H., Purushotma, R., Clinton, K., Weigel, M., & Robison, A. (2006). *Confronting the challenges of participatory culture: Media education for the 21st century*. Chicago, IL: The John D. and Catherine T. MacArthur Foundation, Digital Media and Learning Initiative. Retrieved November 1, 2008, from http://www.newmedialiteracies.org

Joseph, B. (2008). Why Johnny can't fly: Treating games as a form of youth media within a youth development framework. In K. Salen (Ed.), *The ecology of games: Connecting youth, games, and learning* (pp. 253–266). Cambridge, MA: The MIT Press.

Kafai, Y. B., & Resnick, M. (1996). *Constructionism in practice*. Mahwah, NJ: Lawrence Erlbaum Associates.

Kaiser Family Foundation. (2005, March). *Generation M: Media in the lives of 8–18 year olds* (No. 7251). Washington, DC: Program for the Study of Media and Health.

Lankshear, C., & Knobel, M. (2006). *New literacies: Everyday practices and classroom learning* (2nd ed.). London: Open University Press.

Lave, J., & Wenger, E. (1991). *Situated learning: Legitimate peripheral participation*. Cambridge: Cambridge University Press.

Lenhart, A. & Madden, M. (2005). *Teen content creators and consumers*. Pew Internet and American Life Project. Retrieved July 10, 2009 from http://www.pewinternet.org/Reports/2005/Teen-Content-Creators-and-Consumers.aspxMIT

Norman, D. (2008). Affordances and design. Retrieved September 14, 2008, from http://www.jnd.org/dn.mss/affordances_and.html

Pandora Internet Radio. (2008). About Pandora. Retrieved October 1, 2008, from http://www.pandora.com/corporate/

Papert, S. (1991). Situating constructionism. In I. Harel & S. Papert (Eds.), *Constructionism* (pp. 1–14). Hillsdale, NJ: Lawrence Erlbaum Associates.

Peppler, K. A., & Kafai, Y. B. (2007). From SuperGoo to Scratch: Exploring creative digital media production in informal learning. *Learning, Media, & Technology, 32*(2), 149–166.

Piaget, J. (1977). *Psychology and epistemology: Towards a theory of knowledge*. New York: Penguin Books.

Salen, K. (2007). Gaming literacies: A game design study in action. *Journal of Educational Multimedia and Hypermedia, 16*(3), 301–322.

Salen, K., Torres, R., & Wolozin, L. (2008a). *The game school planning document: Draft 1.0*. New York: Institute of Play.

Salen, K., Torres, R., Rufo-Tepper, R., Shapiro, A., Wolozin, L., & Schwartz, A. (2008b). *Quest to Learn: New school PSO and grant application to the New York City Department of Education*. New York: Institute of Play.

Santo, R. (2007). Engaging youth with a new medium: The potentials of virtual worlds. *Youth Media Reporter Journal, 1*(5), 49–51.

Sawyer, R. K. (Ed.). (2006). *The Cambridge handbook of the learning sciences*. Cambridge: Cambridge University Press.

Steinkuehler, C. A., & Duncan, S. C. (2008). Scientific habits of mind in virtual worlds. *Journal of Science Education and Technology, 17*(6), 530–543.

Chapter 10

Augmented Reality Gaming and Game Design as a New Literacy Practice

James M. Mathews and Kurt D. Squire

The emergence of new digital media has altered the way we think, learn, and interact with one another and the world around us. New digital media and the networks and technologies that support them make the world's information available in time and on demand, enable *participation* in complex media practices, including the production and distribution of media content, and provide new avenues for collaboration and creative expression. Together, these factors allow us to engage with one another and the world in new ways that contribute to an *aesthetics of experience* (Gee, 2004; Jenkins, 2006; Squire, 2006; Steinkuhler, 2006).

What might classroom-based instruction developed around this framework look like? This chapter explores the intersection of two key areas of the new digital media landscape, mobile media and game-based learning, and suggests how they might serve as models for learning in a digital age. We provide a brief introduction to each of these areas and then discuss how they might be combined to provide new, innovative learning experiences. We center our discussion on a particular type of mobile-based gaming environment, augmented reality (AR) gaming, and follow the design and implementation of *Dow Day*, an AR game and game-based curriculum. We present our experience implementing *Dow Day* with high school-aged students and then reflect on the potential of AR games and AR game design for learning in general and, more specifically, within the context of new media literacy.

Game-based Learning

Game-based learning is a paradigm that emerged out of situated learning theory. Indeed, video games instantiate many contemporary theories of learning and literacy (Gee, 2007; New London Group, 1996) and provide models for instructional designers looking to develop technology-based interventions for learning (Shaffer, Squire, Halverson, & Gee, 2005). Using a socio-cultural view of learning, Gee (2007) suggests that educational designers have a lot to learn from video games. In particular, designers can borrow models of instruction that guide, shape, and refine learners' conceptual development within rich, deeply situated contexts. They enable designers to confront prior understandings, work through problems in an embodied way, and introduce counter-examples or cases to produce productive understandings. All of this learning can occur through the perspective of particular identities.

These elements of learning combine to enable students to have situated experiences that become the basis for understanding. Galarneau (2007) argues that games are thus best suited for creating *transformative experiences* of phenomena (i.e., experiences that transform or provide a new framework for understanding phenomena). In this way, games allow us to do much more than memorize facts; they allow us to take on new identities, lead investigations, and travel back in time. From an instructional perspective, we might think of games as a pedagogy well suited to presenting complex problems and creating deep transformations in how students think about and interact with the world (Shaffer *et al.*, 2005).

As a simulation-based medium, games challenge both *how* we teach and *what* we teach (Squire, 2008). Already, simulation technologies have transformed how we do science by making *modeling*, a core scientific practice, more accessible to teachers and students (Feurzeig & Roberts, 1999; Wolfram, 2002). Similarly, the particular affordances of new media, such as the capacity to produce historical simulations, provide unique opportunities to transform the teaching of history (Squire, 2005; Staley, 2002). Along with Web-based technologies, which make a wealth of information available in time and on demand, game-based pedagogies threaten the "Trivial Pursuit" style of teaching that dominates schools. In fact, emerging research suggests that teaching information literacy skills may be at least as important as teaching more traditional literacy and content domains in secondary education (Coiro 2003).

Mobile Media

Just as the educational field was preparing to integrate game-based technologies, a new wave of mobile technologies emerged to further challenge educational practices. Mobile media are personalized media that we take with us on the go. Mobile media devices include cell phones, portable music players, gaming devices, portable video players, PDAs, and *smart phones* (i.e., cell phones with broadband Internet access). Such devices have dramatically increased their power and capacity and improved their interface design to a point at which they are now as powerful as computers from just a few years ago. In addition to more "traditional" capabilities, such as communicating via voice and text, today's mobile media devices also have broadband connectivity, real-time 3-D graphic displays, and high-resolution screens for multi-media viewing. In addition, they support new capacities, such as the global positioning system (GPS), which tie multimedia and networked data to specific locations and allow for new types of learning experiences. For example, a tourist walking down Boston's Freedom Trail could now access historical photos and documents, audio guides, or video clips tied to specific locations.

In a sense, mobile media break down traditional barriers that have defined learning in schools. Mobile media enable constant, personalized access to media and information and the ability to participate in social networks regardless of time or place. For example, a student with an iPhone now comes to class with a broadband Internet computer in her or his pocket and with it can access—and even store—as much information and more up-to-date information than is contained in many school libraries.

An upshot of mobile media is that we now live in information-rich spaces around the clock. The portability of mobile devices enables users to document events in real time via a variety of texts, videos, and images. The range of communication needs filled by mobile media range from simple referencing to "liveblogging" (i.e., the use of mobile devices to blog events in real time). A college student can fact-check a professor by looking up information on a cell phone without the teacher even being aware (Foster, 2008). A political junkie can follow liveblogs of political events between errands. A traveler can get directions, traffic reports, or restaurant information delivered in real time.

New mobile media devices such as the iPhone could dramatically expand learning opportunities for youth, but little is known about what specific learning practices will emerge from this medium and how we might design effective learning experiences around them. The few case studies of learning with mobile media suggest that we cannot wholly predict what might emerge when a classroom full of students is armed with mobile media devices (Roschelle & Pea, 2002). Previous research on mobile media suggests that their customizability, portability, connectivity, and sociability (ability to be used without impeding on face-to-face interactions) will lead to new sorts of learning practices that free learners to pursue their own learning interests. However, this will create new challenges for educators to develop and coordinate learning activities (Klopfer, Squire, & Jenkins, 2003; Roschelle & Pea, 2002). To move forward, the field needs to better understand the capacities of mobile media—not just in terms of their technical capacities (like broadband connectivity) but in terms of the social practices they support (Horst & Miller, 2006). That is, it is critical to understand how users *take up, shape, and redefine* technologies as they adapt them to meet their needs.

Augmented Reality Gaming: Location-Based Mobile Media Meets Game-Based Learning

Augmented reality games are a particularly interesting model for learning, in that they layer digital data over the real world to produce new experiences of place. The particular AR game we present here, *Dow Day,* seeks to provide this type of transformational experience by allowing players to role-play as journalists covering a series of anti-Vietnam War protests in Madison, Wisconsin. Through this experience, we hope that players will rethink the relationship between primary sources and the narrative accounts given by corporation-owned media while drawing connections between the reporting of Vietnam protests and contemporary political events.

Dow Day is made possible by an AR gaming engine developed by Eric Klopfer and colleagues at the Massachusetts Institute of Technology. This engine enables players to play AR games on a handheld computer, such as a PDA or similar mobile device that uses a GPS. As players move through the physical world, the devices create a virtual layer (e.g., data, photos, videos, virtual interviews) that *augments* the real-world context. For example, think of an audio tour at an art museum. As visitors travel through the museum, they use an audio player to receive additional information about particular art pieces while standing directly in front of them. Similarly, in AR games, as players explore the physical environment, they can meet virtual people or access virtual data connected to specific locations (Klopfer *et al.*, 2003). During a game about the history of New York City, students might view location-based historical photos or videos depicting urban life in the early 1900s while walking through the same city streets today.

What separates AR games from tours, however, is that they go beyond simply providing information by structuring students' interactions with the place around a *game-based narrative.* As a result, players take on roles to solve a series of game challenges that require them to discern the value of information, reason from evidence, and construct new representations of their understanding. For example, instead of simply taking a tour of an archaeological site, students might investigate the site as a team of archaeologists who have been hired to research the site and produce a museum exhibit about the people who once lived there. Similarly, instead of studying the potential impact of an oil spill on the local environment by reading a textbook or discussing an academic article, students might play an AR game that allows them to role-play as chemists, environmental engineers, and public health officials hired to develop a plan for containing and cleaning up a simulated spill. In this way, AR games seek to situate the narrative and game challenges in real-world places (Holland, Jenkins & Squire, 2003).

Previous research around AR games (Klopfer, 2008; Squire & Jan, 2007) demonstrates their potential to create a *gaming experience* that can emotionally and cognitively engage students and scaffold their learning related to specific learning goals (e.g., scientific argumentation within the domain of environmental science). Squire and Jan present five core design elements that interact to provide students with a rich game-based learning experience. These factors are (1) a compelling task, (2) roles (social configurations), (3) embedded tools and resources, (4) context (or place), and (5) an encompassing activity system. Though their work relates to the domain of environmental science, it provides a framework that can be used to design AR games around a wide range of contexts and learning goals.

Building on the previous work surrounding AR, we designed a new AR game, *Dow Day*, which seeks to use AR gaming as a way to engage students in the process of historical inquiry and develop their *historical thinking* skills. This project goes beyond previous work, however, in three important ways. First, it embeds the AR game within a larger curricular unit that involves pre-game introduction activities and post-game debriefing activities. These activities are closely tied to state and national standards and can be customized to meet specific classroom management and learning goals. Second, it engages students in two key practices associated with New Media Literacy: critique and design. The outcome of *Dow Day* is that players construct a news article to report on events drawing from original sources. Afterward, they critique the reporting on Dow Day at the time and the reporting of contemporary events. As such, it uses design, which is at the core of new literacy studies as a framework for tying together media critique and media production. Finally, it includes an AR design component that allows students to use the underlying technology and design principles to interrogate their own neighbourhoods and tell their own AR-based stories. In this way, they themselves become active producers of new meanings with mobile media.

Dow Day: An Augmented Reality Game-Based Curriculum

Dow Day is an AR game that provides an opportunity for students to experience a specific historical event from a first person perspective. The game revolves around a series of anti-Dow Chemical protests that took place on the University of Wisconsin-Madison campus in October, 1967.

The protests were intended to raise awareness about Dow Chemical's production of napalm and stop the company from conducting interviews on campus. A core strategy used by the protestors was to occupy the building in which the interviews were scheduled to take place. After negotiations between the protestors and university officials stalled, the city police department was called in to remove the students from the building, a controversial action that resulted in violence. In the game, players role-play as journalists who have been asked to investigate the multiple perspectives surrounding the protests and report on why and how they turned violent (Maraniss, 2003; Squire *et al.*, 2007). Taking advantage of the mobility and location-sensitive capabilities of handheld computers, the game takes place at the actual location where the Dow Chemical protests occurred back in 1967. As they walk around campus, players use a handheld computer to conduct virtual interviews, obtain and read primary documents, and view historical video clips and photos.

The game, which takes about 1.5 hours to play, is part of an inquiry-based unit in which students perform as follows:

1   Read and analyze documents (newspaper articles, photographs, charts, graphs, and video clips) that contextualize the historical time period.
2   Develop questions surrounding the protests.
3   Travel to the University of Wisconsin-Madison campus to play at the actual protest site.
4   Write a newspaper article and select two photographs that will run with their story based on the observations and interviews they conducted during the protests. Additionally, the article must be written from the perspective of the newspaper they work for.
5   Develop an additional inquiry question based on their investigations.
6   Conduct further research to answer their inquiry question.

The game and an associated curriculum scaffold the students' inquiry and progressively transition from a highly structured analysis of primary documents to a more open-ended inquiry based on students' individual interests.

Players start the game by receiving two primary documents. The first document lists the on-campus interviews scheduled for October 18, 1967. Dow Chemical is one of many companies conducting interviews that day. This provides an opportunity to ask students to contemplate why Dow has been singled out. The second document, the front page from *The Daily Cardinal* (a student paper), highlights key perspectives surrounding the planned protests. The headlines read, "U Promises Crack-down On Dow Co. Obstructors"; "SRP Defeats Dow Protest Proposal"; and "U

Introduction

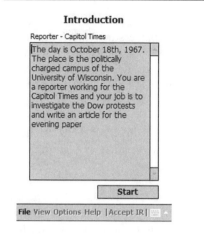

Reporter - Capitol Times

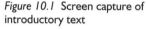

Figure 10.1 Screen capture of introductory text

Figure 10.2 Screen capture of the game map

Activists Disagree On Demonstrations" (*The Daily Cardinal*, October 12, 1967). Together, these documents are designed to provide a context for the protests, create initial entry points into the period, frame the campus as a *contested space* (Holland, Jenkins & Squire, 2003), and introduce students to the idea that the anti-Dow protests and the university's official response were publicly and privately debated, multi-faceted, and not inevitable. This last point is critical in that pre-interviews showed that before playing the game, most students (even those who had previously studied the Vietnam War in school) held non-critical views of the period and anti-war protests in general.

After reading these documents, players are given a GPS-equipped PDA loaded with the *Dow Day* game. The game begins with a brief introductory video and text (Figure 10.1). The video provides additional background on Dow Chemical and highlights events leading up to October 18, 1967, including archival footage of anti-Dow and pro-Dow demonstrations that occurred on campus the day before. The video also includes short interview clips introducing key characters whom players meet later in the game, including the chief of the university police force, the chancellor, a Dow Chemical supporter, and students opposed to Dow's presence on campus. From a narrative standpoint, this approach is used to draw players into the emotion surrounding the conflict, reconfirm the multiple perspectives surrounding the event, and build dramatic tension (Figure 10.2).

Next, players see a campus map and various icons representing potential interactions (Figure 10.2). The first game character players see on their map is their newspaper editor. By walking to the square representing the editor's location in the physical world, the players activate (or trigger) a virtual interview with him. The editor is a fictitious character who introduces the players to their overall game task (conducting interviews and writing an article in time for the evening paper) and introduces their first quest or micro-challenge. Both of these are delivered via a text-based dialog box.

At one point during the interview, the editor directs players' attention across the street to where a Dow Chemical recruiter is walking. The editor says,

> Hey wait! See that guy across the street in Library Mall? No, the one with the black overcoat. He is one of the Dow representatives. I ran into him yesterday, but he did not have time for an interview. He is talking to one of the reporters from the *Daily Cardinal*. Why don't you run over there and see if you can get any information out of him. When you're done don't forget to head up to the Chancellor's office. Hurry and we'll see you later. Good Luck.

Interestingly, it is not uncommon for players to look across the street in an attempt to see the recruiter who, of course, is not physically there. Instead, the recruiter is represented on the game map as a new (and previously invisible) yellow square. As players walk across the street to interview the recruiter, they see their own icon (a red triangle) moving across the map in the same direction they are walking. Once the player is within range of the recruiter (a predetermined distance set by the game designer), the player hears a chime, and the interview dialog box appears along with a picture of the recruiter. As before, after completing their interview, the player's screen returns to the map view, and several new locations/characters appear. The game proceeds in this manner as players navigate the map based on the locations they want to visit and the people they want to interview. Players are not required to take notes during the game because all of the data, including photos, video, documents, and interviews they gather or unlock during the game, are stored on the handheld and are easily retrievable. Players can also share content they gather in the game with other players by using the IR-beaming capabilities built into the devices.

In addition to conducting virtual interviews, the players can also gather virtual documents (flyers, press releases, etc.) via the handheld computer and physical documents that have been placed in physical locations around campus. They can also watch videos and view photos tied to specific locations and events. Collectively, these are aimed at encouraging players to identify with their role, connect with the storyline, and foster an historical *sense of place*. The content in the game consists mainly of primary documents and archival video and photos. Interview text is built from original newspaper accounts, oral interviews, and official documents released by the university, police agencies, and the state legislature. As such, the game might be considered a historical fiction dealing with historical interpretation, first amendment rights, civil disobedience, and newspaper reporting during times of war.

The game is designed to combine media-rich and location-based content within a game structure so as to shape players' experience in particular ways. The game strives to create the perspective of being a reporter charged with investigating unfolding events in *real time*. Aesthetically, the game attempts to create memorable moments that stand out to participants as being emotionally compelling. As Henry Jenkins (2004) argues, games are less about telling formal stories and more about setting up interactions that result in memorable moments for the player (see also Seldes, 1924). We attempt to facilitate these types of experiences in *Dow Day* by using multimedia and place to link players with the past. For example, allowing players to watch video footage of demonstrations that occurred in the same location where they are literally standing typically elicits strong emotional reactions. These moments make the game challenges and overall narrative seem more authentic and promote a sense of *being there*. Being able to create experiences like these—particularly using media to augment players' experience of *place*— are a key affordance of AR games

Figure 10.3 The initial screen that players see when they trigger a video. Videos are viewed in the same location where they were originally shot.

Figure 10.4 Students viewing the video clip depicted in Figure 10.3

as a medium and help cultivate an appreciation for place (Figures 10.3 and 10.4).

Dow Day in the Classroom

After conducting initial pilot tests and soliciting feedback from teachers (mainly about their needs and concerns related to the game content and anticipated issues surrounding the use of AR games in school), we developed an approach to implementing *Dow Day* into high school classrooms that includes three separate, but interrelated stages. Stage one involves playing the game and completing the activities that encompass the gaming unit; stage two consists of a redesign exercise that invites students to co-design future iterations of the game; and stage three provides students with an opportunity to design their own, albeit much shorter, AR game. The second stage was developed to encourage students to think more deeply about *Dow Day* as a designed experience that, like documentaries and history textbooks, presents an *interpreted* version of the *historical truth*. The final stage was included as a way to explore the potential of developing a longer design-centered curriculum that allows students to produce their own history-based AR game. It is important to note that teachers could choose to play *Dow Day* without participating in the game critique and game design activities but, as we discovered, these follow-up activities proved useful for engaging students and providing opportunities for students to think more critically about the game as a designed experience.

Stage One: Dow Day *Gaming Unit*

The game is situated within a curricular framework on the Vietnam War, a topic area commonly taught in U.S. high school history classrooms. The game builds on these preexisting concepts and content, however, by "taking them out of school" and extending them "into the world." In addition to situating the content in events, places, and stories that students can vicariously experience, it seeks to explicitly shed the "frame" of school and replace it with one of experience.

Dow Day is designed as both a stand-alone historical simulation that can be used in informal learning contexts and as a game-based curricular unit for use in a high school history or journalism classroom. The 10-hour game/curriculum is designed in a modular fashion so that teachers may adapt it to local needs. For example, one classroom that ran on a block schedule completed the game in five school days, whereas another classroom that had 50-minute classes completed the curriculum in 10 school days. Game day, which lasts 2.5 hours, is run as a fieldtrip to the local site and includes set-up and orientation (20 minutes), game play (1.5 hours), and debriefing (40 minutes).

Dow Day *and Historical Thinking*

The primary goal of *Dow Day* is to develop students' historical thinking skills, particularly their ability to select and analyze evidence to develop historical arguments, see history as a *re*presentation of the past, and view themselves as active interpreters of historical events. One way that *Dow Day* attempts to achieve this is by situating players' inquiry around an authentic historical problem. Brush and Saye (2008) argue that "problem-based learning activities provide learners with opportunities to move beyond the memorization of discrete facts in order to critically examine complex problems." They acknowledge, however, that this sacrifices some "coverage" for depth of experience, as it "requires learners to remain engaged in the problem for an extensive period of time, and to weigh competing perspectives, or critically examine various points of view regarding the historical problem."

AR games, and *Dow Day* in particular, can create this level of engagement by inviting students to take on a role that actively embeds them in an unfolding game narrative. By taking on the role of local journalists while playing *Dow Day* the game positions students as *interpreters* and *re-constructors* of historical events, versus consumers of *historical truth*. Though this approach mirrors recent trends in history education that stress the importance of engaging students in the process of *doing* rather than simply *consuming* history (Holt, 1990; Wineburg, 2001), it differs in that the *historical interpretation* is scaffolded through playing a role. By design, the AR game seeks to create a hybrid identity as posited by Gee (2004), built around *academic* roles. Students' post-game comments reflect this. One student felt that the game "was a good way to learn because it made me feel like a reporter." Another said that playing the game actually makes you feel "… as if you are walking around interviewing people."

A key way that *Dow Day* encourages students to identify with being journalists is by contextualizing their role around an engaging game narrative and challenge. The players are implored by characters to listen to *their* side of the story and report on the events from *their* perspective. The game capitalizes on conflicts between the various interests negotiating the protests. Because there is uncertainty as to whether the protests will or will not end peacefully, players became interested in seeing the events through to their conclusion. By exploiting the real-life debate surrounding the events and the controversy about who was to blame for the eventual violence, the initial inquiry question evolves into somewhat of a mystery.

Because each of the characters in the game provides a different take on the events, players need to weigh these competing perspectives to draw their own conclusions. This process proved important in getting students to develop a more nuanced view of the events and helped them develop their understanding of and even empathy for the various perspectives surrounding the events.

Students commented that the active, story-driven nature of the game play, where they take on a role and propel the narrative through their choices and actions, differs from the way they usually study history in school. One student said that the game "... presented facts, but in a more interesting way. It gave like a story or scenario that you could follow, so it kind of made it into a game. You got more engaged than just reading out of the textbook." Students also mentioned that it was a good way to learn because it was "interactive," "gripping," "hands-on," and "active." This seems to be a key point in terms of motivation, considering that a majority of the students listed history as one of their least favorite subjects in school. Even those who liked studying history had a tendency to describe previous school-based learning experiences using phrases and terms associated with passive learning ("lectures," "textbooks," "listening to the teacher talk").

As previously mentioned, it is important to consider the role that place plays in both the game narrative, students' willingness to take on a role, and the overall game experience. By situating the players' inquiry in the actual places wherein the historical events took place, students become active agents who are required to inhabit the same buildings, walk the same sidewalks, and talk to virtual characters representing the people who occupied the same place some 30 years earlier. Students mention this as one of the more engaging components of the game/curriculum experience. One player said, "It was kind of powerful to see the places and you can realize that you were standing there when in the same spot these people were doing all this." Another said that he felt that being in the actual place "... helped us get the point across ... seeing what happened like you were actually living that event." Additionally, many students commented on the game's ability to make them feel like they were actually on campus during the protests. This sense of *being there* is a critical component of historical thinking because it encourages students to reflect on how different people experienced the event, further developing an empathetic understanding of the multiple perspectives surrounding the protests (Figures 10.5 and 10.6).

AR games that foreground local place allow students to connect with, think about, and experience the places around them in new and unusual ways. Some of the students who played *Dow Day* were surprised by the fact that the protests took place so close to where they live. One player

Figure 10.5 Students entering a campus building in order to interview the Chancellor

Figure 10.6 A student reviewing additional evidence before writing her article

commented that, "It was intriguing, at least for me, because it happened here. I didn't know that anything like that happened in Wisconsin. Especially like downtown where I have actually been there in spots where it shows on the video, and I didn't know. It's like, something happened here years ago?" Another girl reported that she "never knew that Madison even had huge protests like this." Still other students were motivated to go home and ask their parents about the protests. One parent reported that this was the first time in recent memory that her daughter had come home from school eager to talk about what she had been studying. This suggests the importance of students' emotional reactions to the learning environment and highlights the potential of using a place-based pedagogy to support inquiry. It also suggests that one affordance of AR games may be that they encourage students to connect academic content to lived experiences, particularly via place.

Another affordance of AR games is that they provide shared experiences that can become the basis of new inquiry questions around similar real-world issues. In *Dow Day*, the gaming experience piqued students' interest and naturally led to new questions about the Vietnam War, such as in the following post-game discussion:

Student 1: I want to know what happened after this protest. I want to know, you know, more like about the war and stuff.
Student 2: Or, more beforehand stuff like what was the Dow Chemical Company all involved in because they weren't just making napalm. They wanted interviews and they said, "I am not working

in the napalm department. I'm working in this department." What are the other departments of the company? Like, have a background thing on the company that was being protested against. That would be kind a cool.

The game also provided a framework for thinking about similar issues and decisions facing today's students. During one game, there were flags set up on campus representing American soldiers who had died in the Iraq War. This sparked conversations about the effectiveness of protesting and cultural differences between the 1960s and the present. Another group played the game during a period when university students were protesting the presence of Halliburton on campus. Interestingly, some of the protestors actually invoked the Dow Day protests as part of their rhetoric. Students drew on their experience playing *Dow Day* to compare the two events and raised questions about how present-day protests were portrayed by the media.

Challenges and Questions

Though the game helped students develop a more nuanced view of the protests and provided a context for developing *historical thinking* skills, students failed to see the game itself as a construction of reality and did not discuss the game as a designed learning experience with its own inherent interpretations and biased representation of the past. Instead, students treated the game in the same way they might treat a historical film or traditional documentary (i.e., as an authorized, sanctioned or official *truth*). For example, students did not question the accuracy of the interviews they conducted but instead saw them as a direct representation of views held by individuals (and groups) during the time period. When they were told that the interviews stemmed from actual newspaper accounts from the period, this further cemented the students' belief that the game was an accurate and unbiased representation of the events that took place. In the end, though students critiqued the game in terms of game-play (especially related to the interface, the length of the game content, and the limited branching narrative) and discussed ways that the technology could be used in other learning contexts, they did not tend to make unsolicited comments about the underlying design values or historical representations that appeared in the game. These examples underscore the difficulty of fostering deep critique into the nature of knowledge and suggest the need for educators in highlighting the "authored" nature of representations.

Stage Two: Dow Day Redesign Activity

After completing the gaming curriculum, each group participated in a one-hour redesign workshop aimed at encouraging students to think about the game as a *designed experience*. We explicitly attempted to leverage students' backgrounds as learners, media creators, and video game experts and made explicit our interest in using their expertise to improve future iterations. The resulting discussions were robust and touched on a number of themes related to game design, including game flow, interactivity, choice and consequences, branching narrative, and so on.

In the end, however, though students were interested in giving feedback related to the game mechanics and game interface, they were less interested in doing the hard work of developing new content for characters or reading background material that would help them better understand the events and/or guide the process of content creation. Although students provided some ideas for new roles and characters, most simply opted to add new content rather than alter the existing game structure. Examples for new roles included a student's trying to interview with Dow Chemical (with game challenges such as locating the interview room, trying to get through the crowded hallway, and avoiding anti-Dow protestors); a protest organizer who needs to negotiate with the administration; and a police officer. Still, students' ability to envision characters and new roles demonstrated their growing understanding of the multiple perspectives surrounding the events as well as an interest in and ability to discuss the game as an authored artifact.

Stage Three: AR Design Workshop

As a culminating activity, we conducted a 10-hour design workshop in which students used multimedia and AR design tools to create digital stories about their own neighborhoods and schools. In a short design workshop, it seemed critical to have students design AR-based stories that did not focus on particular content. Instead, the workshops were designed around a common theme: *different people experience the same place in different ways*. Each of the students' stories was designed to communicate how they experience a particular place.

The design workshop consisted of three components: (1) a planning session wherein students brainstormed ideas for their AR game and wrote brief game summaries or treatments; (2) design labs that gave students an opportunity to use the tools required to build and play AR games (i.e., a game editor who allowed the students to enter game content and the game engine or software program that ran the games on the PDA); and (3) critique sessions that provided a structured forum for sharing feedback on designs. As facilitators of the design sessions, we also engaged students in small-group and one-to-one conversations to provide formative feedback during the design process. In the spirit of trying to create a community of practice, however, we also steered students toward helping each other and cultivated students' previous and emerging skills in order to develop "centers of expertise" (Squire, De Vane, & Durga, 2008).

This activity saw even higher levels of student engagement than the game and redesign stages of the curriculum. This exercise contributed to the learning experience in several ways:

1   *Game design as an activity leveraged students' experiences and expertise as gamers, giving them a new lens for thinking about representations.* By way of analogy one might imagine how avid mystery readers might use their skills, knowledge, and identities to produce a historical mystery themselves. In this case, students used their prior knowledge about games (language, ideas about what makes a "good game," etc.) to inform their designs.

2   *Developing local games recruited students' digital media skills, tools, and Web-based communities that were not ordinarily used in school to complete tasks and manage their workflow.* Much research on technology integration in schools has emphasized the difficulty of bringing such tools into the classroom. The process of creating and modifying existing content, an open-ended task with little precedent, readily recruited such skills. Not all of the students had well-developed technical skills, however, and in fact this exercise suggests how many students are consumers but not producers of digital media. This is an important consideration when thinking about the experiences and literacies students bring with them into the design-learning space.

3   *Using the game editor forced students to think about how their game ideas would interact with the game engine, constraining their thinking in particular ways.* As they recognized how the system limited their designs, students developed strategies for working around these constraints. They also recommended changes to the software that would meet their design needs and create a more robust game engine.

4   *Creating games for an authentic audience deepened the design experience.* As students began to see themselves as designers and recognized how their decisions shaped players' experiences, they became more likely to conduct re-edits. For example, when users did not act in a certain way or experience the game in the intended manner, students were forced to reconceptualize their designs. As such, the production process was highly iterative and full of cycles

of creation, analysis, and revision, a process that is a goal of many literacy classrooms.

5   *The complex, distributed nature of the design task led to the development of particular areas of expertise within the groups.* The experience gave students practice in collaborating in a lab-based design environment. Students quickly began learning from one another and developed identities as experts in particular areas, an idea we have discussed elsewhere as "centers of expertise" (Squire *et al.*, 2008). The idea of "centers of expertise" builds off Crowley and Jacobs's (2002) notion of islands of expertise, but adds an explicitly social and distributed component.

6   *The design workshops provided a space for students to share their own perspectives on the places wherein they live their daily lives.* Students created place-based stories that cut across a range of topics, including: the feeling of isolation as a result of moving into a new neighborhood, the loss of rural land and culture as a result of suburban sprawl, and the overabundance of surveillance in contemporary schools. The last example was the theme of a game that required players to get from one end of the school building to the other without getting caught by virtual and real-life hall monitors. In the process of designing the game, the student wanted to point out areas around the building wherein the surveillance cameras could not see you. He also wanted to present his personal perspective on what it was like to live in what he perceives as a surveillance society. Needless to say, this student got a lot of feedback from his peers, who were more than eager to help him do research.

Dow Day as a New Media Experience

For more than a decade, educational theorists have challenged traditional notions of literacy, arguing for new models of literacy that involve multimodal representations, encourage the production of meaning through representations, and most recently, are participatory (New London Group, 1996). Building on this work, Jenkins and colleagues (2006) posit a notion of new media literacy that considers the new forms of participation enabled by digital media, in particular the confluence of new digital media tools and the Internet. A challenge facing educators, however, is leveraging the potential of new digital media to create deep learning experiences. Many teachers find it difficult enough to bring technologies such as video games, the Internet, or mobile media into the classroom without the added challenge of implementing them in ways that reflect the social values underlying such technologies (Leander, 2007).

Dow Day represents one attempt to capitalize on both the technical and social affordances of new digital media (in particular game-based learning, mobile media learning, and new digital media). As such, *Dow Day* presents an example of how an AR game-based curriculum, *especially one that includes a design component*, can be utilized to help students develop their literacy skills. A critical feature of this design is that the game (and extended curriculum) span traditional literacy, critical analysis, and production/design skills within a new literacy framework (Jenkins, Clinton, Purushotma, Robison, & Weigel, 2006; New London Group, 1996). Restated, students aren't "just designing games." Instead, they are reading complex academic texts for meaning, taking a critical stance toward how media are constructed (including the economics behind production), and then crafting their own media representations to represent their personal views.

Specifically, *Dow Day* builds on several key ideas in new digital media and suggests how curricular experiences could be designed around them. Indeed, *Dow Day* features do not just "update" curricula for the digital age. Instead, they more deeply situate learning in a way that contributes to transformative learning experiences for students:

Mobility–Trans-Spatiality: The game is played across different temporal and physical settings. Not only do the players transverse different physical locations, they traverse different time periods and micro-narratives during the course of the game. At various points during the game they are simultaneously in the past and present. For example, when players enter a building they are in both the current time period and in the simulated past, which creates boundary-crossing experiences in which the past and present are connected. In one instance, just as players were exploring the hallway where the protests took place, classes got out. As a result, the players were caught in the rush of university students heading out of the building. This led one student to comment that the same thing must have happened during the protests. She wondered how this might have impacted the protests and concluded that many of the students standing around when the police arrived must have been bystanders, a point that was later supported by a secondary account she read after the game.

Transmedia –Multi-Modal Representations: The story is told using multiple modes of representation (e.g., audio, video, photos, text). It is also told across different types of media. For example, the game content includes interviews, primary documents, real-world data, television clips, and the like. Meaning does not reside in one particular narrative account but instead is something that *students* create by interpreting many different types of texts (including things happening in the physical world).

Narrative Multiplicity: Students take on a role that encourages them to think through the events from a unique perspective. The players also encounter different characters who tell the same story from different perspectives. There are many legitimate interpretations to make about what happened at Dow Day, and indeed, students are encouraged to piece together defensible narratives rather than latch on to pre-scripted ones. From a historical perspective, the curriculum seeks to exploit this feature by highlighting how narratives are temporally constructed and rooted in the time and place of the "reader."

Non-Linearity: Players navigate the content and *game space* in a non-linear fashion and make choices about what content they want to gather and what experiences they want to have.

Emergent Narrative: The narrative emerges in two ways. First, the narrative "emerges" as it is constructed by students through the various multi-modal pieces of evidence they collect. Different choices lead to different interactions, which lead to different narratives. Second, as the "boundary case" example would suggest, leaving the controlled classroom opens unanticipated, emergent narratives and learning opportunities. Each running of *Dow Day* is unique in that it occurs on a particular day within a particular place and time. In nearly every game we run, we encounter real-world people, artifacts, and events that remediate the experience. For example, people have stopped players to share their own experiences about being on campus during the protests.

Active Participation: The game "content" completely depends on players' actions to be activated. Players are active in constructing media and interpretations of experience as they choose locations to visit, access media, and forge a narrative based on the experience. In addition, they write articles and select photos from particular perspectives as they engage in media creation discourses in the production phase of the curriculum.

Differentiation: Although *Dow Day* is relatively "focused" by digital media and the game content (after all, everyone is more or less studying Dow Day), there are opportunities for differentiation, both in how students traverse through the game and in how they construct media experiences afterward. Students can speed through a video or replay it several times examining small details that they find salient. Students can go in depth down particular paths, examining documents in detail or skipping over them almost entirely. The freedom exists for students to focus on different aspects of the protests and explore different parts of the curriculum based on their interests. Teachers have some flexibility in tightening and loosening the boundaries of the curriculum.

Designing New Digital Literacy Learning Experiences

Over the past few years, hundreds of people have played *Dow Day*, ranging from local tourists to high school students. These field tests, demonstrations, trials, and complete curricular implementations have taught us much about how people experience AR games in general and *Dow Day* in particular. Although there are many themes we might focus on, we will highlight two key issues salient to new media literacies: (1) how to usher students from users to designers, and (2) how to nurture a robust site of collective intelligence that can support the design of local games for learning.

Supporting Design Thinking

A key idea defining new literacy studies is a commitment to *design* (i.e., the notion that literacy involves arranging representations so as to produce social futures in the world). Like The New London Group (1996), we emphasize the importance of understanding existing design patterns (such as grammatical conventions), developing a critical awareness of them, and finally designing new representations that produce one's own desired social futures. The *Dow Day* curriculum adopted a three-phase model for moving toward design thinking: (1) playing, (2) redesigning, and (3) new design. In this example, and across many of our AR gaming projects (Squire *et al.*, 2007), we have observed this progression from user to designer to be a complex developmental process. A critical and perhaps overlooked aspect of this process is learning the representational system and its affordances (in this case, the game engine). This finding echoes those we made working with commercial computer games such as Civilization III, in which it is essential for students to develop systemic level understandings of the game system before tackling the problem of design (see Squire *et al.*, 2008). In other words, players need to be able to play and think critically about games before designing their own.

Over these iterations, we have developed several design strategies for fostering this kind of "design" learning. First, we have altered the designs of the model games that students play so as to communicate their "unfinished" nature. Games produced for large groups of teachers necessarily must exhibit a high degree of polish and be free of glitches or errors (Squire *et al.*, 2007). Though these games work more smoothly for broad audiences, they also leave less room for students to enter the game as *designers*. They communicate a sense of "completeness" rather than an open invitation for participation.

In the case of *Dow Day*, a game that itself is an interpretation of history, students are invited to add their own interpretation to an existing, evolving interactive document. As they add characters, roles, or interactions, they are shaping how history is being interpreted. That is, they are having a say in what is considered to be of value in telling the story of *Dow Day* and what is not. As such, the curriculum invites them not just into the practice of game design but into the practice of historical interpretation. This sort of flexibility could be a core affordance of AR games as an instructional medium. Although one could imagine having students add to or reinterpret documents to be produced in a book or film (indeed re-editing an historical documentary is a great exercise), the process of production in this medium, in particular, invites such reinterpretations.

A final feature of the *Dow Day* curriculum is encouraging students to take the leap and engage in the practices of media design. The curriculum seeks to validate and leverage students' indigenous experiences and knowledge, encouraging them to use new digital media to tell stories about their communities through a cutting-edge medium. Nevertheless, we faced many challenges in supporting this transformation. In particular, many of the students we worked with struggled to conceptualize, organize, and manage their own projects, especially as they became increasingly complex. One reason for this was that most of the students had limited design experience and were unfamiliar with how to use basic design strategies (such as storyboarding, rapid prototyping, and iterative design cycles) to plan and evaluate their designs. In response, we developed scaffolding (e.g., outlines and templates) that guided the students through the design process. In this light, one challenge for educators is providing experiences that scaffold students' learning and develop their ability to *think like designers*, without micro-managing their designs.

Supporting Sites of Collective Intelligence

Developing this kind of design thinking may be difficult within the current social organization of schooling, which is organized around groups of students uniformly progressing toward a set of pre-scripted learning goals. In contrast, research on learning in digital media spaces outside of school (such as self-organizing game design communities) has emphasized the *distributed* nature of expertise within these communities. They work because and in spite of the fact that not every member possesses the same skills; rather, individual members develop deep specialized expertise in particular areas. As members work on collaborative projects, they develop a "sense" for what others in the group know and can do and enlist them as needed to attain their goals. Such forms of social organization may be required to support the development of deep design thinking.

The second, perhaps more overlooked aspect of design thinking, is that learners should be designing their own *social futures*, that is, designing with their vision of the future, including *public* and *community futures*, in mind (New London Group, 1993). This approach to design has an affinity for Pierre Levy's (1997) work, which conceptualizes the Internet as a site for collective intelligence that fosters the development of transformative democratic practices. The idea is that communities, such as collaborative blogs like the Daily Kos (www.DailyKos.com) can bring together thousands or even millions of ordinary citizens, each contributing his or her expertise toward reaching civic goals. Together, such collections of citizenry might challenge the dominant media structures and open avenues for collective action.

Our vision for local AR games for learning is that they would be situated within such a site of collective intelligence. We envision networks of people interested in local places or events linking together to share resources and expertise. These networks could span in and out of school, government, private, and educational sectors. It is not hard to imagine local AR games being linked to various interest groups and communities, just as there is an ecology of blogs, Web sites, and media resources online in other subject areas. For example, one can imagine *Dow Day*, with all of its versions, variations, user-generated characters, and so on, published to a Web site for teachers, local historians, students, and tourists.

The emerging pattern of learning described here is quite different— and indeed at odds with current conceptualizations of schooling, which is dominated by a rhetoric of control. It suggests that learners pursue personally meaningful and educationally relevant questions, self-organize into groups to produce media pertaining to those questions, and solicit feedback on their work from others (both inside and outside of the local school community). Critically, such organizations involve consequential participation (Lave, 1988) that seek to dissolve the historical lines between schools and the "outside world" that have characterized schools for the last 100 years (Tyack & Cuban, 1997).

Future Directions

Dow Day serves as one example of how local AR games for learning might be employed within structured school settings. Though we will continue to develop *Dow Day* and look for additional opportunities to assist teachers and students in the design of their own AR games, our research is turning more toward the broader use of mobile media as they expand across multiple contexts, both inside and outside of school. Unfortunately, much of the current discussion surrounding the use of mobile devices in schools centers on how to keep students from using them during the school day.

Though concerns about inappropriate use and equity are valid, it is equally important for educators to seek new opportunities for integrating mobile media technologies into the classroom, especially as more and more students come to school with handheld devices already in their pockets. On the basis of these trends, we believe that ubiquitous access to new computing and communication technologies will place implicit pressures on educators to move beyond retrieval-type pedagogies.

References

Brush, T., & Saye, J. (2008). The effects of multimedia-supported problem-based inquiry on student engagement, empathy, and assumptions about history. *The Interdisciplinary Journal of Problem-based Learning, 2*(1), 21–56.

Coiro, J. (2003). Reading comprehension on the Internet: Expanding our understanding of reading comprehension to encompass new literacies. *The Reading Teacher, 56*(5), 458–465.

Crowley, K. & Jacobs, M. (2002). Building islands of expertise in everyday family activities. In G. Leinhardt, K. Crowley, & K Knutson (Eds.), *Learning conversations in museums* (pp. 401–423). Mahwah, NJ: Lawrence Erlbaum Associates.

Feurzeig, W., & Roberts, N. (1999). *Modeling and simulation in precollege science and mathematics education*. Secaucus, NJ: Springer-Verlag New York, Inc.

Foster, A. (2008). Professor considers laptop ban after reading about distracted student. *Chronicle of Higher Education*. Retrieved July 10, 2009, from http://chronicle.com/wiredcampus/article/3023/professor-considers-laptop-ban-after-reading-about-distracted-student

Galarneau, L. (2007). Productive play: Participation and learning in digital game environments. *Advanced Technology for Learning, 4*(4).

Gee, J. P. (2004). *Situated language and learning: A critique of traditional schooling*. New York: Routledge.

Gee, J. P. (2007). *What video games have to teach us about learning and literacy*. Second revised and updated edition. New York: Palgrave Macmillan.

Holland, W., Jenkins, H. & Squire, K. (2003). Theory by design. In M. J. P. Wolf & B. Perron (Eds.), *Video game theory reader* (pp. 25-46). London: Routledge.

Holt, T. (1990). *Thinking historically: Narrative, imagination, and understanding*. New York: College Entrance Examination Board.

Horst, H., & Miller, D. (2006). *The cell phone: An anthropology of communication*. Oxford: Berg Publishers, Inc.

Jenkins, H. (2004). Game design as narrative architecture. In N. Wardrip-Fruin & P. Harrigan (Eds.), *First person: New media as story, performance, and game* (pp. 118-130). Cambridge, MA: MIT Press.

Jenkins, H. (2006). *Convergence culture: Where old and new media collide*. New York: New York University Press.

Jenkins, H., Clinton, K., Purushotma, R., Robison, A., and Weigel, M. (2006). *Confronting the challenges of participatory culture: Media education for the 21st century*. Chicago, IL: The MacArthur Foundation.

Klopfer, E. (2008). *Augmented learning: Research and design of mobile educational games.* Cambridge, MA: MIT Press.

Klopfer, E., Squire, K., & Jenkins, H. (2003). *Augmented reality simulations on PDAs.* Paper presented at the national American Education Research Association (AERA) Conference, Chicago, 2003.

Lave, J. (1988). The practice of learning: The problem with "context." In S. Chaiklin & J. Lave (Eds.), *Understanding practice: Perspectives on activity and context* (pp.3–32). Boston, MA: Cambridge University Press.

Leander, K. (2007). "You won't be needing your laptops today": Wired bodies in the wireless classroom. In M. Knobel & C. Lankshear (Eds.), *A new literacies sampler* (pp. 25–48). New York: Peter Lang.

Levy, P. (1997). *Collective intelligence: Mankind's emerging world in cyberspace.* Trans. by Robert Bononno. New York: Plenum Trade

Maraniss, D. (2003). *They marched into sunlight: War and peace Vietnam and America, October 1967.* New York: Simon & Schuster.

New London Group. (1996). A pedagogy of multiliteracies: Designing social futures. *Harvard Educational Review, 66*(1), 60–92.

Roschelle, J., & Pea, R. (2002). A walk on the WILD side: How wireless handhelds may change CSCL. In G. Stahl (Ed.), *Proceedings of computer support for collaborative learning 2002* (pp. 51–60). Hillsdale, NJ: Erlbaum Associates.

Seldes, G. (1924). *The seven lively arts.* New York: Harper & Brothers.

Shaffer, D., Squire, K., Halverson, R., & Gee, J. (2005). Video games and the future of learning. *Phi Delta Kappan, 87*(2), 105–111.

Squire, K. (2005). Changing the game: What happens when video games enter the classroom? *Innovate: Journal of Online Education, 1*(6). Retrieved July 2009, from http://www.innovateonline.info/index.php?view=article&id=82

Squire, K. (2006). From content to context: Videogames as designed experience. *Educational Researcher, 35*(8), 11.

Squire, K. (2008). Video games and education: Designing learning systems for an interactive age. *Educational Technology, 48*(2), 17–25.

Squire, K., & Jan, M. (2007). Mad City Mystery: Developing scientific argumentation skills with a place-based augmented reality game on handheld computers. *Journal of Science Education and Technology, 16*(1), 5–29.

Squire, K., Jan, M., Mathews, J., Wagler, M., Martin, J., DeVane, B., *et al.* (2007). Wherever you go, there you are: Place-based augmented reality games for learning. In B. E. Shelton & D. Wiley (Eds.), *The educational design and use of simulation computer games* (pp. 265–296). Rotterdam: Sense Publishers.

Squire, K., DeVane, B., & Durga, S. (2008). Designing centers of expertise for academic learning through video games. *Theory Into Practice, 47*(3), 240–251

Staley, D. J. (2002). *Computers, visualization, and history: How new technology will transform our understanding of the past.* Armonk, NY: Sharpe.

Steinkuehler, C. A. (2006). Massively multiplayer online videogaming as participation in a Discourse. *Mind, Culture & Activity, 13* (1), 38–52.

Tyack, D., & Cuban, L. (1995). *Tinkering toward utopia: A century of public school reform.* Cambridge, MA: Harvard University Press.

Wineburg, S. (2001) *Historical thinking and other unnatural acts: Charting the future of teaching the past.* Philadelphia, PA: Temple University.

Wolfram, S. (2002). *A new kind of science.* Champaign, IL: Wolfram Media. Inc.

Index